Using Science in
Cybersecurity

Highly Recommended Titles

Cybersecurity and Legal-Regulatory Aspects
edited by Gabi Siboni and Limor Ezioni
ISBN: 978-981-121-915-3

SecureCSocial: Secure Cloud-Based Social Network
by Pradeep K Atrey and Kasun Senevirathna
ISBN: 978-981-120-591-0

Cyber Security Practitioner's Guide
edited by Hamid Jahankhani
ISBN: 978-981-120-445-6

Data Science for Cyber-Security
edited by Nick Heard, Niall Adams, Patrick Rubin-Delanchy and
Melissa Turcotte
ISBN: 978-1-78634-563-9

Dynamic Networks and Cyber-Security
edited by Niall Adams and Nick Heard
ISBN: 978-1-78634-074-0

Data Analysis for Network Cyber-Security
edited by Niall Adams and Nicholas Heard
ISBN: 978-1-78326-374-5

Using Science in Cybersecurity

Leigh Metcalf

Carnegie Mellon University, USA

Jonathan Spring

Carnegie Mellon University, USA

NEW JERSEY · LONDON · SINGAPORE · BEIJING · SHANGHAI · HONG KONG · TAIPEI · CHENNAI · TOKYO

Published by

World Scientific Publishing Co. Pte. Ltd.

5 Toh Tuck Link, Singapore 596224

USA office: 27 Warren Street, Suite 401-402, Hackensack, NJ 07601

UK office: 57 Shelton Street, Covent Garden, London WC2H 9HE

Library of Congress Cataloging-in-Publication Data
Names: Metcalf, Leigh, author. | Spring, Jonathan M., author.
Title: Using science in cybersecurity / Leigh Metcalf, Carnegie Mellon University, USA,
     Jonathan Spring, Carnegie Mellon University, USA.
Description: First. | Hackensack, NJ : World Scientific, [2021] |
     Includes bibliographical references and index.
Identifiers: LCCN 2021009781 | ISBN 9789811235856 (hardcover) |
     ISBN 9789811235863 (ebook for institutions) | ISBN 9789811235870 (ebook for individuals)
Subjects: LCSH: Computer networks--Security measures. | Computer security.
Classification: LCC TK5105.59 .M496 2021 | DDC 005.8--dc23
LC record available at https://lccn.loc.gov/2021009781

British Library Cataloguing-in-Publication Data
A catalogue record for this book is available from the British Library.

For any available supplementary material, please visit
https://www.worldscientific.com/worldscibooks/10.1142/12247#t=suppl

Desk Editor: Amanda Yun

Printed in Singapore

Contents

Chapter 1

Introduction

There have been prominent calls for improving cybersecurity through making professionals more academically rigorous as early as 2001 (National Science Foundation, 2001). These calls shifted to pleas for more "science" in security around 2008 in the upper levels of the US Department of Defense (DoD), as documented by MITRE Corporation (2010). Within just a few years, the Air Force, Army, National Security Agency (NSA), and US federal civilian government had joined this chorus, with some minor variation. The governments of the United Kingdom and Canada were using similar language by 2012. The first textbook aimed at giving security professionals a crash course in essential scientific methods was Dykstra (2015). By 2017, academic security researchers (Herley and van Oorschot, 2017) and top professional information security events (Evron, 2017) were discussing what it would take to make security more scientific.

We have written this book to provide an accessible, actionable path for anyone who wants to do cybersecurity work well. We say "well" and not "scientifically" because the only point of doing the work scientifically is that it is done well and that others can trust that it was done well. There are other ways to conduct good cybersecurity work; it's not our way or nothing. But the scientific methods, properly applied, have proven over the past few centuries to be the best way humans have for understanding and solving problems. Engineers' pride may be hurt by this. However, they should not fuss over whether science or engineering comes first; you cannot do science without tools and engineering, and you cannot do modern engineering without knowledge and methods from science (Dear, 2006; Vincenti, 1990).

We have been involved in bringing scientific and mathematical principles into our cybersecurity work for some time. We have been collaborating on using these mental tools to solve cybersecurity problems since 2010. The first few years were focused on the problems, but a pattern emerged. We brought our backgrounds (philosophy of science and mathematics) to the cybersecurity work and our practice matured alongside our awareness of the broader science of security. We have unique perspectives to share. Of course, we think they are better perspectives. There are important gaps in teaching cybersecurity professionals how to reason about an incident or any problem they face (Spring and Illari, 2018b) and the science of security folks are not filling them (Spring *et al.*, 2017). Leigh wrote a book on applied mathematics for cybersecurity (Metcalf and Casey, 2016), and Jonathan has written almost as much on applying scientific reasoning and logic in cybersecurity. Along the way, we have applied and tested our thinking with results that have changed the way people use and think about blocklists, for example. But we have not laid out a how-to, with examples, explaining the mental tools and practical steps someone can take to practice cybersecurity ~~well~~ scientifically. Or *had* not. Until this book.

Most of the publications in the field are merely emphasizing the fact that scientific principles are necessary, but there are very few guides that aim to uncover these principles. The aim of this book is to begin developing the scientific method for cybersecurity, taking into account the vagaries of the data and the difficulty of the task. We will do this by using extensive examples and also take the time to point out the pitfalls and fallacious thinking that can arise.

We want the reader to learn the basics of how to perform a good study in the field of cybersecurity. We do this by discussing the various studies that are possible for a investigator and how to frame a question appropriately to gain a useful and applicable result.

Cybersecurity is an ever-changing field, which means the results of today may not be the correct results tomorrow. It is also a very broad field, encompassing computers, society, law, economics, and more. It is also a human-created field, unlike biology, for example. The artifacts and events that occur in cybersecurity were created by humans and are not naturally occurring.

But the fact that they're created does not mean they are any easier to understand or more accessible than those in the life sciences. There is no one person or group of people who are wholly responsible for how the Internet or computers work. Some have passed away, but more importantly, there are just too many people who have contributed. And new people are adding new technology and behaviors every day. Cybersecurity is like the life sciences in that there is no creator that we can ask how the systems work. Practitioners have to study the situation and learn what they can through what tools and information is available. And at least in the life sciences, the viruses cannot read doctors' publications and directly learn what capabilities they need to subvert human defenses.

Cybersecurity is also an inherently practical field. Practitioners who use research want the results to be applicable to their very real and current problems. Usable results, that is. The results of a scientific study in cybersecurity should be usable beyond the study itself.

The chapters of this book are intertwined. We have arranged them in the order that we believe introduces the topic best, so the suggested reading order is Chapters 2 through 8. The last three chapters are examples of applying the principles discussed earlier in the book.

Chapter 2 is a catalog of data found in cybersecurity. We have often noticed that researchers are focused on a single area and aren't necessarily aware of other data sources that can help them. For example, knowing how the data were transported can be as important as the network flow. Route injection can mean that the data originated from a location other than what the Internet Protocol (IP) address suggests. The chapter is not a catalog of all the data available, but attempts to discuss the major data sets, how they work, and what useful information they may contain.

Chapter 3 is about setting goals. The goal in cybersecurity is usually knowing something about the data well enough to support or inform some action. When you know such a thing well enough, you know a truth. When someone goes in search of truths, they should be searching for adequate or satisfactory explanations that constrain and integrate with the other satisfactory explanations that people know about the topic. The chapter describes what this looks like, from both computing and practices in other scientific fields, to establish the goal for practicing a science of security.

Chapter 4 describes the desirable properties of studies and observations that are more likely to lead to this goal. Since cybersecurity crosses so many interrelated disciplines, it cannot simply take the desirably properties from just one other field. Parts of cybersecurity are like physics, parts are like psychology, and parts are like ecology. Chapter 4 works to respect and encourage this diversity of methodology while still usefully guiding how you can design studies in any part of cybersecurity.

The basics of exploratory data analysis are covered in Chapter 5. Statistics is a deep and extensive field; the chapter focuses on introducing the reader to the ability to take a data set and quickly analyze or visualize it. We discuss what the statistics mean, what the visualizations can do for you, and how to create a good visualization depending on the data.

A common problem in cybersecurity is the amount of data that is available to analyze. It isn't always possible to analyze an entire data set, so sampling is often used. Chapter 6 discusses the basics of sampling and uses examples to illustrate the various kinds. Good and bad examples are given.

Chapter 7 ties the prior six chapters together into advice on types of structured observations to design in cybersecurity. Later chapters will demonstrate examples of designing studies of different types. There are always trade-offs among Chapter 4's study properties; no study can have all the desirable properties. Thus, the second part of Chapter 7 introduces designing research agendas composed of multiple studies whose strengths compensate for each other's weaknesses.

We discuss the goals and pitfalls of research in Chapter 8. The pitfalls can negate or reduce the impact of your research while the goals are what you wish to achieve in the research. This chapter covers these by looking at the data, the process, and the results. We also discuss common logical fallacies and how they can affect the research.

Chapters 9 through 12 use data drawn from open sources to put the principles discussed in the book into action. We look at Domain Name System (DNS) traffic, network traffic, malware, and humans.

The end goal of this work is to encourage research in the field as well as to discuss how to do it in a scientific manner. We want the reader to walk away with a greater understanding and practical help to ensure their research contributes to the field.

Chapter 2

Data in Cybersecurity

An arborist studies trees, so their catalog of available data to study includes a list of trees, the ecosystem a tree is found in, the soil, and other tree-related information. Similarly, cybersecurity research studies events and trends in the Internet, so the data catalog that a cybersecurity researcher would use includes security and Internet-related data. It also includes additional data sets that have been created by external sources. The problem with data created by external sources is that there is no way of knowing how good these data are nor what the provenance of them are. In general it's known that an event happened and data was collected.

This chapter covers common data in cybersecurity. Using the arborist analogy, it's the equivalent of a catalog of trees and their ecosystem that the arborist could use to start a research project. The catalog attempts to list common sources used in cybersecurity research, but it isn't exhaustive. It might seem disconnected as well, and that is mostly due to the nature of the work. DNS data are different and usually distinct from malware data, which is different (and distinct) from data used in Internet routing. Unlike trees, which have the basic connection of "tree," cybersecurity data runs the gamut from human-created to machine-created.

Again, this isn't comprehensive. It should be used to learn how to think about data and the pitfalls in using some of these data sets. Some people tend to focus on a single data set without being aware of the other possibilities available. Part of the goal of this chapter is to expand your knowledge of the available data sets.

It's possible to create a data set for research, but it's necessary to examine the potential problems in that set. No data set is perfect by any means; it's the imperfections that make the research interesting and sometimes difficult.

2.1   Domain Names

DNS is one of the core protocols that makes the Internet run. At its heart, it is the association of IP addresses with domain names. It allows users to type www.google.com rather than memorizing a series of numbers. DNS is the engine behind content distribution networks and allows the owner of a domain to change IP addresses without notifying users.

The protocol was designed to be a hierarchical directory (Liu, 2002). Instead of a single phone book with every domain to IP address listed, it's a telephone book that lists other telephone books that lists other ones. The resolution follow its way through the telephone books until the one that contains the information is found. This means that no one server, known as a *name server*, knows everything, they just know where to ask.

The process of finding the IP address of a domain is called domain resolution, and it works in reverse order by starting with ., moving to `com`. then to `google.com`. and finally, to `www.google.com`. In each step, the name servers associated with that step are asked for the answer, and they either give the answer or point the computer to the next server to ask.

DNS is used for more than just the domain name to IP mapping, it has almost forty different types of records. It can be used to determine what domain to send email to (`MX` records), storing information about the domains themselves (`TXT` records, `SOA` records), for security (both for DNS and mail), and more. DNS has been used to send signals as well, which means that the application looks up a domain and, based on the response, has some action.

DNS-based block lists (DNSBLs) (Levine, 2010) create domain names out of either IPs or domains by prepending them to the DNS blocklist domain. If the DNSBL is `example.com` and we're interested in `badguy.info`, then the look up would be `badguy.info.example.com`. The IP address is reversed, so that means `192.0.2.99` would have the look up `99.2.0.192.example.com`. The response from the query is a signal as to whether the IP address or domain has been tagged as bad by the blocklist owner. The responses should be within the 127.0.0.0/8 loopback network, and each application should have its own numbering specification for the results of the query.

In the original specification of the DNS protocol, there was no security built in. Instead, it is a network of trust. The computer trusts that the name server it queries will return the correct response. To resolve www.google.com, there were a minimum of three queries before a response was returned that contained an IP address. Every step could give the wrong result, and the computer would never know.

Attempts have been made to add security through extensions, known as DNS security extensions (DNSSEC) (Kolkman and Gieben, 2006). As mentioned above, when www.google.com was resolved, it took a minimum of three name servers before any IPs that were associated with it were determined. At any point in the process, those answers could have been subverted and incorrect ones could have been given. To prevent this attack, DNSSEC was proposed. It uses cryptographic signatures to add a verification step to DNS resolutions. It is up to the owner of the domain whether or not to use it, so it isn't used everywhere.

2.2 Routing Data

Routing is the method that sends data through the Internet from the source to the destination. In the days when the Internet began, it wasn't large, so this process was relatively simple. Every router could know the location of every other router. As the Internet grew, the original protocols could no longer support it, leading to the development of two kinds of routing protocols, interior routing protocols and exterior routing protocols. Interior routing protocols are the protocols used inside of an organization; exterior routing protocols are the protocols used between organizations.

Border Gateway Protocol (BGP) (Caesar and Rexford, 2005) is an exterior routing protocol which is designed to route collections of networks between organizations. These collections are called Autonomous Systems (AS) and are denoted by an autonomous system number (ASN). A company is assigned an ASN by their regional Internet registry (RIR).

ASN is associated with a collection of networks; there doesn't have to be a physical location tied to the ASN. The networks associated with an ASN can span multiple countries as well, depending on the networks.

Each ASN has peers with which it shares information. They want their peers to route traffic to its networks, so they do this by telling the peers that they have the networks, known within the protocol as announcing the networks. Technically speaking, for each network the ASN has, it announces to its peers ASN NETWORK. In BGP speak this says that "I, ASN, have these networks." For example, a potential announcement could be:
64496 10.0.0.1/24

This tells the peers of 64496 that it has this network. Each of our ASN 64496's peers will tell its peers their ASN prepended to this announcement.

It looks like:

`PEER 64496 10.0.0.1/24`

This tells their peers that to access an IP address in 10.0.0.1/24, then they first must go to PEER which passes them to 64496, which owns that network. This does not mean that there is a device with that IP address, just that that combination of ASNs in that order will allow traffic to flow to that ASN that owns the IP address. This combination of ASNs in the given order with a network at the end is called a route.

Peering with multiple ASNs allows redundant routes to be present in the virtual ASN network. If the only route available is:

`ASN_A ASN_B ASN_C ASN_D NETWORK`

Then that is the only route that traffic can traverse. If there are multiple routes, then there must be a method by which the route is chosen. The Request for Comments (RFC) (Rekhter *et al.*, 1994) specifies the criteria for choosing a route and it includes:

- the shortest ASN path.

- the most specific network announcement. This means the network with the fewest number of IPs in it will win.

- the highest local preference. This is a value set by the router to determine which peer is preferred.

The other important part about multiple routes is the amount of control that the originator of the traffic has, which is to say very little. The source of the traffic chooses the peer to which it wants to send the traffic to. At that point, the source loses all control of the traffic. The peer chooses its next destination based on its own criteria, not on the origin's criteria. So while the router can say which path it wanted its traffic to take, it doesn't know what the actual path is. This can also be affected by filtering. An organization's peering agreement with another organization may include not announcing certain routes to its other peers, so the data may traverse a completely unknown route.

BGP also has no security built into the protocol (Murphy, 2006). This means that anyone can announce any network, and there's no inherent verification that this ASN is allowed to announce it. An Internet Routing Registry (IRR) is a mechanism (Bates *et al.*, 1995) where the owners of networks can register who announces those networks, but there is no requirement that autonomous aystem (AS) operators respect these. Another method used to secure BGP is Resource Public Key Infrastructure (RPKI) (Cohen *et al.*, 2015). These certificates are used to authenticate announcements, but there is no requirement that the certificate is used.

2.3 Full Packet Capture

Full packet capture (Koch, 2018) is just what it sounds like. Every packet that traverses a network is captured, meaning copied, and saved for future study. A sensor is placed on the network that collects and stores this data.

Every action a user makes on the Internet is apparent, with some caveats. First, it completely depends on where the sensor is placed. If somehow the user is outside of the coverage of the sensor, that user's actions won't be recorded. The user can also encrypt their connection. If, for example, they visited a secure website, the website they visited would be recorded, when the visit was, how long the visit lasted, and the encrypted data.

On the other hand, if the website was unencrypted, everything would be recorded, from what they typed in to what they received. This means that if the website was used to deliver malware, then the malware can be extracted from the traffic. Every domain and IP address they access is recorded, every Uniform Resource Locator (URL) they click on, every email they receive, and every system they connect to.

The downside to full packet capture is that storing the data can take up a lot of disk space, depending on the size of the organization. Think about how much web surfing a typical user does in a day. Now imagine storing every bit of traffic sent to the Internet and received. Now, multiply that by the number of users in an organization. Add in traffic to the organization's webserver and mail server. In short, this means a lot of data to store.

In 2016, an estimate (Koch, 2018) was made of how much space would be required for 72 hours of full packet capture on a 1 gigabit (Gb) link. The computation determined it would take at least 24.3 terabytes(TB) of space. Not only is storing that amount of data difficult, but searching it becomes an untenable task.

2.4 Network Flow

If full packet capture is "catch everything as it goes by," then network flow is "take the trace of what went by." Think of full packet capture as capturing all the animals that visit a watering hole whereas network flow is examining the footprints left behind. Similar to full packet capture, a sensor is placed on the network and the data is collected.

Network flow captures (Gates *et al.*, 2004):

- Source IP address

- Source Port

- Destination IP address

- Destination Port

- Protocol

- Start time

- End time

- Number of Packets

- Number of Bytes

- Transmission Control Protocol (TCP) Flags

It's a trace of what the user did without storing what the user did. It clearly uses less space than a full packet capture, and so storing more data than full packet capture is possible, making historical analysis possible. However, context is lost. The fact that an IP visited a web server and downloaded 10M of data is recorded, but there's no clear context of what happened during the session.

2.5   GeoIP

GeoIP is the geographic location of an IP address (Holdener, 2011). There are many companies that sell this data, each claiming to be more accurate than the others. This is one of the problems with the data. Researchers must rely upon the company supplying data to tell them the right thing, but there is no way of double checking it short of going to the longitude and latitude given and trying to determine the current IP address. Companies will declare that their data is accurate, but they don't explain how they determine the location of an IP address, nor how they verify that they're right.

It's been known (Hill, 2016) to be very wrong, to the point of 600 million IP addresses pointing to a Kansas farm house due to a lack of precision.

Relying upon GeoIP to locate the origin of traffic has its own issues. Suppose the IP address a researcher is examining is malicious. It could because it is part of a botnet, so the true origin of the traffic is unknown. The owner of the system may not know that their system sent malicious traffic. Using GeoIP to locate this system gets the researcher no closer to the actual location from which the traffic originated.

In summary, GeoIP data can be used to geographically locate systems, but take the result with a grain of salt, and be careful how it is used.

2.6 Blocklists

Blocklists are collections of any or all the following: IP addresses, domains, URLs, MD5s, and more. We discussed them briefly in Section 2.1, discussing those that were delivered via DNS.

The elements on a blocklist are generally called indicators, in that they indicate malicious behavior. The creators of these lists are looking for malicious behavior and provide them to the public either as open source or for purchase. Organizations then use blocklists to filter traffic, both inbound and outbound. They don't want spam (that's one blocklist to buy) nor do they they want their users to visit sites associated with malware (that's another one). Analysts use blocklists when investigating an incident as well.

In general, the creation of these lists is a black box. Someone decided that an indicator was associated with malicious behavior and added it to their list. If a list is bought from a company that tracks spam, then clearly anything on that list was associated with spam. Unfortunately, there's no direct knowledge on how the spam was created and by what process email was tagged as spam. The only knowledge we have about the list is that the company collected spam email in some way and pulled this information out of it.

Studies of the blocklist ecosystem have shown that there is very little overlap between the lists (Metcalf and Spring, 2013b). Even between lists that collect similar data, like spam lists, there is very little overlap. This could be related to the different methods each list owner uses to create their blocklist, but since the methods aren't disclosed, it's impossible to verify. The blocklist studies also looked at data related to the domains and IP addresses, like name servers or Autonomous Systems, to determine if there was agreement —very little was found.

Suppose a researcher's task is to find malicious domains, and after much research they've created a method to do this. They know that the domains found in their method are malicious because they found a blocklist that had every single one of the domains on it. Since there's very little overlap between lists, what the researcher has done is figured out how to recreate the list.

There can also be an issue with blocklist quality. Private IP addresses, that is, the addresses listed in RFC 1918, shouldn't be routed on the Internet. This means they also shouldn't show up on a well-tended blocklist; however, they often do. This can mean that the blocklist owner isn't performing due diligence before adding elements to their list. Well-known domains can also end up on blocklists, usually due to the ad network that they are using. If the ad network is known for serving up malware, then the well-known domain can be tagged as malicious. Any domain can be used maliciously.

Blocklists can be great sources for malicious behavior, but researchers must be careful when they use them. There's not an indication of why things are necessarily tagged as bad, just that they are on the list. Since the companies producing the blocklists don't share their methods, all researchers can say is "I found a domain that's on a blocklist, so it could be bad" not "it is definitely bad."

2.7   Log Files

Log files are records that applications and operating systems keep of their operation. For example, when an application starts, it can log the time at which it started and the steps it took. An operating system could log every time a user logs in or logs out. It is common for applications and operating systems to log errors, such as when a user attempts to log in, but fails to give the correct password.

Log files are local information. They are concerned only about the system from which they originated but nothing about any other system. If two webservers have similar configurations, it's expected that they have similar logs. On the other hand, if it is one webserver and one nameserver, then the logs would be different.

Logs are often subject to availability. Sometimes, the owner of a system configures logs to store everything, sometimes, they don't.

2.7.1   *Application Log Files*

Suppose a Linux® server is running an ssh daemon that is open to the world. One day the system administrator checks the log files and see a list of failed attempts to log in remotely via ssh. The attempts cycle through a list of user names, most of which are not on the system, and each of them fails. This is a direct attack on a system and the sysadmin is happy to see that they all failed. If they had noticed that one succeeded, then the system would have been compromised.

Application developers (DeLaRosa, 2018) are the ones that determine what an application will record in log files, so if the ssh daemon developers had not decided failed logins were important information, then the intrusion detect wouldn't have been found in the ssh log files. This means that researchers are dependent on what the application developers find worth logging and in general, researchers don't have any say in what gets logged.

Researchers are also dependent on the log retention schedule, which is a predetermined length of time that log files are kept. If log files are only kept for a week, then anything past those seven days is lost. If they are kept for much longer, then it becomes a disk space issue. This is usually determined by the administrator of the system, not necessarily with security in mind. Another issue is that the administrator may determine that some events should be logged and saved whereas other events are not. A mis-configured logging system can lose important security events, preventing later analysis.

Another factor in log files is that the log message format can change, depending on the operating system. The ssh failure on one system can have a completely different format than the message on another. In other words, there's no consistency of the data.

2.7.2 *Firewall Log Files*

Firewall log files (Winding *et al.*, 2006) are a specialized form of the log files discussed in the previous section. They generally have the same issues discussed in the previous section, but also have additional features and issues as well. Firewalls can be in multiple locations. A single host can be running a firewall or a network device may act as a firewall.

When a firewall sees a connection, it has two choices. It can `ALLOW` the connection through or it can `DENY` it. Depending on the configuration of the system, either or both messages can be logged. If a firewall `ALLOW`s a connection, then the connection is allowed to the destination. In the section on network flow, we discussed how the same data is collected. In other words, this is somewhat redundant information. Network flow knows about the connection, the firewall knows about the connection, and it has been recorded in both locations. If network flow is collected, it does seem extraneous to also be collecting the `ALLOW`ed connections from the firewall.

On the other hand, the DENY connections are where it gets interesting. Remember that to collect network flow, a sensor is needed. If the sensor placement looks like Fig. 2.1, then network flow will record that a connection occurred, even though the firewall denied the connection. By reversing the placement of the sensor and the firewall, network flow will no longer

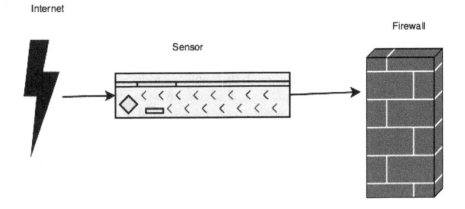

Fig. 2.1   Sensor Placement

record the connection that didn't occur. This means that when analyzing either firewall log files or network flow, sensor placement is key and knowing where the sensors are is important because it can affect results.

2.7.3 *Proxy Log Files*

A proxy is an interface between the users of an organization and the outside Internet. A common proxy is the web proxy, which allows the organization to enact content filtering. Proxies can also cache results and share them between multiple users, which can save bandwidth.

The log files of a proxy server (Fei *et al.*, 2006) are records of what web servers the users of an organization are contacting. Like all log files, they're dependent on the configuration of the appliance as well as the retention policy. If a new form of malware is discovered that's originating from `http://www.example.com/` and the proxy logs only go back 24 hours, then the research is limited. Similarly, if there is a mis-configuration and not every user is required to use the proxy, then if those users visited the site, no one would know.

2.7.4 *Certificate Transparency Logs*

Not every log is on a per-system basis. The *Certificate Transparency Log* is a public log of Transport Layer Security (TLS) certificates as they are issued. (Dowling *et al.*, 2016). No one can modify the logs after they've been written; they can only have log messages appended to them. This is ensured using a cryptographic mechanism. Anyone can download and use these logs as well.

The logs contain the domain, the issuing authority, the certificate, the issuing date, and more. Any domain can get a TLS certificate, even names generated by a domain generation algorithm (DGA) (Metcalf, 2018b). The difficult question is why.

These logs are freely available and a valuable research tool.

2.8 Windows Registry

The Windows registry is a collection of low-level settings for Windows (Carvey, 2005). It is a hierarchical text file that controls various aspects of the system, such as device drivers. Malicious software often modifies the registry so a savvy investigator will analyze it for clues. There's also no such thing as a standard Windows registry; it's generally a per-system configuration.

These registries are very useful in research, but researchers need to be aware of the details of the system from which they collect them as the details can affect the entries in the registry. One registry may have an entry that another one doesn't because of system configuration. At this time, there is no way to centrally collect windows registries from group of systems; they must be collected one at a time.

2.9 Domain Registry

Suppose a researcher found a domain associated with malicious behavior, and they want to find the owner. Maybe they want to know what other domains they owns to see if they're malicious, or they want to create a report on the malicious domain, or they want to send this information to law enforcement. There are any number of reasons to look for the owner of a domain.

Luckily, this information is available. It's possible to search the registry operator for the top-level domain (TLD) of the domain, or use the command whois to query the owner. This should return the name of the organization or person that registered the domain, their address, and contact information as well as the name servers that serve that domain. That's the good news. The bad news is that many domains are protected by private domain registration. This means that rather than getting the name of the organization or person that registered the domain, a corporation that specializes in private registrations is returned as the response. This allows domain owners to maintain their privacy, but at the same time, it hides the owners of malicious domains. The name servers are not obfuscated, though. They must be known for resolutions for that domain to work.

It is also possible to look for the owner of an IP address by using the whois command as well as by searching online. There is no privacy protection for owners of networks and the result also indicates the allocation that the IP address belongs to. For example, 8.8.8.8 is Google's open DNS server. If the command run is

    whois 8.8.8.8

then the result shows that network is 8.8.8.0/24 and it is owned by Google. The result will also include that it is a subnet of a larger block owned by Level 3 Communications.

Unfortunately, it is not possible to search by owner. It's not possible to ask, "Okay, Mr. BadGuy owns that domain, now what are the other domains he owns?" There are companies that sell that information though, so it is possible to buy the data.

2.10   TLD Zone Files

A zone file is a configuration file for a name server. If an administrator is running a name server for an organization, it will contain the domain names used by the organization and the mapping to the correct IP address. Remember, most name servers don't know this information, but rather where to find it out. The TLD zone files are a good example of this. They contain a list of domains that are registered within the TLD, and the name servers associated with them. So, a typical line within the file could look like:

    MYDOMAIN IN NS NS1.EXAMPLE.COM.

If this is the COM TLD, then there is a problem. To go to NS1.EXAMPLE.COM, then a computer would have to look up the name server for EXAMPLE.COM. If it happens to also be NS1.EXAMPLE.COM, then that information implies that to look up example.com a look up has to be done for example.com. To solve this problem, the A records for all name servers whose TLD matches the TLD in question is saved within the file. In other words, in the bottom part of the file is a line that looks like:

    NS1.EXAMPLE.COM. IN A 127.0.0.1

Doing this tells the TLD name server that when looking for the IP address for *NS1.EXAMPLE.COM*, the result is directly in the file and no further resolutions are necessary.

Gaining access to these files generally means entering an agreement with the TLD registrar. There is nothing in the original agreement that says that the registrar must make them available; however, the new TLDs do have this requirement. In general, it is possible to gain access to most generic top-level domains (gTLDs), but not to country code top-level domains (ccTLDs) (ICANN, 2013). ccTLDs operators have no requirement at all to share such information, and some countries consider that private information.

Not every domain in the file is active. Some organizations register place-holders, either for future plans or to prevent other organizations from using the same domains. Adversaries can register a large swath of domains and then only use a few at a time. However, when the file is downloaded, it contains a definitive list of domains registered at that time. The nature of domain registrations means that even a minute later, that file could change. If the file is downloaded at noon on Monday, it won't know what domains were registered at 12:30.

2.11   Passive Operating System Fingerprinting

Passive Operating System Fingerprinting, also known as Passive O/S Fingerprinting, is the process of determining the operating system at a given IP address without obviously probing the system (Faircloth, 2016). Active probing can alert an adversary to the presence of their adversary, which is a bad idea. Instead, the hope is to use clues left on the network by the host to determine what operating system it is running.

There are as many methods for accomplishing this as researchers on the topic. For example, analyzing network traffic that originates from the IP address is a method commonly used. Examining the DNS queries that originate from the IP address is another method of analyzing the operating system. None of these methods are 100% effective, rather they give a probability of a particular operating system at that IP address. This means it's not possible to definitively say what operating system is at a given IP address. It's only possible to say with the degree of certainty that the chosen method gives.

Work has been done to defeat passive fingerprinting. This means that combined with the uncertainty of the methods used in Passive O/S Fingerprinting, it's not possible to definitely say what operating system the host at an IP address is using without active probing. It's an educated guess backed up by math and knowledge about how the different operating systems function.

2.12   Vulnerability Reports

A vulnerability report is just what it sounds like, a report that a vulnerability exists. The Common Vulnerabilities and Exposures (CVE) is a method created to share publicly known vulnerabilities using a standard dictionary and numbering format. The numbers look like CVE-YYYY-NNNN where YYYY refers to the year the vulnerability was discovered and the NNNN is the vulnerability number.

The Mitre Corporation (MITRE) (MITRE Corporation, 2012) oversees the CVE process. They hand out the CVEs upon request, but rather than overseeing the process for all vulnerabilities, they have granted certain organizations called a CVE numbering authority (CNA) the ability to assign CVEs. Some of these organizations only handle CVEs for software within their purview. For example, Microsoft only assigns CVEs to Microsoft products. Others are granted the privilege to hand the CVEs out for any vulnerability they choose to coordinate, such as the CERT® Coordination Center (CERT/CC). Once a computer network attack (CNA) has handed out a CVE, that vulnerability is considered to exist. There is no overriding vetting process for vulnerabilities other than what the CNAs have put in place.

The centralized location and standardized method of CVEs is useful; however, it is dependent on the vulnerabilities reported. A malware author isn't going to ask for a CVE for the 0-day vulnerability they have discovered that could allow them to steal information. Similarly, an organization might decide to hide the vulnerability they discovered in their hardware that would leave a customer open to attack. There is no requirement for vulnerability reporting, so the list of vulnerabilities available in the CVE database is not comprehensive. It's only what people happen to report.

2.13   Fuzzing Reports

Vulnerability reports are a passive tool. When a vulnerability report is made it doesn't necessarily include how the vulnerability was found, just that it was and someone deemed it important enough to share. Fuzzing (Godefroid *et al.*, 2005) is the art of looking at software and attempting to find vulnerabilities. It is a black box testing technique, meaning context is lacking. In other words, the tester only has the program, not the source code of the program.

A former co-worker once told us that they let their four-year-old beat on the keyboard as a last test before releasing software. They would start the program, set the kid in front of the keyboard and tell them to go to town. The logic was that if the four-year-old mashing random keys couldn't break the software, then it was stable. Fuzzing is the art of automating the four-year-old's actions. In technical terms, it is the continuous automated process of sending mutated input to software and recording the result. If a combination of random input causes the software to fail, then that string is recorded.

Fuzzing testing is not comprehensive. This means that every combination of characters isn't tested to determine the result because otherwise it would never finish. The results of fuzzing are also not applicable across versions of software. It could break in version 1, be fixed in version 2, but crash again in version 3. The automated testing is clearly much faster than allowing the four-year-old to test, but it is still very slow.

2.14 Incident Reports

In a well-run security operations center (SOC) each security incident has a report written about it (Cichonski *et al.*, 2012). These reports should contain information relevant to the event, such as IP addresses, domains, URLs, hashes relevant to the event, the time at which the event was discovered, the time at which the event ended, the effect of the event to the organization, and anything else the investigator finds interesting. They are a record of an event, so rather than inferring that something occurred, there is direct evidence.

As they are generally written by humans, they are a messy source of information. Extracting the relevant information is the first step to using the data effectively.

Depending on the methods used to create the report, information can be missing. While it is a record of an event, it is not necessarily a complete record. Similarly, it's not possible to assume that every security event at an organization was discovered and a report was written. Incident reports are a collection of "we found this," but not necessarily a complete record of what was found nor a record of everything that occurred. Human error is a concern in analyzing incident reports.

2.15 Network Inventory

Network inventory is just what it sounds like. The inventory of all the devices on the network. If a network is the focus of a study, then a list of everything on the network and its relative location would be useful. For example, the knowledge of where all network sensors are located for network flow and full packet capture, assuming those exist. A list of all servers and routers is also important. This should be easy; a well-run organization should have this information available.

But don't be surprised if this isn't available or is incomplete. Some organizations have sensors recording data, and they're not even sure where the sensors are. It's not possible to assume that any inventory is complete without further investigation, and sometimes, that investigation is not possible. There are many reasons this inventory is not complete, almost all of which involve human error.

2.16   Signatures

A signature is an indicator of a pattern of behavior. It's called a signature because it should be created so that it matches only one specific behavior, like how a written signature should be unique to the person with the pen.

Signatures are used in cybersecurity to find patterns of behavior, whether it is in networks or software. This could be a hash of a file or a known string in a binary that indicates maliciousness. It could be more complex than a single string, such as the indication used for network behavior.

No matter what they are used for, they have a common issue. The signatures will only find patterns that are known; they will not find new patterns. They also need to be kept up to date. Having a collection of signatures that were good last year does not mean that the set is useful this year.

Signatures are also highly dependent upon the pattern chosen. If the pattern is too broad, then it will match everything and can't be considered useful. If it is too narrow, then it won't match anything. Also, signature sets are not a complete set of "every possible malicious pattern," but rather a set of known malicious patterns. It's not possible to know how good the set is or how complete it is; it is just known that someone found this pattern, decided it represented malicious behavior, and added it to the set of signatures. This means that someone must find a pattern before it can be added to the signature set. This does sound obvious, but it also just reiterates the point that the set is a collection of things people found and until someone finds it, it won't be there.

Suppose someone defined a signature for an intrusion detection system (IDS) (Roesch, 1999) as a simple access to a web server. Then every access to a company web server will generate an alert. This is not a useful signature. An old denial of service attack was to send initial Transmission

Control Protocol/Internet Protocol (TCP/IP) packets with the SYN bit set. By looking for just this set of circumstances, it's possible to find this attack.

Another use of a signature set is in the open source tool YARA (French, 2012). YARA's tagline is, "The pattern matching Swiss knife for malware researchers (and everyone else)" (yara). It uses signatures to match software to find malicious software, like the function of anti-virus software. It is useful in that it is a binary signature, meaning it will match against compiled software. This means it's possible to find malicious software without having the source, just by knowing a binary string that is found within the software.

To summarize, signatures are only as good as the creator and aren't a static resource. Using a file hash as a signature for malware will only find that malware that is an exact match. If the malware changes, the signature will no longer work.

2.17   Humans

"Humans" is a much broader category than the preceding sections. In this book, we focus on technical data sources. But everything a computer does at some point traces back to something a human designed or instructed it to do. The human might not have known full consequences of their design choice or instruction, but everything starts with human intentions. Especially when understanding why a computer has done something, security analysts find it useful to understand human behavior or goals.

The kinds of data on or about humans are diverse. You might collect interviews with users about why they prefer not to use encryption, or economic data about how attackers cash out stolen credit cards. A researcher could collect data on how long it takes software developers to use secure coding techniques, or test SOC analyst performance between two versions of a security product interface. Chapter 12 provides examples of how to work with these kinds of data.

2.18   Lessons Learned

Data in cybersecurity has a wide range of possibilities, from data used in and by the network to human-created data such as signatures and incident reports. All of them can be used to research cybersecurity and all have their drawbacks.

It's important to not only understand the process that created the data, but to also understand the potential problems with it. Those problems can cause issues with the research, the method, and the result. Without careful analysis, your research could be for naught.

Cybersecurity makes great use of convenience samples. Almost every data set discussed in this chapter is a convenience sample. We just happened to collect DNS. We just happened to see those incidents and make a record. We just happened to create a signature to add to our IDS to find a network traffic pattern. These are not populations of all the incidents, DNS, or signatures available, they are just the set we happened to run across.

Remember this in your research.

This chapter hasn't been a complete catalog of all possible data that could be used in cybersecurity research. Your research may lead you to using data that isn't listed; you should always analyze the data carefully and ensure that it is complete, comprehensive, and relevant.

Chapter 3

In Search of Truth

"Ground truth" refers colloquially to the actual state of affairs. We think the term is a military or emergency response loan word, where "on the ground" means where the soldiers or responders actually are and what they are actually experiencing. "The ground" contrasts sharply with the plan or the situation room view, which often goes awry. An accurate picture of the ground truth is what any security analyst wants. An analyst's goal should be to accurately understand the situation of interest. Applying scientific methods should get the analyst to ground truth faster, more consistently, or both.

There are several problems with loaning the term "ground truth" into cybersecurity and into scientific practice. Questions about the nature of truth are a classic philosophical quagmire. However, this chapter will pick out just those questions about truth and cybersecurity that end up having a material and important change on what a practitioner should do or expect. It is convenient to split this discussion into those parts related to cybersecurity that it inherits from logic and computing (Section 3.1) and those parts from scientific practice that should be adopted by cybersecurity (Section 3.2).

The consistent result from both parts of the discussion is that *there is no single, unique truth about a cybersecurity event or set of events.* Many people find this conclusion uncomfortable. But science and logic can provide plenty of advice on what an adequate or satisfactory description and explanation of a set of events should contain and provide advice on how to find or produce such explanations. No single, unique truth does not mean anything goes; on the contrary, each satisfactory explanation should constrain and integrate with every other satisfactory explanation. The term for this is *integrative pluralism* (Mitchell, 2003): "pluralism" because there are multiple true viewpoints, and "integrative" because those viewpoints should successfully interact. A practitioner that understands and accepts integrative pluralism will be more flexible and better able to work with the messy reality that is cybersecurity.

3.1   Truth in Cybersecurity

The problem about determining cybersecurity ground truth from looking at computers is that, on their own, computers do not have too much to tell us about cybersecurity. This claim seems strange on its surface. "Cyber" is only about computers, or at least so the popular understanding goes. But "cyber" is much more than about computers, and so is cybersecurity. Cyberspace, if we take the term seriously, is about the shared social construct we humans have built with technological assistance (Pym, 2018).

Whether or not an event is a security event is determined by the organization's security policy.[1] No person can do cybersecurity work without some security policy in mind. A security policy is about what actions are acceptable or not. In one environment, a given configuration of bits on a computer may be a security event, while in another environment, the exact same bits are not a security violation.

It may seem obvious that context matters, but the consequences to the importance of context are both far-reaching and under-appreciated in cybersecurity operations in 2020. "A given configuration of bits" sounds clinical, so let's be more specific. A domain name, say `evil.example.com`, is a given configuration of bits. An IDS signature that identifies a valid File Transfer Protocol (FTP) connection outbound to that domain name identifies a different configuration of bits. Should you use that signature to block traffic? Well, that depends on your security policy. There is not one unique, ground truth answer to the question. That fact makes it rather difficult to evaluate whether an analyst should buy and deploy a set of IDS signatures from this or that vendor; at least, not without declaring that the organization's security policy is merely defined by the vendor's list. Such a declaration may be an efficient risk management decision, or it may be very stupid. It all depends on the context.

Formally, security is a semantic property and "a given configuration of bits" is a syntactic property. To evaluate a semantic property, such as security or truth, we need context (formally, we need a model in which

---

[1] If pressed, we are using these terms with their meanings from IETF RFC 4949. But almost every other security glossary or standard presents a similar story.

we can interpret the syntax). In formal logic, "True" has a very specific meaning (Boolos *et al.*, 2002). Since computers are logic machines, the specific meaning in logic is relevant to cybersecurity. And due to some strange turns in the history of the sciences, formal logic has also influenced how sciences use the term "True." So it is worth a short digression into how formal logic uses the term before discussing ground truth in the sciences.

In a formal logic system, sentences are written in a syntax. A sentence is comparable to a "configuration of bits" mentioned earlier. A sentence can be valid or invalid, which is an evaluation of whether it follows a specified set of rules for which symbols can follow other symbols. This set of rules is the logic's *syntax*. A sentence cannot, quite importantly, be true or false. Almost all logicians follow Tarski and Vaught (1956), who defined truth in terms of model theory. To determine whether a sentence is true or not, one must first specify a model by which the sentence will be interpreted. Formally, a model is a mathematical structure with specific properties. The main point, though, is that the same sentence can be interpreted by different models to reach different truth values. There is no single, unique truth value for a sentence; it depends on the model to bring the appropriate context.

So what does it mean to be logical? The word is often used in a way that implies there is one unique ground truth. However, when someone colloquially talks about whether a person is being "logical," the speaker has specified neither a language nor a model. In common usage, they are probably thinking of Aristotle's predicate logic as the language and the model as the rational numbers. There are other languages and other models that might be reasonable to choose, and they will not all give the same truth values. And Aristotle predates Tarski by a couple of millennia, and Tarski and other logicians have updated what it means to be logical in that time. Those logicians famously include Alan Turing, who dreamt up the idea of the modern computer as a thought experiment to solve a problem in mathematical logic (Turing, 1936).

Computers are logic machines, and there is no unique ground truth in logic. So there is no unique ground truth on computers. There are security policies, which are agreements between humans. Given a security policy and a fully specified computer system, there should be a unique answer to whether the system contains a security violation or not. More specifically, the security policy would need to be complete and well-defined; in practice many policies are neither. And an analyst usually does not know the full specification of every state that a computer system has been in during its

Models in Logic

One example where logic models are relevant to cybersecurity is improving the memory management of programs. The operating system (OS) stack is a set of sentences: move this pointer here, add 1 to the value there, etc. Compilers can catch errors in syntax. They can check whether a line of C code (that is, a sentence) is valid. But we cannot know whether running the program on the stack will have memory leaks or a null-pointer dereference by analyzing the stack. These questions depend on the values the stack variables take during program execution. Memory management checks must be done in the context of what values the variables can or did take. The logic model in which we interpret the stack variables is the heap. A heap gives values to all the variables in the stack, so it functions like a logic model.

There are other ways to construct a logic model (Apt, 1981; Kripke, 1965; Girard, 1987). In fact, there are different ways to construct a logical model of heaps in computer OS's (Calcagno *et al.*, 2011; Bornat, 2000). But we cannot determine semantic properties, such as truth or whether there is a security violation, without a model. The word "model" is used in science and engineering differently than in logic. But the differences are smaller than they appear. A good logic model for this program verification task should represent how the computer OS actually works, just as a good scientific model should represent something about how the system of interest actually works (Pym *et al.*, 2018).

whole history, either. This situation is messy, but that is OK. The sciences have good tools for dealing with messy truths, as long as we do not expect the sciences to magically resolve a messy situation into one unique ground truth.

3.2   Truth in the Sciences

When Americans are taught science in elementary school (or Brits are taught science in primary school), the curriculum is almost always around *the* single scientific method, and how that method leads to *Truth*. This relationship between science and absolute *Truth* is an inheritance from a philosophical movement known as logical empiricism. This idea of "capital T truth" is not the same as the contextual, semantic definition of truth (lowercase T truth) that Tarski defined for logicians. Programmers are familiar with this lowercase version of truth from `if/then` statements. As with cybersecurity, in science a contextual, model-dependent understanding of truth will be more helpful.

Because so many people have had basic science in early education, and that early education is generally still based on logical empiricist ideas, it's worth thinking about what assumptions the logical empiricist movement both requires and provides. Section 3.2.1 provides this historical background and examines two dangerous assumptions within logical empiricism. Section 3.2.2 introduces the viewpoint we will take in this book, which is the prevailing viewpoint in the life and social sciences today.

3.2.1 Philosophy of Science Primer

Philosophy of science[2] is a field that has developed as a discourse on top of science: a reflection upon the operation of the sciences (Uebel, 2016). For three centuries, the scholars we now recognize as scientists were called "natural philosophers," and there was no separate group of philosophers of science. In inter-war Vienna, a group of thinkers who identified as "the Vienna Circle" came to challenge both the prevailing metaphysics and political Romanticism (i.e., the Church and European facism). This movement emphasized themes of observation of the world, trust in science, high value on math and logic, and modernism. A key movement of the Circle has come to be called *logical empiricism*, for its reliance on logical rules based on empirical observations.[3]

We briefly introduce two of the main tenets of logical empiricism: (i) empiricism and verification, and (ii) unity or reduction of scientific fields (Creath, 2014). These tenets coalesced in the 1930s, were refined through the 50s, and by 1970 had suffered ample critiques to be changed beyond recognition. This historical trajectory makes it intellectually dangerous to rely upon logical empiricist arguments or concepts uncritically. Yet, those who rely on our early education's presentation of science often do unknowingly and uncritically rely on these concepts.

Empiricism and verification. Statements testable by observation were considered to be the only "cognitively meaningful" statements (Uebel, 2016). Although logic and mathematics are the most reliable forms of reasoning, logical empiricists did not take them to rely on observation, but instead accepted them as true by definition, following Russell and early

---

[2]This section is a modified version of a similar section from Spring *et al.* (2017).

[3]Logical empiricism is closely related to logical positivism and neopositivism; we will not distinguish these at our level of analysis (Uebel, 2016; Creath, 2014).

Wittgenstein. Therefore, according to the logical empiricist view, the key scientific challenges are how to verify a statement is in fact about the world, and how to meaningfully integrate observations into logic and mathematics. Historically, this is all well before Tarski, so a logical empiricist tends to think of logic as *True*, rather than the model-theoretic and contextual version of truth that is used today. A logical empiricist would view integration between observation and logic as necessary for science to be useful. Integrating observations into deductive logical statements is also a response to David Hume (see the box on Hume's complaint), two centuries earlier, and his famous problem of induction. Hume, in broad strokes, argues that no matter how many times we observe the sun to rise, we cannot prove (in the sense of deductive proof) that the sun will rise tomorrow based on the observations.

In modern terms, induction might be better called "generalization." Justified generalization is still what any cybersecurity analyst wants to be able to do. If you want to know whether some DNS requests are representative of some specific malware command and control (C2) channel, the question is about whether it is justified to generalize from the particulars (the request) to a piece of general knowledge (description of the C2 channel). The premise of this book is that knowing how other sciences have handled this problem of justified generalization should help cybersecurity practitioners. The conclusion of this subsection will be that logical empiricism does not handle it well, which is dangerous because popular understanding often equates science to logical empiricist tendencies.

Empiricism is closely related to verification of empirical facts. Consistent with logical empiricism, Rudolf Carnap proposed a method for *verification* by working on atomic elements of logical sentences, and expanding observational sentences based on rules from atomic observations (Creath, 2014). The goal of empiricism is to be grounded in observations. The goal of verification is to integrate those observations into a framework of general knowledge, in the form of statements in first-order logic, that can justify predictions. Carnap thus links induction and deduction, bypassing Hume's complaint.

Yet it became clear that verification might not always be achievable. It is against this backdrop that Popper proposed the more limited objective of *falsification* (Popper, 1959), which claims we cannot verify logical state-

Will the sun rise tomorrow? Hume's complaint

In 1777, Scottish philosopher David Hume influentially wrote about human understanding. Although he did not have all the answers, Hume has been influential for the questions he raises. For example: What is the difference between perception and knowledge? When do we "know" something rather than think or believe it?

Security practitioners are still asking these questions, though with a bit better nuance. We want to assess whether what we "know" is ground truth, and with what degree of certainty we can use that knowledge to intervene on our systems to prevent or respond to incidents.

Sunrise is the famous surprising example of not-knowledge:

> *"That the sun will not rise to-morrow* is no less intelligible a proposition, and implies no more contradiction than the affirmation, *that it will rise.* We should in vain, therefore, attempt to demonstrate its falsehood. Were it demonstratively false, it would imply a contradiction, and could never be distinctly conceived by the mind."
> (Hume, 1902, §4, §§21; emphasis original)

Hume claims knowledge is Logical and Logic is "conceived" by any mind; observation is not Logical because it involves facts that are neither true nor false ahead of time. These are problematic claims. There is not just one logic (see Section 3.1). In particular, temporal logic evaluates claims about tomorrow (Manna and Pnueli, 1992).

Furthermore, Hume's goal is that perceptions should be True or False, rather than adequately fit a model for a purpose. However, *the sun will not rise to-morrow* is inadequate given our model of the solar system and orbital mechanics; it does not serve the purpose of planning when to wake up. Within this view, *the sun will rise tomorrow* readily counts as (scientific) knowledge.

Yet Carnap and the logical empiricists met Hume's challenge in Hume's view. Many elementary school science classes inherited this limited perspective. Thus Hume's complaint—we cannot readily link perception to absolute "True" law-like generalizations—influences our conception of science. But, as we describe in this chapter, this view is more rigid than is necessary, and that excess rigidity harms our ability to learn.

ments at all. Instead, Popper asserts that the best we can do is hope to falsify them.[4]

In 1962, Kuhn demonstrated that even the more limited goal of falsification is untenable (Kuhn, 2012). Kuhn refutes the premise that scientists operate on logical statements. Rather, he argues that key examples, literally "paradigms," are scientists' operative cognitive model. Later work in the philosophy of science has refined the shape of these cognitive models— one prominent method is as *mechanistic explanations* (Glennan and Illari, 2017)—and improved understanding of how data are processed to provide evidence for phenomena (Bogen and Woodward, 1988).

Even ignoring Kuhn's socio-scientific critique, falsification is about mapping observations into logic. Popper is silent on designing reliable observations and choosing what logic or conceptual framework in which we should reason. These two problems provide more actionable advice than whether something is falsifiable. More useful than falsification are modern discussions of investigative heuristics for scientists (Bechtel and Richardson, 1993), models of when a conclusion from observations is warranted (Norton, 2010), and accounts of causation that make use of intervention and statistics rather than logical implication (Woodward, 2003).

Reduction of science to first principles. Another dangerous tenet of logical empiricism regards the unity of science or the reduction of science to single first principles. There are two senses of unity here that are not often properly distinguished: methodological unity and unity of content by reduction to a single set of models. A unity of methods would mean that, although individual sciences have distinctive approaches, there is some unifying rational observation and evaluation of evidence among all sciences. This view was de-emphasized within logical empiricism. With confusing terminology, modern arguments often return to this idea under mosaic unity or pluralism: the sciences are about widely different subjects, but there are important shared social and methodological outlooks that unify science as an enterprise.

The traditional idea of reductionism is that the set of laws of one science can be logically reduced to that of another (Nagel, 1979). This notion requires the conception of laws as logical rules of deduction. As famously

---

[4]Popper published the idea in German in 1935. The English translation appeared in 1959. Carnap's 1956 work is in part a reaction to Popper. Verificationists against whom Popper reacted include Wittgenstein as early as 1929 (Creath, 2014).

critiqued by Cartwright, the laws of physics are not true explanations of the world, but rather of the models we build of the world (Cartwright, 1983). If laws are about models, and models can be diagrams or small-scale physical replicas, it is unclear how reduction could be defined. Bickle (2008) defines reductionism (in neuroscience) as when a lower-level mechanism contains all the explanatory power necessary to intervene on a higher-level mechanism. Merits of Bickle's view aside, he has disposed of all logical-empiricist ideas of laws, deduction, and verification; he uses the modern concepts of mechanistic explanation and intervention.

Reductionism is dangerous because it tends to blind us from using the appropriate tool for the job. If everything reduces to physics, then we just need a physics-hammer, and everything looks like a nail. But we shall need a more diversified toolbox in a field such as cybersecurity. Social sciences play a role equally important as technical sciences (Anderson and Moore, 2006). The modern terms in philosophy of science are *integrative pluralism* (Mitchell, 2003) or *mosaic unity* (Craver, 2007). The core of these terms is that fields cooperate on adding constraints to coherent explanations according to their particular tools and expertise to painstakingly build out more general knowledge of groups of mechanisms (Spring and Illari, 2018a). Such interfield explanations are what is valuable, not reductions (Darden and Maull, 1977).

Take understanding how a botnet extracts money from its victims as an example of interfield explanations with mutual constraints in cybersecurity. Psychological methods contribute part of the story about how people are deceived by phishing emails. Network science methods contribute to understanding the fast-flux network used to deliver the phishing payload. Software engineering methods contribute to understanding how the vulnerability in the software can be exploited. International finance contributes to understanding which transactions the botnet owners will avoid or seek. Criminological methods contribute constraints on the motivations and organization of the thieves. International law contributes to understanding what methods are available to apprehend and punish the criminals. None of these contributions can be reduced to any of the others, and each of them improves the clarity and detail of the whole model of botnet money laundering.

3.2.2 *Science as a Process*

Science is not a destination. Scientists do not inevitably arrive at Truth. Science is a process. It is a process that, more often than not, gets us better and more useful results than anything else we know of. But it is a process that will have to adapt to cybersecurity. What this process should be, in different contexts, is the primary topic of the rest of the book.

A common pitfall is to treat the terms "scientific" and "correct" as synonyms. Science is a process; a process that yields answers. Answers may be correct or not, based on facts of the world. However, one calls a process "correct" if it follows an agreed-upon, human-defined form. To avoid confusion by overloading the word "correct," we will instead ask whether a process is satisfactory in efficiently producing adequate answers. We should not assume answers are reducible to one "correct" answer; many answers may adequately satisfy a purpose (Simon, 1996). Conflating "scientific" with "correct," and "correct answer" with "adequate," is a result of logical-empiricist assumptions.

If we take this approach, then we do not have to make cybersecurity look like physics in order to talk about doing cybersecurity scientifically. A science of cybersecurity should borrow from other scientific disciplines. But its main focus is to gather evidence about which processes of inquiry and reasoning lead to satisfactory results. Cybersecurity is a diverse discipline, and we expect there to be a diverse pluralism of processes whose results will integrate with and constrain each other.

The idea of all science as a contextual process smooths the adoption of science in cybersecurity. Cybersecurity has to deal with active adversaries. Adversary intent is an important part of the relevant context. We should find it easier to integrate science into cybersecurity if cybersecurity borrows from scientific processes and goals that already are sensitive to context. Such scientific practices are more often found in the life sciences, economics, psychology, and history than they are in physics (of course, there are exceptions to this generalization). In an unfortunate twist of fate, many, if not most, folks in security that are scientifically trained were trained in physics. So the views we present in this book may not be the most commonly espoused science of security views, but for the reasons explained above, we believe they are the most useful ones.

This book follows Spring and Illari (2018a) for the definition of the goal of a scientific process. The goal is knowledge that is somehow general. This takes the form of "clusters of multifield mechanism schemas related along four dimensions" of activities and entities, phenomena, organization, and etiology.

But the practical question practitioners may be more interested in is "when do I stop trying to learn more." There is no easy answer to this question, and it is essentially a question of the economics of information. The question could also be stated as "how much is reducing my uncertainty worth." This question can be modeled formally (Letier *et al.*, 2014; Akerlof, 1970), but the following chapters will help the reader get a heuristic feel for answering this question in different contexts.

We have so far avoided answering the thorny philosophical question of how one verifies that they have ground truth knowledge of a situation of interest. Very loosely, if you can use your understanding based on your model to intervene on or change the system of interest, and in all relevant cases your model accurately predicts the effect of your intervention, then your model is good enough. In cybersecurity, interventions often take the form of access control lists (ACLs), filters, blocking, authentication methods, or other security controls. Interventions may also be remediation actions after an incident to free the system from adversary control. The predicted effect is usually something like the system continues to provide expected services at the expected level, which it presumably would not do if an adversary successfully attacked it.

Science will not provide a cure-all, a panacea, or a silver bullet. Because context matters, a security practitioner can never be sure they have considered all the relevant contexts, or that the way their policy defines an adequate system state is actually what the users of the system will find adequate. There will always be doubts. But an appropriate scientific approach will help you understand and communicate to others when those doubts are justified.

3.3 Recap

From both a computer science perspective and a scientific perspective, there is no single, unique truth about a cybersecurity event or set of events. Instead, the question is whether your model of the situation is satisfactory for your goals. A satisfactory model should respect both the logical and scientific constraints on cybersecurity.

From a logic perspective, an important mistake is when an analyst makes claims without the proper context. Specifically, trying to make semantic (that is, security) claims with only syntactic (that is, a configuration of bits) information. To evaluate security claims, the analyst needs an appropriate or representative security policy. In logic terms, an appropriate model is necessary to provide an interpretation. There are multiple possible logics, and each has multiple possible models; which one is most suitable depends on the analysis goals. There is not a preferred logic which provides the one unique truth of falsity of a statement.

From a science perspective, an important mistake is when an analyst assumes there is just one scientific method that will arrive at just one correct model of a situation. This mistaken view was promoted for years by the historical school known as logical empiricism; many readers likely received some version of this problematic view during early school years. This fact makes it doubly important for any analyst to examine their assumptions about what makes a process an adequate method to arrive at reliable and satisfactory knowledge of a situation. A thorough understanding should integrate results from multiple disciplines and multiple viewpoints.

Chapter 4

Desirable Study Properties

Designing a structured observation is a complex task. This chapter will describe some general properties of structured observations: consistency, generalizability, transparency, and containment. Similar to the consistency, availability, and partition tolerance (CAP) theorem for databases, no one study can provide all of these properties; there must be trade-offs. To fully understand a situation, even in the limited sense of "intervene on or change the system of interest, and in all the cases you care about your model accurately predicts the effect of your intervention" defined in Chapter 3, requires designing multiple structured observations with compensating strengths and weaknesses. While this chapter introduces the properties of a study, Chapter 7 introduces the different types of study that can be designed to accomplish compensating strengths and weaknesses.

Note that while structured observation is a nice formal term, it is a bit of a mouthful and we will often use the term study. These two should be treated as synonyms here. If we mean a case study, we will always say "case study" in full. Case studies are a type of study (that is, structured observation).

This chapter is loosely inspired by the "prudent practices" described by Rossow *et al.* (2012) and desirable characteristics for experimentation in computing (Hatleback and Spring, 2014). The names of the four desirable properties are intentionally broader than those in this prior work. Cybersecurity requires a wide variety of study designs, so we have made an effort to avoid language that implies a certain kind of study. The properties represent ideals and norms about how study design should be done. There are lots of ways in which modern studies may not meet these criteria in every way described here, but these criteria are what should happen. Ideally, any trade-offs for other properties, such as lower cost or expediency, should be clearly and transparently explained.

We will call the person who sets up and conducts the study the "designer." Even with observational studies, the observation is structured and designed. A term like "experimenter" would not capture the role played by the designer in natural experiments or simulations. A term like "researcher" might miss the practical application, but is also a bit passive. The designer of a study must take an active and conscientious role in making sure the study properties meet the designer's needs, whatever they happen to be.

The chapter is organized in four sections, one for each desirable property. The biggest topics are consistency, generalizability, and the tension between the two. Section 4.3 discusses transparency and enumerates the different parts a study should have. Section 4.4 covers the fourth property: containment, or the management of potential harms.

4.1 Consistency

Consistency goes by different names in different types of structured observations. In an experimental setting, it might be called "internal validity" (Hatleback and Spring, 2014). Psychological studies may discuss the related term "construct validity" (Cronbach and Meehl, 1955). The common theme in consistency, or these other terms as appropriate, is that *the study is measuring and responding exactly and exclusively to what the designer believes it to be measuring and responding to.*

To improve consistency, the designer aims to insulate the study from unintended and unknown influences. Consistency can be assessed across time (via repetition) and across space (via reproduction). Some common aspects of a study where consistency can be corrupted are in the study's tools or designer's model of the examined phenomenon. Insulation tends to be antagonistic to generalizability, but the trade-off is somewhat flexible. The rest of this section will discuss each of these aspects in some more detail.

4.1.1 *Insulation*

Insulating a study from external influence means the only factors influencing the results of the study are part of the study. The amount of insulation that the designer needs changes with the type of study. But in all cases, adequate insulation is much easier if the designer knows how the system of interest works. This dependency is problematic because usually the designer wants to study the system precisely because they do not sufficiently understand how it works.

Perhaps the trickiest aspect of evaluating consistency is that the study needs to be insulated from all *relevant* external influence. What is or is not relevant may not be obvious. For studies focused on observation, adequate insulation is achieved when all the relevant observations are recorded with adequate precision and frequency. For studies focused on intervention, adequate insulation is achieved when the intervention is the only factor that influences the outcome. In both of these cases, perfection is never possible. Good practice is to assume there are unknown factors and to analyze the results to estimate the net total influence of any factor that the study did not record. This practice is not foolproof—two unknown factors could be canceling each other out—but it provides important context and a measure of how well insulated a study was.

To design a well-insulated study, it helps to know what other people have found in related scenarios. This strategy helps the designer make new mistakes, rather than just repeat the old known mistakes. Academic studies collecting these insights are called literature reviews or "systematization of knowledge" papers; always consult them on the topic of interest if a relevant one exists. But cybersecurity science is practiced in industry as well, and a study designer should also search the public proceedings of industry consortium events, such as those organized by the Forum of Incident Response and Security Teams (FIRST), the Anti-Phishing Working Group (APWG), the Linux Foundation, and the Internet Corporation for Assigned Names and Numbers (ICANN). If your industry sector has an Information Sharing and Analysis Center (ISAC), your organization is part of an Information Sharing and Analysis Organization (ISAO), or you are in the constituency of a national computer security incident response team (CSIRT), use those resources to learn details specific to your work context.

A designer should approach study design expecting there to be mistakes in insulating the results from expected influence. These can be valuable scientific results! Taking consistent notes, tracking code changes, etc., is the key to pinpointing the exception when it arises. The difference between a useful result and a failed study is whether the designer can pinpoint, or at least suggest, why the study results were impacted by a mistake in some specific aspect of the study. Getting in the habit of taking good notes and documentation from the very beginning is hard. But your future self will appreciate it.

4.1.2 *Consistency Across Time*

Part of consistency is that if the same people use the same equipment to run the same study again at a later time, then the results are all mutually consistent. That is, the result can be replicated. "Mutually consistent" does not mean exactly identical. Rather, it means that they are not at odds with or contradict each other.

One common theme in scientific literature is repeatability. Consistency across time (replication) is only one kind of repeatability: when the same designers use their same equipment, it is replication of the study results. Reproduction is covered under consistency across space, and corroboration is covered in Section 4.2. Repeatability, replication, reproduction, and corroboration are sometimes (unhelpfully) used interchangeably, so when colleagues or authors use the terms, ask whether they are distinguishing between consistency across time, consistency across space, or comparing related studies.

Replication of a result provides evidence of consistency across time. Replication aims to ensure that the design of the study and the tools and instruments used have a stable interaction with the world. This kind of consistency mostly protects the study designer against mistakes, flukes, or some bad assumptions about how the instruments work (Cartwright, 1991). These are basic checks, and while we need a lot more to build solid knowledge of a system or situation, without these basic checks there is nothing upon which to build.

Replication can be challenging in cybersecurity because the network, popular applications, social expectations, and global regulations are constantly changing. These reasons provide plausible explanations for why a network study from 10 years ago will not replicate exactly. But recall that consistency across time means "mutually consistent" results, not identical results. If two studies 10 years apart are not well-insulated from other changing factors in the environment, then we should expect these external factors to influence the results. The two replication attempts may run the same code from the same computer with the same IP address within the same ASN. But to know what results are expected in the later attempt, the designer needs to know how trends in at least six different fields will change the results. If the designer is naïve and does not expect these changes, the replication attempt will produce surprising results. But a better way to think about these two studies is whether they corroborate each other (see Section 4.2). If the environment of the study has changed so much in between attempts, the designer is not actually replicating the old study. They are testing whether their results generalize to the new environment the Internet has evolved into in the intervening time.

An important question for any study is to know the environment's rate of change. Specifically, how much time passes before the designer should be thinking about their work as corroboration rather than replication? There is no simple answer to this question; see the box on stepping in the same river twice. For particle physics, we expect the answer is measured in billions of years. For clandestine Internet marketplaces exchanging stolen goods, the duration may have been two years in 2001 and six months in 2019. For cybersecurity, even the duration that some system is stable may itself not be stable. If you want to use your results to inform future planning or security policy, then it helps to have a system to regularly attempt to replicate them and test to see if they remain stable. In cybersecurity, it is dangerous to assume any results are stable.

4.1.3 *Consistency Across Space*

Consistency across space is maintained if different people in other settings use the same tools and follow the same study procedure and the results are all mutually consistent. That is to say, the results can be reproduced. As with replication, "mutually consistent" does not mean exactly identical.

Reproduction is about trying the study in another setting that should be equivalent to the first setting, based on our models and knowledge of the system of interest. For example, consider a study to test whether a particular IDS signature detects Zeus C2 traffic. The analyst replicated the test on their network over the last week, and for that time period, the results are stable and promising. To reproduce the study, they could share the signature with other similar organizations. If the analyst works at a healthcare provider with multiple hospitals, likely equivalent settings include other healthcare providers in the same region. Equivalence would also expect a similar network architecture for the placement of the IDS and an IDS that uses the same signature format language. The peer hospitals can then reproduce the study on whether the IDS signature adequately detects the C2 traffic.

Reproduction is barely broader than replication. Even so, it provides two important services that are importantly different from replication. Reproduction provides additional witnesses to the result; this increases the credibility the result is a stable interaction between the instruments and

You can't step in the same river twice

Space and time are related, and so consistency across space is related to consistency across time. Any attempt to conduct a study in different places will necessarily also conduct it at different times and vice versa. If we wanted to be excessively pedantic, the Earth is moving rather quickly around the sun, so to conduct a study in the same place would require a rocket ship. But here, again, the word is *relevantly* the same, not identical.

There is a famous phrase attributed to the Greek philosopher Heraclitus (Turkish philosopher, really; he lived in Ephesus). There is some disagreement about his actual words, but the gist may have been *one could not step twice into the same river* (Graham, 2019). The river is defined by change and flux: it is not a lake or a dry riverbed, but flowing water. To be in the same place—the river—at a second time necessitates in some sense that one is not in the same place: the river has changed. Our bodies have a similar nature.

So when this chapter differentiates "consistency across space" from that across time, focus on the relevant similarities. Across time focuses on the same designer trying the same study again. Cross back over the same river again. Across space emphasizes different designers trying the same study in a different "place," where place should more accurately be understood as a different segment of a population that is expected to be the same for the purposes of the study. Cross the river in the same way just a bit upstream or downstream of where the last test was.

Computers and computer networks are also constantly changing at many different levels. Sometimes it is useful to focus on the stability, such as farmers who want to know when the Nile River floods every year. Sometimes it is useful to focus on the changeability, such as a ferry pilot who wants to know the currents and eddies today. When evaluating whether a study in cybersecurity has the right amount of consistency, keep the goals of the study in mind.

the world and also not outright fraudulent. Before buying a product, look for evidence that their marketing claims can be reproduced on your systems.

Secondly, reproduction helps confirm what entities the designer considers to come from the same population. In the IDS example above, there are multiple populations in the study: Zeus malware (as opposed to other malware families), network traffic at the organization-Internet boundary (as opposed to local area network (LAN) traffic or files on a local file system), and healthcare providers (as opposed to other industry sectors). C2 is a network phenomenon, so if the test population were a file system, we would not expect the study to replicate. But some populations are not so easily defined and distinguished. For example, when a malware sample is part of the Zeus family. It is probably too rigid to say Zeus is exclusively the open-source implementation available on GitHub. But how many changes make a sample a different family is a difficult question. For the purposes of the IDS signature example, any change to the C2 protocol would be relevant to the results, whereas wholesale changes to other code sections might not be.

As with replication, a reproduction attempt may be a signal that some-things we expected to be relevantly the same actually have relevant differences. While learning relevant differences would mean the reproduction "failed" in a strict sense, such a finding is a successful improvement of knowledge. The only truly failed reproduction is when the designers cannot distinguish whether the discrepancy is in the study design or in the system of interest. Again, detailed notes and documentation along the way are vital. But if the problem can be localized to the study design, it can be improved. If the problem can be localized to the system of interest and what had been expected to be a single relevant population, then those populations can be studied as separate. However, a sloppy study design would be a failure because then we cannot distinguish these scenarios. Tools, statistics, and models will help avoid sloppy study design, as well.

4.1.4 *Consistency of Tools*

How can anyone tell whether the results of a study are an accident of the tools being used to make the observation or a genuine reflection of the system of interest enabled by those tools? This problem goes back at least as far as telescopes ($\sim$1625 CE) and microscopes ($\sim$1660 CE). But mathematics and logics are also tools, albeit intellectual rather than physical ones (De Millo *et al.*, 1979). So this problem really dates to thousands of years ago, at least to when Euclid and Pythagoras used the idea of a circle or a triangle to study and plan how to make bridges and catapults. But the first person credited with observing micro-organisms (Antonie van Leeuwenhoek in 1676) certainly highlighted the problem. Everyone rightly behaves as though micro-organisms are real, but no one has seen a microbe without the assistance of a tool.

Science and engineering are not actually so separate. If we think of science and engineering as integral, inseparable parts of each other then the question about trusting tools becomes less mystical and more pragmatic (Dear, 2006). The view in a good microscope yields observations that allow people to change the world or create new technology. If the changes or technology function as anticipated, that increases confidence that the observations are true. The microscope itself is a tool, produced by optics and lens crafting, and we have increased confidence the tool will work as expected because we believe the observations and models of optics to be true. Technology promotes science and science promotes technology. Neither the instrumental/pragmatic view nor the philosophical/alethic (the nature of the truth of the statement) view are primary. The instrumental (technology promotes science) and philosophical (science promotes technology) views of science are mutually reinforcing.

Like microscopes, to trust a tool in cybersecurity you should build up interconnected, multidisciplinary sets of evidence based on both pragmatic results and the established models of other areas. The problem is perhaps exacerbated in cybersecurity because everything in the system is a human artifact: the computers themselves, the cultures of security compliance, the criminology of money laundering, the system of network identifiers. To the extent possible, differentiate the objects of study from the tools used to study them.

The tools for studying a system of interest tend to improve iteratively with knowledge of the system. A useful example is the interaction between engineering airplanes and formal fluid dynamics (Vincenti, 1990). The earliest airplanes were not just engineering achievements; they performed in ways that were not explainable by contemporary knowledge. Early airplanes were both tools for moving humans around and tools for probing models of fluid dynamics. The two disciplines improved each other for decades, such as understanding how and why round-head rivets cause turbulence. So we do not expect cybersecurity tools and our understanding of system behavior to reach a steady place any time soon. However, if you have created a new tool, test that it works as expected in some relatively well-known situations before trying it to demonstrate something new.

4.1.5 *Consistency of the Designer's Model*

In order to design and analyze a study adequately, the designer should have three things: (1) a conceptual model they want to improve, (2) methods to avoid systematic biases in the execution of the study, and (3) appropriate formal modeling tools for the analysis. Each of these three topics could be its own book, and these three ideas recur throughout this book. We will briefly address each of them directly in turn here.

In a study, the designer often wants to refine or confirm some aspect of their model of the system of interest. Part of study design is evaluating whether the system model to be tested is internally consistent in the first place. An example of inconsistency would be to expect a malware sample to require a C2 channel to install some specific code, but expecting that code to be necessary for establishing a C2 channel. This would lead to an unresolved dependency in the malware function. It would be a waste of time to design a study to see if this fictitious model described some malware family because the model itself is inconsistent.

The most suitable methods for building and checking conceptual models of systems for cybersecurity are often those from the life sciences. Although the devil is in the details, the heuristics from the life sciences can be summarized as decomposition and localization (Bechtel and Richardson, 1993). Decompose the system of interest into expected or known entities. Localize the expected or known operations or properties of the system to those entities. Then, attempt to isolate the entities and observe to what extent they exhibit those operations or properties. Organizing the entities and understanding similarities are useful further steps (Glennan and Illari, 2017), but decomposition and localization are the start.

Humans have a tendency to unduly anchor on the first piece of information or idea they have about a situation. This tendency can cause problems in various kinds of analysis. In a scientific endeavor, it may mean the designer anchors on their initial hypothesis and will not let it go even though the study results indicate the hypothesis is not supported. It might mean anchoring on early promising pilot results even though a later, more comprehensive study indicates there is no reliable result. In cybersecurity, as in other adversarial analysis, it might mean the analyst believes what their adversary wants them to believe rather than what a full reading of the facts would indicate (Heuer, 1999).

Pursuing science must be, at its core, a humble endeavor. Although history contains many examples of pompous scientists, this is not the path to good science. Humility means, among other things, always being open to being mistaken. Accepting mistakes gracefully, and surrounding yourself with others who do, helps to avoid getting stuck on the initial hypothesis or initial result. To produce a consistent study and consistent results, a designer must make use of the best available data, not the first available data.

The most important page on the Internet

The page title, *List of cognitive biases*, is unassuming. The distinctive Wikipedia template is not flashy. It is an exacting and exhaustive list of the ways in which your brain will fool you. If your response to the preceding sentence is, "I am my brain, it could not fool me," or "I am a very learned and rational individual who does not fall for any tricks," then you have not spent enough time reading the resources cataloged there. Have a look now: `en.wikipedia.org/wiki/List_of_cognitive_biases`.

What is your model of how your own thinking works? Do you think of your brain as a computer, rigorously and carefully moving from one logical statement to its implication? For better or worse, brains do not work that way. Probably for better; many of the biases likely are heuristics developed over the course of evolution because they kept humans alive. If a 100% accurate answer takes 5 seconds to compute, but there is only 1 second before the predator attacks or the prey escapes, it is explainable that a 90% solution calculable in half a second has become the dominant way brains work. Psychologists have documented hundreds of these heuristics/biases for as many diverse situations.

If a person is going to do anything—solve a cybersecurity problem, navigate a job interview, or overcome a traumatic life event—it helps to know how a brain works. We cannot generally change how it works wholesale. But we can be aware of when the brain's heuristics are working with us toward our goal, and when the brain's biases will work against our goals. In the latter case, formalizing methods and procedures that will lead to the goal are valuable. Statistical analysis properly established is one example. But there is no replacement for self-awareness. Cognitive biases are often unavoidable, but the only way to question and check our thought process is to be aware of how it can go awry and seek to mend it.

We discuss common logical fallacies in cybersecurity in Section 8.6.

There are many important aspects of formal modeling of a study and its results; the relevant aspect for consistency is that the formalism itself is repeatable by others. This property is distinct from replication or reproduction of the study itself, and is often discussed as *statistical reproducibility* (Stodden, 2015). Statistics play an important role in generalizability and corroboration, which is the focus of the next section. Here, the point is just that the statistics or formal modeling themselves need to be consistent and repeatable; what these statistics indicate about the repeatability of the study as a whole is another matter. Even this seemingly small matter can be exceedingly tricky.

For the model to be consistent, if someone else performs the statistical or formal analysis of the study, they should get mutually consistent results. There are many analysis choices, such that even different groups of professional statisticians who analyze exactly the same data can reach incompatible conclusions (Silberzahn *et al.*, 2018). Therefore, the designer must not only make these choices carefully, but document them so that others can understand the modeling choices. This discussion and care are particularly important when developing a machine learning (ML) model (Spring *et al.*, 2019).

4.1.6 *Relationship to Generalizability*

Generally, more focus on consistency of a study means less focus on its generalizability. The reason is that more consistency usually means more control and more insulation from external factors. Generalizability involves connecting the study results to external factors. However, this trade off is not one-to-one; while insulation and connection are opposed, aspects of consistency such as that of tools or models are not directly related to whether the study's results are more generally applicable. Aspects of consistency related to repeatability do not directly support generalizability, but they do enable further studies to probe the extent to the which the results apply.

Certain types of study are optimized for high insulation. Highly insulated studies are often valuable, but they are most valuable when paired with different studies that are optimized for connection. Certain traditional types of study design occupy different places on this continuum between insulation and connection. Section 7.2 will discuss types of studies. But there are three more desirable properties of scientific studies to introduce first.

4.2 Generalizability

Generalizability is a cluster of related and overlapping concepts, and it may have different names in different types of structured observations. *External validity* is specifically about whether the results of the study apply outside the study, whereas *ecological validity* is about whether the topic of the study is something that actually occurs in the world. Transferability is a related term sometimes used about case studies. The common theme of generalizability is *the study provides results that are applicable to the world outside the study in a clear and reliable way.*

To improve generalizability, the designer connects the study with the part of the world that is of interest as much as plausible. Such connection tends to reduce insulation from unintended and unknown influences, and so is antagonistic to consistency. Generalizability can be assessed by comparison between results of different studies; one indicator of generalizability is how specifically and carefully the designer has stated the target population to which the results are intended to generalize. Some places a study might have problems arise with generalizability are mismatches between the study's population and the target population or errors reasoning with the results of the study. The rest of this section will elaborate on these topics.

4.2.1   *Connection to External Factors*

The general goal of connection is to make sure that the results of the study are not merely an artifact of the study design. This goal applies to all types of studies; some examples of how results can be an artifact of study design are as follows. In a case study or interview, often the mere presence of an observer changes the behavior of the people being studied. For surveys, there are a variety of well-known ways that the structure, order, and phrasing of questions influence the outcomes (Diamond, 2011, §IV). A simulation may not apply to any real scenario. a randomized controlled trial (RCT) intentionally creates an artificial setting, disconnecting aspects of the system from external factors; in such cases, it usually requires a separate study to evaluate whether the insulated laboratory results are in evidence outside the laboratory (that is, the *ecological validity* of the RCT).

Connection to external factors is also about actively connecting the results to the world, not just about avoiding a situation where the result is an artifact of the study. This connection takes a variety of forms in cybersecurity. For example, in studying the usability of security measures, it is important that the study subjects have both a primary task and a realistic experience of risk (Krol *et al.*, 2016). Otherwise, the study will be too disconnected from the real situations in which users make decisions; such disconnection means the results cannot generalize to any situation outside the study. A similar disconnect happens if network traffic data or host activity in studies or personnel training exercises are not simulated to very carefully mimic actual traffic. Anonymization of network traces disconnects the traffic from the real world for privacy reasons. How to anonymize in a way that preserves the important functional and reputation information an analyst can often derive from the real identifiers remains an open research question.

The rest of this generalizability section continues the theme of actively connecting a study to other contexts, contributing to and supporting more general knowledge. Corroboration is related to the concepts of replication and reproduction that were covered in Section 4.1, but an attempt at corroboration is an initial probe of whether the results generalize to similar contexts. Defining the extent of expected generalization is a way of describing what populations the designer expects their results to connect to and those to which they do not expect to connect. There are formal and conceptual tools that help structure and test generalization and avoid human cognitive biases; we discuss statistics and mechanism schema as two important examples.

4.2.2 *Comparing Studies*

One kind of evidence that the results of a study generalize is whether other independent but related studies corroborate it. Studies can be designed intentionally to corroborate a prior study; in this case, corroboration is a kind of repeatability test (Feitelson, 2015). Corroborating studies do not use the same equipment, the same people, or exactly the same study design; rather, they examine either the same system of interest in a slightly different way or a slightly different system of interest in the same way. If the results are mutually consistent (that is, they do not contradict each other), then the two studies corroborate each other. Corroboration does not automatically mean both studies are true, but it is a positive piece of evidence.

Systematic errors in study design can sometimes manipulate the appearance of corroboration even though none of the interrelated studies are actually generalizable. For example, animal models, such as mice, have systematic limitations in emulating human cancers, and so research on human cancer in animals is often unsuccessful and the research's successes systematically (though accidentally) leave areas unstudied (Mak *et al.*, 2014). In cybersecurity, erroneous corroboration results may result from un-careful use and comparison to blocklists (Metcalf and Spring, 2015). If the blocklist architect changes what activity they are looking for or where they are looking from, the identifiers to block change almost entirely. This result indicates that judging whether one account of malicious activity corroborates another by merely looking for shared identifiers on a blocklist is implausible without a lot of other information about why those blocklists should be the

same. Usually blocklists are not the same; that is, they are not expected
to overlap.

Systematic corroboration should be encouraged. In situations where
extensive RCTs are viable, a meta-analysis of comparable RCTs provides
statistical tools for assessing the extent to which a hundred or so studies
inter-corroborate each other. Cybersecurity is not currently suited to such
analysis; cybersecurity may never be suited to meta-analysis of RCTs given
the rapidly changing technical state of the Internet, diversity in cultural uses
of different parts of the Internet, and diversity of security policies for evaluating the risk of events. At least, setting an adequately shared scope would
be a serious challenge. For this reason, we encourage the use of more conceptual generalization tools. Re-situation of results through metaphors (Morgan, 2014) and generalization via clustering mechanism schema (Spring and
Illari, 2018a) are two options (see Section 4.2.4).

4.2.3 *Extent of Generalization*

Generalization is about arguing that the results observed on the study population apply to populations outside the study. Let's call the population
outside the study the *population of interest*, which we wish to learn about
by conducting the study. There are three useful steps in arguing the population of interest is included within the extent of generalization of the
study results. Firstly, precisely and accurately define the population of interest. Secondly, carefully and transparently select the population in the
study when designing a study. Thirdly, argue why the selected population
is representative of the population of interest in all the ways relevant to the
study's results.

A population is any collection of units that are part of some collection
and can be enumerated. This formal definition expands the elements of
a population beyond people to include computers, network packets, pay-
ment attempts, etc.; any group of equivalent units will do. Precisely and
accurately defining a population of interest can be tricky. Precise means
exclusively the units of interest are included by the description. Accurate
means all the units of interest are included by the description.

Consider an example population of interest, "all servers owned by the
organization," and the example description "all open ports lower than 1023
found by an nmap scan of the corporate network on Friday." The description may not be precise if workstations or devices owned by visitors
mistakenly have those ports open. The description may not be accurate
if there are cloud-based or other off-premises servers owned by the organi-

zation. Network scanning accuracy in particular can also be impaired by filtering policies, timing, odd protocol interactions, and scanning methodology (Bano *et al.*, 2018). Determining the adequacy of a description of the population of interest may deserve its own small pilot study before moving on to designing the selection of the study population.

The way that the study designer selects the study population sets a kind of upper limit on the extent of generalization, though other aspects of study design (discussed in this section) could further restrict generalizability. The extent of generalization possible is primarily dependent on the selection method, sometimes called a sampling plan. We prefer "selection" methods here to help keep population selection methods distinct from sampling methods used in statistical analysis discussed later. That selection is actually executed properly in accordance with the method and such practical things are also necessary, but we focus on the basic selection method types. There are situations where each method can be appropriate, but random selection methods (stratified or simple random) have more generalizability from the study population to the population of interest. Chapter 6 has more detail on executing sample selection methods.

Volunteer selection means publicizing the existence of the study and soliciting volunteers to participate. The resulting population will not inherently generalize at all. At best it is a sample of those that received the notification of the study, and there is rarely a way to link that population to the population of interest. Participants also get to choose to participate, which introduces variable effects of inducements or payments (people with less wealth may be more likely to respond) as well as non-participation choices based on any number of personal situation, comfort, ability, or emotional variables. Volunteer sampling is appropriate in a situation where the volunteers themselves are a meaningful population of interest and/or the main goal of the study is to demonstrate that an effect exists at all, not the extent to which that effect generalizes.

Convenient selection is characterized by the study designer including whatever participants are convenient. In a retrospective or historical study, this choice may be based on the limits of data collected in the past. Similar to volunteer selection, convenient selection is best when the study population itself is of interest or the goal is to demonstrate the possibility of a result. If enough information is collected about the study population it may be possible to make very limited or tentative generalizations at least as hypotheses to test in future studies.

Snowball selection starts with an initial population item, studies it, and uses that member of the population to find new members to study. Snowball selection (or sampling) is often used to access hard to reach populations of interest (Faugier and Sargeant, 1997). Such populations are resistant to accurate random sampling methods for various reasons. Snowball sampling is the term in sociological research, but the concept is similar to "indicator expansion" or "pivoting" used by threat analysts to start with one suspicious indicator and use network or host logs to connect to further suspicious indicators (Spring, 2013). As with volunteer and convenient selection, it is not usually possible to generalize from a sample collected by snowball selection. For something like threat hunting, generalization is not the goal. The population of indicators found via indicator expansion *is* the population of interest.

Simple Random selection takes the whole population of interest and systematically selects a subset of the population in which each member of the population has the same likelihood of selection into the study population. If all these conditions are met, then the results on the study population can be generalized within well-defined statistical bounds to the population of interest. However, two points require a lot of care to execute properly: (1) enumerate the population completely and (2) ensure each member of the population has equivalent likelihood of selection.

Stratified selection involves separating the population of interest into distinct, non-overlapping subgroups (called strata) and then conducting a simple random selection within each stratum. The criteria on which the strata are separated are some features that are expected to influence the outcome of the study. The purpose of stratification is to have balanced or proportional representation of these features in the study population when a simple random sample would not deliver it.

Census is a selection method where the study is performed on all members of the population of interest. Actually reaching an entire population is a large challenge; for human populations it tends to require resources on par with a national government. Organizations such as `shodan.io` and The Measurement Factory attempt to conduct censuses of different Internet-accessible devices. The extent to which they have actually captured the whole population of interest is an open research question. Despite the challenges, the clear benefit of a census is that, by definition, the results apply to the population of interest.

The final step is to argue the extent to which the study population relevantly represents the population of interest. This step is important because the population from which the selection was taken is almost never exactly the population of interest. For example, there are systematic differences between how a phone survey, Internet survey, and survey of viewers of a particular media outlet represent the population of citizens of a country. For example, phone surveys are sampled from everyone who has a landline and answers calls from unknown numbers, which is different from people with cell phones and different from all citizens (Kennedy *et al.*, 2016).

Handle with care any study that claims to generalize to *all* people, networks, computers, etc. Section 4.2.5 will help identify where such broad claims often go awry.

4.2.4 *Generalization Tools*

Formal and conceptual tools help structure generalization. Formally, the usual tool is statistical reasoning and inference. Fitting to mathematical models more broadly is an important strategy, but statistical tools are particularly important because they are the main method for measuring how well the data or study results match the mathematical models. The conceptual tool we describe as an example is mechanistic reasoning about which decompositions and organizations of the system of interest are supported by the study results.

Statistics, at heart, is a way to express and quantify uncertainty (Kadane, 2011). Statistical tools help a study designer manage and process the uncertainties in any given study. To do so, the designer must be able to carefully express specifically what they are uncertain about. To express uncertainty well requires a kind of honesty with oneself, but it is only through such honesty that uncertainty can be expressed, measured, and understood.

This book cannot give even a basic introduction to statistics; see for example (in order from most philosophical to most applied) Kadane (2011), Gelman *et al.* (2020), Metcalf and Casey (2016), or Davidson-Pilon (2020).

Instead, our goal is to situate statistical tools within their role in study design and hopefully impart why it is important to use them well and appropriately in Chapter 5. In brief, every aspect of consistency and generalization we discuss, and containment in Section 4.4, has some aspect of uncertainty. Insulation, replication, reproduction, corroboration, connection: the extent to which any given study meets these criteria is uncertain. Statistical methods are valuable tools for managing that uncertainty. This chapter focuses on study design principles because a designer needs to know what principles are important before they can determine whether statistical analysis about those principles is necessary.

To some extent, a study designer need not know how to craft the statistical tools, just how to understand them. Especially if the designer is lucky enough to work with a professional statistician. If you do take this route, and effectively outsource this aspect of your study design to a colleague, then make sure you consult them during your study design and not simply after you have done your data collection. Statistics is not magic; it will not fix a "garbage in, garbage out" sort of problem.

Mechanistic generalization is a way of creating connections between systems of interest based on their entities, activities, organization, the system schema, and/or the history of the system (Spring and Illari, 2018a). It is a predominant mode of reasoning in the life and social sciences (Glennan and Illari, 2017). As such, like statistical tools, we can only introduce the basic purpose here. See Parkkinen *et al.* (2018) for an accessible introduction. We believe that mechanistic reasoning is appropriate for security because, like the life sciences, cybersecurity studies complex, interconnected, idiosyncratic systems, it studies nested layers of organization, and it studies regulatory feedback loops.

In loose terms, data or files are an entity and executing code is an activity (Hatleback and Spring, 2018). These terms are loose because any conventional executing code was a file at some point. So, as with logics and truth, context matters in analyzing generalizability as well.

Mechanistic reasoning is a helpful generalization tool because it allows the analyst to flexibly incorporate context. It also mimics the programming principle of encapsulation. Any system of interest can be modeled as simply an entity with its input/output activities or more complexly as an organization of entities and activities that produce those behaviors in specific ways. The schema is the more general shape of entities, activities, and organization, abstracted away from their particulars. Generalization can be sought as other situations where the same schema applies, though it is filled in with different details or other situations where nearly the same schema applies. If cybersecurity were just about bits on disk, this may not add much, but since mechanistic reasoning has a history in the social sciences, it allows us to integrate the human, economic, and technical aspects of the system of interest in one conceptual toolbox.

The goal of a scientific enterprise usually includes knowing how a system of interest works. What does it mean to know it, though? One adequate way to know a system is to have a complete, fully specified mechanism for it. So in an important way, each aspect of this chapter is to help a study designer have better mechanistic knowledge of the system of interest than before the study.

4.2.5 *Common Generalization Errors*

Before moving on to transparency, we touch on three common mistakes in study design and analysis related to generalization. These are far from the only mistakes one could make, but they are three of the more costly ones: (1) systematic bias in the available population data, (2) mistaken assumptions about the population of interest, and (3) abuse of statistical tools.

The population available to study may not adequately represent the population of interest. A stratified selection method can help resolve such problems, but the study designer needs to know the relevant factors on which to stratify the selection ahead of time. As ML becomes more popular, this problem is ever more present. The main examples are from non-security ML examples so far, but they are instructive of what uncritical generalization from the study population can lead to. For example, an image processing study to "identify all images with wedding dresses" will have linguistic and cultural difficulties. Usually, the English word "wedding dress" would be associated with a white garment because Queen Victoria popularized that fashion in the mid-1800s. But many wedding dresses are red (Zou and Schiebinger, 2018), and these are systematically under-represented in common image training sets. Therefore, a study on white, Victorian wedding dresses will not actually generalize to *all* wedding dresses. Two solutions should both be applied: stratified selection for data-intensive studies and more precise and restrictive descriptions of the population of interest.

A related problem is mistaken assumptions about the population of interest. Psychology is battling an entrenched version of this mistake at present that directly affects how cybersecurity practitioners should understand and interact with system users. Psychological studies tend to be conducted on people from Western, educated, industrialized, rich, and democratic (WEIRD) populations (Henrich *et al.*, 2010). WEIRD populations are systematically unlike other populations, and psychology has for a long time mistaken findings culturally specific to WEIRD as universal human traits (Nielsen *et al.*, 2017).

Cybersecurity studies and advice have inherited this generalization error from psychology (Krol *et al.*, 2016). Any claim that all users behave a certain way are suspect. But even a more restricted claim, such as 62% of users do something silly, should be interrogated. Ask questions such as which kinds of users, how were they selected for the study, with what demographics, etc. Ergonomics has known for a long time that, although one can calculate the "average" features of an "average person," or even specifically an average US Air Force pilot, no individual actually matches that "average" person (Hertzberg *et al.*, 1954). Systems should be designed to fit a variety of body types and mental types. We expect that although there may be an "average" Windows installation, there is actually a wide variety of fielded systems. Cybersecurity will need to accept and handle this diversity of both humans and machines rather than trying to collapse it to a universal average and then generalize.

The most widespread abuse of statistical tools involves significance testing and p-values; the problem is so widespread that the American Statistical Association has requested scientists stop using these concepts in studies (Wasserstein *et al.*, 2019). "Statistically significant" has a precise meaning within statistics that is almost never used correctly in studies. Any time statistical methods are used as an up-and-down test of whether study results are true or should be accepted is an abuse of statistics. These abuses of statistics lead to a mistaken belief that the results of a study generalize to a larger population than is actually the case. A more in depth discussion about how to avoid these problems can be found in Chapter 8.

This section has presented a complex, nuanced description of generalizability and some of the study design features that can provide it. There is no easy statistical method to either reduce that analysis to a single number or test whether it has been achieved.

4.3 Transparency

There are many aspects in which a study should be transparent: the design methodology, the study design itself, the data collection, the results of the study, how the results were analyzed, and the interests the authors or their funders may have in the results of the analysis. Transparency is a multifaceted concept within each of these aspects. The facets are captured well by borrowing from the oath for sworn legal testimony: we want the true description, the whole description, and nothing but the true description. Transparency is generally from the researcher to their audience, but it also might mean members of the research team are transparent with each other, or a researcher taking good notes and being transparent with their future self. This subsection focuses on each of these facets of transparency in turn, exploring particular ways that a good researcher might nonetheless come to undermine them.

4.3.1 *Design Methodology*

An accurate or true design method description should include how the study designer identified the problem, a clear statement of the research question(s), what problems are related but how they are different, how related problems have been addressed in the past, and why the study design is reasonable based on this past work. This should go without saying, but the study designer should not fabricate the description of the method. A true description includes documenting any mistakes or oddities that arose during the execution of the method.

Capturing the whole method is less intuitive. Any exploratory study or pilot study conducted to inform the final study design should be included. Such intermediate results not only shaped the design process, but also could highlight ways biases were introduced or eliminated from the study population.

Avoiding extraneous details helps the clarity of the description. When reporting or discussing a study, it is good practice to have the method as a description separate from the results; the results should also be separate from a discussion of the meaning or usefulness of the results. The different parts of the methodology (study design, data collection, etc.) should have their own sub-parts of the methodology description. This regimentation serves two purposes. First, and most importantly, it serves as a checklist for the study designer to make sure they have considered and clearly conceptualized each necessary part of the study. The second purpose is to explain to others transparently. It is vital that research be reported to others, but a vital purpose of this explaining is simply that the study designer will have to order their thoughts in order to explain to others, which is tremendously helpful ensuring a good study design in the first place.

4.3.2   *Study Design*

Transparency in study design means explaining the mechanics of the study. The necessary mechanics to describe are dependent on the study type. For details about what should be described for each study type, see Section 7.2. The basic idea is to describe how the study properties of consistency, generalizability, transparency, and containment are expressed in the study.

4.3.3   *Data Description and Collection*

The most transparent description of the data used in the study is to provide all the data open-source. To discuss the data, the designer should provide some summary description of what data are available, how they were collected, how the study population was selected from the available population, the relationship to the population of interest, and any errors or anomalies in data collection.

There are various reasons why it may not be possible to share the whole data set. When interviewing users, it is may be acceptable to share sanitized transcripts of the interviews, but researchers should not share the personal information of the study participants. Technical artifacts may also consist of sensitive data that has some legitimate reason not to be shared. If this is the case, the designer will need to explain what that legitimate reason is, why the study is valuable anyway, and how the provided description is transparent enough that a reader or listener can both understand all the important aspects of the data and be assured that the study designer has in fact competently completed the study. These considerations apply to case studies, natural experiments, and intervention-based trials equally.

In addition to the data and the whole description of the data, it is important to describe what is excluded from the study. If outlier data points have been excluded, this needs to be clearly stated along with the method for how outliers were identified, preferably in enough detail that someone else could do the outlier detection and reach equivalent results. In interviews or surveys, excluded data are not "outliers," but partially or erroneously completed forms. But as with outliers, these should be described with reasons and enough detail that someone else could repeat the decisions.

4.3.4   *Study Results*

A transparent accounting of the results should provide the end-product of executing the study method. The exact form this takes will vary based on the study type. Many researchers are tempted to only include the "interesting" results when reporting. This bias in reporting results introduces myriad subtle problems. Limiting results to the "interesting" ones takes those results out of context. Manipulating the context makes results look more interesting than they really are; it also makes them misleading and deceptive.

Cherries are tasty, but cherry-picked results are awful

Suppose you've created a method to detect malware. After much work, you determine your method is 99.9% effective. That is, out of 1,000 pieces of malware, it identifies 999 correctly. This is a very good method.

However, when you test it against samples that aren't malware, it identifies it as malware 10% of the time. You have a 10% false positive rate for your method. If you omit reporting this result, then you are manipulating your results and only reporting the interesting fact that your method is correct in identifying known malware 99.9% of the time.

The problem with selective reporting of results like this is that both values, along with the base-rate at which malicious files occur in the real environment, are necessary to know the alarm error rate (Axelsson, 2000). Alarm error is a question about alerts that an analyst gets in their queue or dashboard: if the malware detector produces an alert, what are the chances it is actually malware and not a false positive?

Say the system scans 1 million files. If it is quite a high risk system, it might see 1% (10,000) that are actually malware. From the remaining 990,000, at a 10% false positive rate the system will produce 99,000 alerts and correctly ignore 891,000. The system will also correctly alert on 9,990 of the malicious files. So there will be 108,990 alerts, 91% (99,000) of which are a waste of time and resources. The system is basically useless, despite its seemingly impressive 99.9% detection rate. If you plan to buy or use a system, ask about the alarm error first.

A results section is not the place to comment on how the results related to the research question. The results should be presented as neutrally as possible, and the analysis of the results is where to discuss the status of the research question(s) in relation to the results. This regimentation serves the same two purposes as the rest of the transparent description. It is clearer for a reader or listener. But more importantly, it helps keep the psychology of the study designer separated from the results themselves. This separation helps make space for careful analysis and gives the study designer a chance to reflect on potential anchoring bias or other disruptions to clear reasoning (see Section 4.1).

4.3.5 *Analysis of Results*

Transparency in the analysis, first and foremost, should give a clear answer about the status of the research question(s). Clear does not necessarily mean decisive. A clear answer will indicate which aspects of uncertainty about the research questions have been constrained, why that conclusion is justified, and which aspects of uncertainty remain for future work.

To provide the whole analysis, a study designer should be honest about what did not work and when the results cannot be used as hoped (to bear on the research question). Such shortcomings may actually lead to insights about the system of interest or study design in the situation that were not previously understood. It is also possible the study design was not up to community norms, in which case the study designer will need to be honest, take it as a learning opportunity, and improve for the next study.

Most research raises more questions than it answers. This phrasing of an analysis of results sounds dismissive, and we prefer a different phrasing. Reducing uncertainty about a broad research question usually means localizing remaining uncertainty into other, better defined questions. Although in some strict sense there are more questions than the start, the quality of the questions and what we know about the system of interest have both improved. If uncertainty about the research question(s) has been reduced or constrained, then the study was a success.

Finally, part of transparency should include explaining why anyone should care about the results. Explaining the study itself is the primary point of transparency. But how the results should change current behavior or beliefs is also important.

4.3.6 *Conflicts of Interest*

Studies are rarely conducted without funding. And studies are done by real humans, with real interests. These can never be eliminated, so the study designer should be transparent about them. In general, it's good practice to be skeptical if a study's results align too neatly with the interests of those funding it. The study itself may be adequately designed and executed while lacking context because organizations tend not to choose to fund studies that may yield results contrary to their interests. Such patterns are discernible in larger bodies of funded work as long as funding and conflicts of interest are declared.

4.4 Containment

Containment is about containing harms: both limiting harm the study, especially experimental interventions, does to participants and limiting harm to the wider world that the study may cause. The best source for guidance on containment in cybersecurity is the Menlo Report (Dittrich and Kenneally, 2012). It's based on the landmark report that established experiment design review for the life sciences. The four principles the Menlo Report identifies and adapts to cybersecurity are respect for persons, beneficence, just and fair distribution of effort and harm, and respect for law and public interest. A prerequisite for all of these is identifying stakeholders. We add a sixth topic, which is a cautionary tale about the risks that secrecy or secretive studies pose to adequate containment.

If a study will be done by university faculty or staff, many countries require prior approval by a research ethics board (REB) or Institutional Review Board (IRB). This approval is that containment is adequate. However, many cybersecurity researchers do not work in environments where formal review is required. And even in academic institutions where it is required, the REB or IRB likely predominantly deals with studies in the life sciences and may not have deep expertise in cybersecurity. Ultimately, the study designer is responsible for proper containment of harms. Lack of formal or effective review does not absolve a designer of this responsibility.

4.4.1 *Identifying Stakeholder Perspectives*

Stakeholders are anyone potentially affected by the study. Stakeholders include some obvious and some less obvious groups. Those directly affected by the study may include the researchers, human study participants, and users of computer systems being studied. Especially if a study will test or probe an operational system, the owner, operator, and users of that system should be consulted (perhaps in the form of the system's acceptable use policy).

Stakeholders do not just include those who might be affected by the execution of the study, but also by the publication and dissemination of the study results. Users of a service may be affected by a change precipitated by a study involving the service, for example. Malicious actors, government organizations, and society at large are also each potentially affected by studies, especially those studying misuse, abuse, or criminal behavior involving the Internet. But mathematical research in cryptography has potentially a broad set of stakeholders as well.

Within this broad set of stakeholders, a designer should take special care to identify vulnerable stakeholder groups. Containment of harm is not simply additive, by which we mean it is not enough to ensure the average harm is low enough. If harm falls unfairly or unjustly on some stakeholder group, the designer needs to adequately consult and protect that stakeholder.

4.4.2 *Respect for Persons*

The minimum expected respect for persons involves two tenets: treat humans as individual autonomous agents and adequately protect those persons with diminished autonomy. The key research practice that embodies respect for autonomy is *informed consent*. The Menlo Report defines informed consent as a "process during which the researcher accurately describes the project and its risks to subjects and they accept the risks and agree to participate or decline" (Dittrich and Kenneally, 2012, p. 7). In human subjects research, seeking informed consent can get tricky, but when the affected users are occasional users of a remote computer network, seeking informed consent may be difficult. If research results are expected to affect a wider aspect of society, the study designer should also consult with some representatives of that group; depending on the harms to an organization or group, some authorized representative (such as general council or the CEO) may also need to consent. Nonetheless, difficulty of obtaining consent is never a valid excuse for violating that consent.

In cybersecurity studies involving human participants, one challenge involves providing a realistic risk to make the evaluation of the participant's security behavior realistic enough to be worth studying (Krol *et al.*, 2016). Realistic risk may mean not fully informing the participant about the goal of the study in advance. There is a body of ethical norms around when it is acceptable to deceive study participants, but they always involve prior approval and carefully debriefing the participants afterwards. The process involves not only telling the participants the true nature of the study, but also monitoring that the stress or deception involved has not in fact unduly harmed participants. If it has, the study will have to be stopped, redesigned, and restarted.

Users of any system under study should also give consent. In general, this means a study should not interfere with any system operations. As a specific example, malware research should not wantonly allow malicious code to replicate and infect the Internet (Rossow *et al.*, 2012). If a researcher discovers a vulnerability in a system, it should be disclosed to whoever is best able to fix the system. If those parties are unresponsive, third party vulnerability coordinators such as CERT/CC should be contacted for assistance. For guidance on coordinated vulnerability disclosure, see Householder *et al.* (2019).

A study may also collect information that discloses private or sensitive information about persons. It is generally not possible to obtain consent from every person who might be identified by a data set or collection of data. The appropriate containment strategy in such situations is to restrict access to the data or only share anonymized data. Since this protection is at odds with transparency (Section 4.3.3 in particular), and anonymization is at odds with generalizability (Section 4.2.1 in particular), there is no easy answer to this balance.

Some aspects of containment should seek the informed consent of the group within society. For example, when ML algorithms are deployed to make decisions related to a population, that population should be consulted. If the impact of the work is localized to members of an organization, such as a labor union or users who enter into terms of service, then it's possible to seek informed consent through those mechanisms. As Section 4.4.4 will discuss, this is not always possible. If a study or tool will impact a section of society from which informed consent cannot be effectively obtained, then the study designer has a duty to actively demonstrate that harm is prevented.

4.4.3 *Beneficence*

Beneficence, in broad strokes, means the study does more good than harm. However, this simple statement hides extensive complexity; discussion of beneficence consumes more space in the Menlo Report than any of the other principles under discussion. The main questions are: (1) What stakeholders are expected to realize what benefits? (2) What stakeholders are expected to realize what harms? (3) How are benefits maximized? (4) How are harms minimized? (5) What are the plans to mitigate a harm when it does occur?

Benefits and harms should be identified systematically. Section 4.4.1 discussed stakeholder identification. Good stakeholder identification is a prerequisite for systematic identification of benefits and harms. "Systematic" here means that the study designer should be able to write out or express their search procedure for identifying benefits and harms. As with other methods within a study, this transparency provides others an ability to comment, but more importantly, the act of forcing oneself to explain a method helps the designer improve the method.

Identifying harms include jurisdiction-sensitive decisions. In general, violating a law or legal requirement is a harm. Since jurisdictions can and do have conflicting laws, a designer will need to specify in which jurisdiction's laws and norms they have considered harms and benefits. Insofar as the Internet is global, some respect is due for a variety of jurisdictions and norms.

Maximizing benefits and minimizing harms is partly a question of study design. The benefits are improved knowledge or reduced uncertainty about the system of interest. That is, the benefits are explaining consistency, generalizability, and transparency. Protecting some stakeholders from harm involves some trade-offs with these. But such trade-offs have been the subject of this whole chapter. There is no faux numerical score we can provide to score a study's benefits and harms based on the principles in this chapter. But the chapter provides the language for which aspects are important, so a study designer can be clear about what aspects are in tension. Harms, to each of the various stakeholders, need to be weighed and balanced as well.

The best laid plans often go astray. But having a contingency plan to address and mitigate a harmful situation that may occur during the study can significantly reduce the harm. Each of the potential harms identified in the systematic analysis should have an accompanying mitigation plan for if and when it occurs. Such planning is basic risk-reduction best practice.

These five questions and their answers should be integrated into the study design. Exactly what that looks like depends on the study type (see Section 7.2).

4.4.4   *Justice: Fairness and Equity*

Justice has two aspects in the Menlo report: fair selection of topics of interest and study populations and equity in the distribution of benefits and harms. Neither fairness nor equity mean equality. As with other aspects of study design, context is important for justice.

Fair selection of topics of interest is easy to see as a funding issue. In that regard, it is directly related to conflicts of interest (see Section 4.3.6). Any individual study probably cannot be assessed in relation to a fair topic selection. But especially to the extent that the demographics of scientists and researchers do not match the demographics of society as a whole, some care is needed to ensure the interests and questions of those under-represented groups are tackled with equitable fervor by the research establishment.

Fair selection of the study population, on the other hand, is directly a matter for the individual study. Section 4.2.3 introduced six population selection methods. For selection to be fair, no stakeholder group or protected category of persons can be excluded from selection. Protected categories include anything based on, but not limited to, the following: religion, political affiliation, sexual orientation, gender, health, age, technical competency, national origin, race, and socioeconomic status (Dittrich and Kenneally, 2012). Zou and Schiebinger (2018) presents evidence of such unfair study population selection in the context of harm done by various deployed ML algorithms. The excessive targeting of WEIRD populations essentially for the mere convenience of the study designers, as discussed in Section 4.2.5, also violates fairness.

In cybersecurity, an equitable balance of benefits and harms has at least two important aspects. Firstly, the study and its results should benefit stakeholders allied with the study designer more than the study benefits their adversaries. In the intelligence analysis world, this trade-off is well-developed under the term equities analysis; though "equities" means something entirely separate from "equitable" despite sounding similar (Spring and Stoner, 2015). A strategic containment of harms would mean only disclosing or using study results where the adversary's expected response can be managed at least as well as the status quo. Worries about adversary responses should not lead to so much secrecy that they either create other inequitable distribution of harms or so much secrecy that containment becomes secondary to secrecy (see Section 4.4.6).

The other consideration is whether the distribution of benefits and harms in the study population or society are equitable. There is a huge danger in embedding the cultural norms or biases of the researcher or system architect into the software product (Noble, 2018). Such embedding both hides and increases inequitable distribution of harms. The inequitable distribution of harms has been well documented in ML in general (O'Neil, 2016), but the problem is not strictly limited to stochastic algorithms like ML. Security research often makes or supports sensitive decisions: who is permitted, what is private, etc. Any algorithm supporting cybersecurity should, from the outset, be built to ensure an equitable distribution of benefits and harms.

4.4.5 *Respect for Law and Public Interest*

Research is not an excuse for illegal activity. While most cybersecurity researchers are not also lawyers, ignorance of a law is not an excuse for breaking it. The public interest is a broader concept than simply illegal behavior and ties to beneficence (see Section 4.4.3). Two heuristics cover what a study designer should assess in respect for law and public interest: compliance and accountability.

Compliance means abiding by relevant laws in the jurisdiction(s) where the study will take place. Cybersecurity research can easily come into contact with regulations around fraud, privacy of persons, intellectual property, child sexual abuse material, and civil rights and liberties. For example, any research study into suspending abusive accounts on some service should conduct some basic due diligence about how such a study will interact with each of these aspects.

Accountability is ensuring that the study designer and other research staff are incentivized to behave responsibly. Transparency (see Section 4.3) enables accountability. The overall goal of an accountable system is to build trust between the research community and society. It is on the basis of accountability to conduct studies thoroughly while containing harms that science can enjoy the prestigious status is has in modern society (Dear, 2006).

4.4.6 *Risks to Containment From Secrecy*

Secrecy changes the way science is conducted. The best examples of this principle that are documented come from declassified documents on biological weapons testing from the 1950s (Balmer, 2013). British researchers accidentally exposed the crew of a fishing vessel to anthrax spores. At the time, it was an open research question as to whether the exposure concentration would cause humans to catch the deadly disease. But the research was secret, so the fisherman were not told. Instead, they became unwitting research subjects. Since none of them contracted the disease, they never knew they had been in a study.

While this ethics choice seems rather stark and appalling today, we are all subject to experiments without our knowledge or consent on the Internet. Some are trivial, such as our packets are routed differently because an Internet service provider (ISP) is testing different routing configurations.

You can't say that! Suspending accounts

Anyone who has been on the Internet for 30 seconds knows that unsolicited bulk messages are a part of any space. Unsolicited advertising has been a tense subject on the Internet since the 1970s (Brunton, 2013). Let's take as an example a study to identify accounts that conduct deceptive information operations on a social media platform. Or, less politely, trolls.

This study would likely touch regulations around each of fraud, privacy of persons, intellectual property, child sexual abuse material, and civil rights and liberties. What counts as fraud in the jurisdiction matters, but also what rights a fraudulent account has may also matter. In most jurisdictions, criminal behavior is not subject to the same privacy protections. Which naturally brings us to ask what protections personal privacy has in the first place. Privacy influences study design through which aspects of the data can legitimately be processed and stored. Intellectual property cuts two ways: can the study designer own the detection algorithm and can a troll claim copyright of their material to prevent copying and analysis. Usually, yes to the first and no to the second. If the study will crawl social media, the designer's obligations and liabilities if they crawl child sexual abuse material are an unpleasant topic, but an important one. In some jurisdictions, even unknowingly copying such material is a crime.

But the biggest concern around deciding what is and is not an abusive account is civil liberties, such as freedom of speech. Unless the topic of the study is very narrowly defined "information operations," such as foreign interference in elections in the US or UK (Caulfield *et al.*, 2019), deciding who gets to speak and who does not is an enormous legal topic. Thorny legal issues around this topic contribute to the continued prevalence of unsolicited bulk email (Brunton, 2013). And subtle algorithmic choices can dramatically harm stakeholders (Noble, 2018). Although for most cybersecurity research the designer can get by without consulting a lawyer in the design, if there is real potential a study will be used to censor civil liberties, seeking a lawyer's advice on the study design is probably warranted.

And though some packets may drop, that is part of most service agreements with an ISP anyway, so even though the study is secret, there are few ill effects. Others are concerning. Until 2014, Facebook routinely conducted experiments on as many as 500,000 users at a time to see if they could manipulate their emotions by changing which posts the users were shown

(Goel, 2014). It remains unclear whether social media companies have stopped such emotional manipulation, but they tend to argue to the US Congress that it is permitted by virtue of curating the platform.

There are less insidious but still important aspects of cybersecurity science that are effected by secrecy in unknown ways. Consider filtering unsolicited bulk email (that is, spam). Imagine a mailbox owner researches some useful spam detection. There is a legitimate imperative to secrecy here, so the whole method will not be published publicly. The designer should still maintain good transparency so that trusted peers can review consistency, generalizability, and containment. But this spam detection method becomes a system of interest that the spammer will now research, also secretly. Any countermeasures they produce become a new system of interest for the mailbox owner to study (Brunton, 2013). And so on.

This cycle of legitimately secret research is having unstudied effects on scientific norms within cybersecurity communities. Our hypothesis is the primary one is a breakdown of accountability (see Section 4.4.4) as any excuse to remove transparency can be misused as a shield to prevent normal peer review. It also drives researchers into two camps: (1) academic researchers who study more abstract problems and therefore can be totally transparent and (2) applied researchers who have some legitimate need to do part of their work in secret. Although the desirable study properties are the same in both situations, difficulties in communicating across these boundaries has resulted in diverging conceptions of science in different cybersecurity communities (Spring *et al.*, 2017).

Secrecy may legitimately change the way we talk about scientific studies. But it should not change the desirable properties of a study. How a community of practice can accommodate these ideas remains an open problem. One goal of this book is to provide a language and a scaffold with which such communities could be built.

4.5 Summary

This chapter has ranged widely to cover the four desirable study properties of consistency, generalizability, transparency, and containment.

Consistency ensures that the study measures and responds to exactly and exclusively what the designer believes it to be measuring and responding to.

Generalizability ensures that the study provides results that are applicable to the world outside the study in a clear and reliable way.

Transparency ensures that the important aspects of the study are described accurately, completely, and without distracting or distorting detail; these aspects are the design methodology, the study design itself, data collection, the results of the study, how the results were analyzed, and the study's funding.

Containment describes both limiting harm that the study does to participants and limiting harm to the wider world, analyzed through the concepts of respect for persons, beneficence, just and fair distribution of effort and harm, and respect for law and public interest.

Chapter 5

Exploratory Data Analysis

Suppose an arborist's particular study is on tree growth patterns. The arborist doesn't just guess how much each tree has grown, rather, they use a tool to measure the height of the tree exactly. Guessing height isn't repeatable by someone else, so the tool is a requirement. The time at which the measurement is made is important too. The arborist picks a time and repeats the measurement at that time. That way, someone else can repeat exactly what they did because the observations the arborist made were structured.

This process applies to cybersecurity as well. Researchers don't just guess how much traffic is seen in a day, they measure it. It's also measured at the same time every day. The observations should be structured and repeatable.

It's not enough to collect structured observations; they must be used. An arborist wants to determine if the tree growth follows a certain pattern; researchers would like to know if the network traffic has a pattern, too, or if malware is changing, or if the domain name length of malicious domains is growing. Researchers want to answer questions about the data and the future of the data.

The methodology of statistics drives answers to these questions. Statistics allows researchers to make inferences about the data collected. It is a useful tool in research and understanding what can be learned from statistics is more important than learning the formulas that drive it. Chapter 4 provides an introduction to what can be learned through statistics through talking about generalizability of research.

This chapter is not filled with formulas, but discusses how to explore the data visually. Formulas can be looked up in books if you understand what they mean. It's not possible to discuss statistics without formulas, so there will be some, but we spend more time explaining statistics, as a concept, than formulas.

5.1 Definitions

In order to learn a new field, it's necessary to learn the terms used in that field. Terms can have different meanings depending on the field, such as a virus in cybersecurity means something different from a virus in medicine. Context matters; in this case, the context is statistics. This chapter will begin with some basic definitions.

Statistics begins with a *population* to study. For example, a population can be the set of all domain names, a set of network traffic, all malware collected in a day, or the users of a network. A population can be huge, like the set of all domain names, or small, like the malware collected in a day.

The things in a population are *units*. If the population is all malware, then the unit is a single piece of malware. A unit has *properties*. These properties are features the units have. For example, a property of a domain name is the IP address or addresses it points to. Many units have more than one property.

A *sample* of the population is usually taken and that is studied rather than the entirety of the population. A sample is a subset of the population, discussed in Chapter 6. In that chapter, we discuss the variety of ways to take a sample, for now, we'll assume a subset of a population rather than the full population. We do this because sometimes, it's infeasible to study the entire population.

The measurement of a property of a unit is a *variable* or a *statistical variable*. For example, if the unit is a domain, then one property to consider is the domain length. Then, the variable is the length of the domain.

Counting the number of times a domain length appears in results is the *frequency* of the variable. The frequency of each variable can be counted and a table can be created of the results. This table is also known as the *distribution*. A distribution is a concept we'll use over and over. It's the summary of the data in a form that can be used to analyze the data.

For example, suppose the measurement is the number of IP addresses a domain in our set points to. Starting with a set of 1894 domain names, for each one, the number of IPs is counted. This can be summarized by looking at the number of times each length appears in Table 5.1. The table summarizes the number of IP addresses with a frequency greater than 5 to

Table 5.1   Example of a Distribution

Number of IP addresses	Frequency
1	1034
2	801
3	45
4	10
More than 5	4

shorten it. It would have been just as easy to list a row for each of the frequencies 6, 34, 45, 52 though.

Returning to variables, there are two kinds, *categorical* and *quantitative*. Categorical variables have fixed categories for the data —quantitative variables are numerical. For example, the destination port for TCP traffic is categorical whereas the amount of traffic recorded during a fixed time window is quantitative.

If the categorical variables cannot be ordered, they are referred to as *ordinal*; otherwise, they're *nominal*. It's possible to order the destination ports for TCP traffic, but it isn't necessarily possible to order malware in a meaningful way.

Quantitative data that can take any value is *continuous*. If there is only a distinct set of values that the data can take, it is *discrete*. For example, the amount of traffic that can be measured in a day can take any value, depending on the sensitivity of our measurement. The length of a domain name is measured in the number of characters in the domain, and can't be longer than 255, so it is discrete.

The length of a domain name is a *static* value, measuring it repeatedly won't change the result. No matter how many times the domain google.com is measured, the answer won't change. However, the amount of traffic that that domain receives changes from day to day, so it is necessary to measure it repeatedly. This is known as a *repeated measure*.

Measurements can have errors. For a simple example, suppose a tool is used to measure a metal bar. Every time the bar is measured, the value changes. It shouldn't, the bar doesn't change between measurements, but the value from the tool changes each time. These variations are called the *measurement errors*.

5.2   Summary Statistics

Analysis almost always begins with a distribution once there is a population, a sample, and chosen units. Then, a measurement is taken of some property of those units and used to create a distribution, like in Table 5.1. The next step is to study that distribution. In order to understand and describe the distribution, it has to be studied.

To begin with, we'll consider some summary statistics. That means we'll take the distribution and try to summarize it in a few numbers that give us information about it. Let's start by looking at a distribution that has been studied a great deal and use information about it as a starting place.

The normal distribution, also known as the bell curve distribution, is a very common distribution. It is very common in describing grades. Teachers want a lot of Cs, fewer Bs and Ds, and even fewer As and Fs. Fig. 5.1 illustrates the curve.

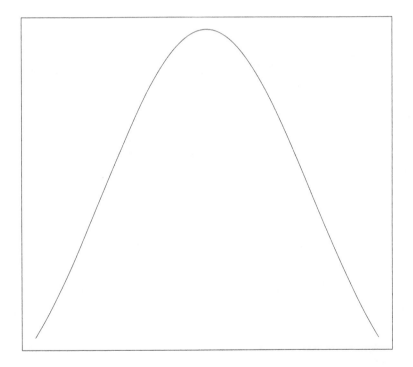

Fig. 5.1 The Normal Distribution

The middle of the curve is where most of the values lie, and as the curve spreads out, the distribution of values is smaller. There are three statistics

Table 5.2   Distribution of Protocols

Port Number	Frequency
80	1500
443	898
25	134

that can summarize the center of the distribution, the *mean*, *median*, and the *mode*.

The *mean* of the data, or *average*, is the absolute midpoint of the data. Think of it as balancing a seesaw; there is an equal amount of data on either side of the mean. It is a bit fickle though. If a few of the variables are very large, and the rest of them are very small, then the mean can be skewed towards the large numbers. If this happens, it isn't representative of the distribution. It's the center of the data when it is summed up, but not the middle of the data.

The average of the distribution in Table 5.1 is calculated:

$$\frac{1 * 1034 + 2 * 801 + 3 * 45 + 4 * 10 + 6 + 34 + 45 + 52}{1894} = 1.56$$

which says that the average number of IP addresses each domain points to is 1.56.

The average is over the frequency of the measurement across the sample. Averaging domain name length is an understandable concept, but averaging network traffic protocol isn't. For example, let's look at the Distribution Table 5.2.

We could average the frequency each port is used:

$$\frac{1500 + 898 + 134}{3} = 844$$

however, there is no such thing as an average port in Table 5.2. Even though the ports are labeled with numbers, they are categorical values. Calculating the average port would be like trying to compute:

$$\frac{HTTP + HTTPS + SMTP}{3}$$

There's no way to compute this equation. It's not possible to average categorical variables. The reason is that addition is not defined on the categories, and this is true even if the labels for the categories are numbers. Trying to calculate averages of categorical variables is an unfortunately common mistake. For example, Common Vulnerability Scoring System (CVSS) version 2 and 3 make this mistake (Spring *et al.*, 2020).

An alternative to the mean is the *median*. To find this, first sort all the data, then count from either the top or the bottom until the middle of the data is found. The median isn't affected by the large values like the mean is, but if there are a lot of repeated values it can move it towards them. It's a counting exercise to find the midpoint of the data. Looking at Table 5.1, the median is 1. It is skewed towards the 1 because of the overwhelming number of them. Returning to the data in Table 5.2, it's not possible to determine a median of it either. Ordering protocols doesn't make sense, even if they are labeled with numbers.

The *mode* is the most commonly repeated value for a variable. It can show where the median is skewed. In Table 5.1, the mode is 1.

In the normal distribution, the median, mean, and mode are the same value. If the mean and median aren't close, then that illustrates that the frequency of the data doesn't follow the normal distribution. Unfortunately, it illustrates nothing else.

The *variance* of data is the spread around the mean. It's computed by summing up the square difference between the mean and each data point, then dividing that value by the number of data points in the distribution. It's a summary statistic of how far things are from the mean, on average. The formula considers all of the possible distances between each value and the mean, sums that up, then creates the average.

If the variance is very large, then most things are far apart from the mean, since it is an average of the squared distance. If it's low, then things are clustered together. From Table 5.1, the variance is 3.24. That implies that the data are spread out from the mean. The visualization already demonstrated that, but now it's been shown statistically.

The *standard deviation* is the square root of the variance. It is a measure of how varied things are in the data set; in Table 5.1 it is 1.8. One thing about the normal distribution is that 95% of the data is within two standard deviations of the mean.

The summary statistics we've discussed in this section revolve around the normal distribution, where everything is concentrated in the middle. They are useful for summarizing the data, but shouldn't be the only analysis.

5.3   Basic Data Visualizations

It's possible to analyze a distribution by creating a spreadsheet of the data and examining that. If there are only a few variables to look at, then it is easy to find a pattern in the spreadsheet. Table 5.1 is an example of a small distribution that's easy to analyze in a simple table. Once the results spread off a single page, looking at a spreadsheet is less useful. A better way to work is to create a visualization, and let the eyes become the decision maker rather than staring at a column of numbers. It's much easier to see a pattern in a picture than in a list of numbers.

There are different visualizations for different kinds of data. The next sections will examine some of the common visualizations and what can be learned from them.

5.3.1 *Bar Plot*

Visualizing categorical data is often done by using a *bar plot*. On the x-axis of the plot, mark a container for each category. Now, mark a height for the frequency of that category and draw a box. In Fig. 5.2, the categories of protocol from Table 5.2 are summarized. Protocol is a nominal variable because there is no definitive order for the various protocols. Alphabetical order of the protocols means just as much as the order of the age of the protocols, meaning the researcher can use any order that they see fit.

Fig. 5.2 illustrates that there is a lot more TCP data than Internet Control Message Protocol (ICMP) data, while User Datagram Protocol (UDP) occurs in the middle. Is this standard for the traffic on a network, or is this something different? That can only be answered by further study and repeated measures.

If the data are ordinal, then it makes sense to order the categories on the plot. For example, putting ports in order from 0 to 65536 does make reasonable sense even if it can make for a huge plot if the goal is plotting all ports.

The plot in Fig. 5.2 is vertical, but it could have made a horizontal plot instead. It depends on which method is preferred and makes more sense. A visualization is created to aid in the analysis process, so it depends on the user of the visualization.

5.3.2 *Histogram*

For discrete quantitative data, a *histogram* is used, which looks like a bar plot, but is created slightly differently. Creating a histogram starts with separating the items into bins, or ranges, usually of equal size. For example, three bins could be 0 to 3, just over 3 to 6, and just over 6 to 9. When counting whole numbers of items, each bin might be just one value, such as 17, 18, 19, and so on. Now, count the number of elements in each bin.

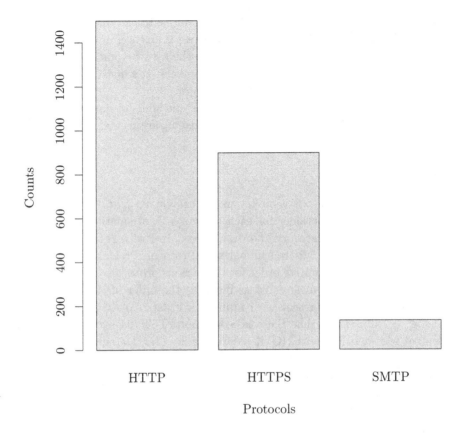

Fig. 5.2   Bar Plot

Create a rectangle on the graph whose base is the size of the bin, and the height is the number of elements.

Fig. 5.3 illustrates a histogram for domain length. The figure used a width of one for each bin, but that isn't a requirement.

The distribution in Fig. 5.3 is *unimodal*. That means there is exactly one mode. It's apparent in the bin that starts at 21 and extends to 22 which means there are more domains of length 21 than of any other length. The visualization makes the mode apparent.

Another method occasionally used for this data is the pie chart. This is a bad idea. It's not possible to see the pattern as effectively as with the histogram, and the pie chart can obscure two frequencies with similar

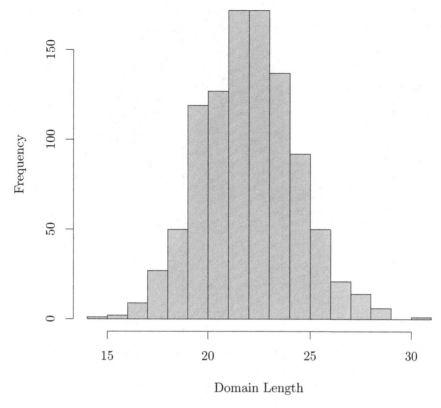

Fig. 5.3   Histogram for Domain Lengths

sizes. It is quite apparent which is taller in a histogram while it may not be readily apparent in a pie chart.

The shape of the histogram can immediately illustrate information about the data, whereas the pie chart just illustrates a sum of parts of the data and doesn't show the shape of the data. Fig. 5.4 illustrates a classical symmetric distribution, where the mean equals the median, just like the normal distribution.

The symmetric distribution has most of its values in the middle of the distribution with smaller amounts on the ends. If the distribution is symmetric, then it's possible to use a little math to show how likely it is the values will stay in the middle and avoid the outsides.

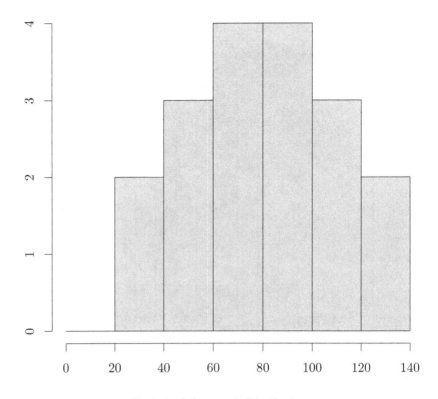

Fig. 5.4   A Symmetric Distribution

A *uniform distribution* is when the frequencies all have the same value as shown in Fig. 5.5. A uniform distribution is also a symmetric distribution; it's one where the frequencies are equal.

If the distribution is uniform, then every possible result is equally likely. For example, if a particular virus has a uniform distribution when considering the systems it could infect, then it is equally likely any system could get the virus.

If a distribution has two modes, it is *bimodal*, as illustrated in Fig. 5.6. Bimodal distributions can mean that the distribution has two groups in the data where each group is centered around the mode. If that is the case, the data should be examined closely to figure out why. For example, suppose the experiment involves looking at connections to ports. After the connections are counted and the graph is created, it's determined that the distribution is bimodal where the two modes are at port 80 and port 443.

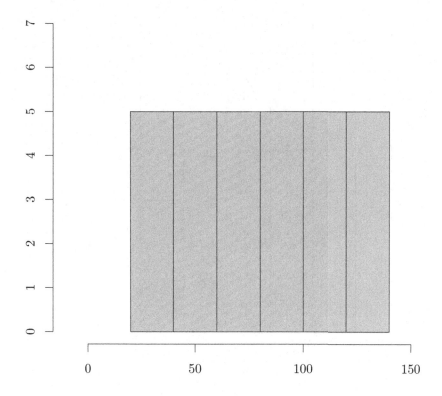

Fig. 5.5   A Uniform Distribution

In other words, there is an equivalent amount of web traffic to both http traffic and https traffic.

By plotting the frequencies, it's clear if the distribution is symmetric, uniform, or bimodal. Eyes are the analytic engine in this case, by examining the plot they can determine the shape of the distribution. This isn't a mathematical determination, though, and should never be labeled as such.

5.3.3   Density Plot

In discrete data, there are only so many values that can have frequencies. If they are divided into bins, it is easy to create bins of equal size. In continuous data, there's a range of values, any of which can have a frequency. If the wrong place is picked to create an interval for the bins, then it is possible to miss a dip or a peak because it straddles two bins.

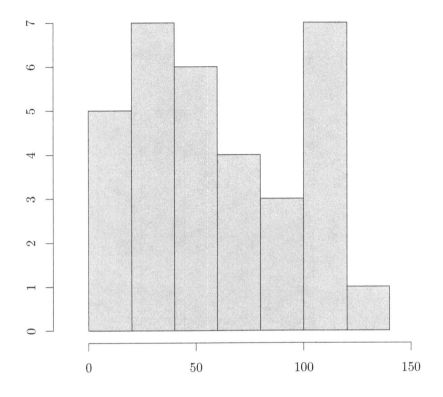

Fig. 5.6   Bimodal distribution

Instead of drawing bins, a smooth line is drawn. These are *density plots*, as illustrated in Fig. 5.7. Using a density plot means the visualization isn't vulnerable to the bin size, unlike in histograms. It also illuminates the shape of the data. Fig. 5.7 looks sort of like the normal distribution. However, it's skewed a little on the right. Without more statistical analysis, that's all that can be said.

5.3.4   *Box Plot*

An alternative to the histogram and the density plot is the *box plot*. While a histogram and density plots give a general impression of the shape of the distribution, the box plot summarizes the data. It looks at features of the data, including the median, as well as the spread of the data. This can give an idea of how symmetric the data is or isn't.

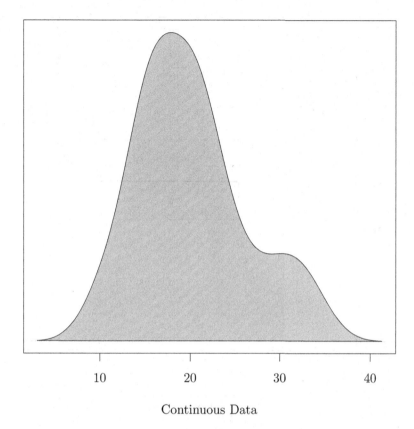

Continuous Data

Fig. 5.7 A Density Plot

Go half way through the first half of the data, then that is the *first quartile*. Halfway through the second half of the data is the *third quartile*. Between the first and third quartile of the data is the *spread*. The box plot is created by making a line at the first quartile, a line at the third quartile, and connecting the lines. At the median, draw a line across the middle of the plot. To finish the plot, draw a line at the minimum value and one at the maximum value. Then connect those lines to the box with another line. The final plot should look like Fig. 5.8.

Fig. 5.8 was drawn using data from a normal distribution, so it is symmetric. The height above the median and below the median is the same, and the height of the maximum and minimum values is also the same.

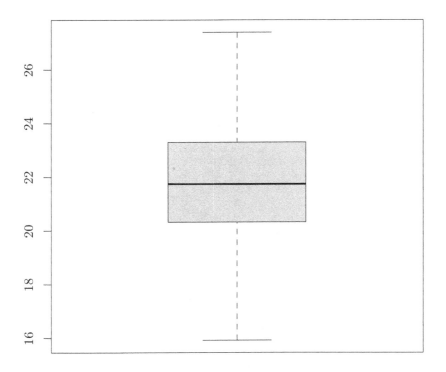

Domain Length

Fig. 5.8   A Box Plot

The box plot in Fig. 5.9 is asymmetric. The median is closer to the first quartile than the third quartile, and the maximum is further away from the spread than the minimum.

The box plot is also useful for comparing distributions visually.

In Fig. 5.10, there are two different distributions. The distribution on the left appears more symmetric than the one on the right, while the one on the right has a larger spread. This is an example of using a visualization as an analytic for the eyes, letting judgement compare distributions rather than using a mathematical method.

A statistical method is still best for reinforcing the point though.

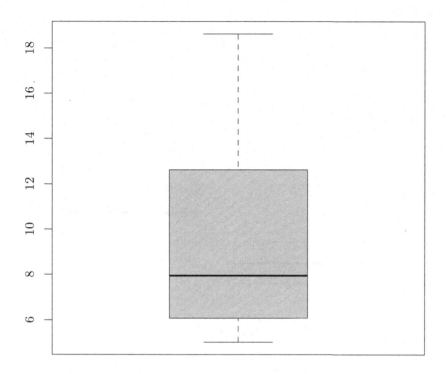

Domain Length

Fig. 5.9 An Asymmetric Box Plot

5.4 Random Variables

A *probability distribution* is a function that gives the probability of getting any particular value between 0 and 1. It describes how likely it is to get a given value. For example, the normal distribution in Fig. 5.1 is a probability distribution, and it's more likely to get values in the center of the distribution, that is around 0.5, than values that are closer to 0 or 1.

Using the probability distribution, a *random variable* can be created. It is a variable whose value is determined by the probability distribution. This is different from the variable defined before, where it's given by the result of an experiment on data. With a random variable, something is known about the probabilities that isn't necessarily known about the experimental results. Educated guesses can be made about future values of results using

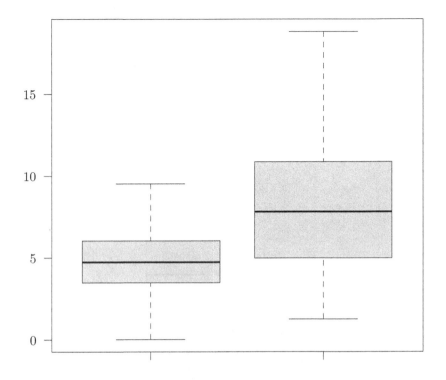

Fig. 5.10   Comparing Box Plots

the probability distribution that can't be made with the experimental result because a lot is known about standard probability distributions.

The goal, then, is to be able to show with a good degree of certainty that the distribution from the experimental results is "close" to a known probability distribution. Those values can be used to make inferences about the experimental results, including predicting future behavior, analyzing current behavior and finding weird behavior that doesn't quite fit.

A mathematical model is a description of a real world event using mathematical terms. The mathematical model can be asked questions like, "what should we expect given this event?" even though it's not possible to query an experimental distribution the same questions because it doesn't have any way to determine the answer. By finding a known probability distribution that the data is reasonably close to, then the data can be modeled with this distribution.

We already used the mean to summarize the distribution of sampled data. We can also use this to study our random variables. In this case, it's known as the *expected value*. This is often written as $E(X)$, and it is the value that we *expect* to occur. The function that defines the probability distribution is the *probability mass function*, and it's written as:

$$f(x) = P(X = x)$$

That means in calculating $f(x)$, the result is the calculation of the calculating the probability that x occurs for the distribution.

5.5 Discrete Distributions

Discrete probability distributions are just like the discrete distributions we discussed before. They're a function with only a limited number of results and they can be enumerated.

An experiment with only two possible outcomes is a *Bernoulli trial*. The most common Bernoulli trial is flipping a coin, but they are often seen in cybersecurity as well. For example:

- Is a computer on?

- Is the system under a distributed denial of service (DDoS) attack?

- Is it running a web server?

These questions have only two answers, so they qualify as Bernoulli trials. If the question is "How much traffic occurs during a DDoS?", then the answer can be any number of packets, depending on the severity of the attack. This isn't a Bernoulli trial. However, the idea of the Bernoulli trial can be used to build other probability distributions.

5.5.1 *The Bernoulli Distribution*

The Bernoulli distribution models the Bernoulli Trial. If the probability of one event occurring is p, then the probability of the event not occurring is $1 - p$. For example, the probability of a heads in a coin flip is 0.5 and the probability of not-heads, or tails, is 0.5.

The expected value of the Bernoulli distribution is p and the variance is $p(1 - p)$. Another way of looking at it is if it is expected that the result will happen $p\%$ of the time and to not happen $(1 - p)\%$ of the time.

For example, if it is known that 2% of the computers fail when turned on, then that can model that with the Bernoulli distribution. The probability of it failing is 2%, the probability of not failing is 98%. The Bernoulli distribution is concerned with the single event, not any subsequent events.

5.5.2   *The Geometric Distribution*

While the Bernoulli distribution only considers a single experiment, the Geometric distribution wants to answer the question: What is the probability that success will be on the jth trial (Solomon, 1987)? In other words, if a coin is flipped ten times, what's the probability of getting heads on but not until the 4th flip?

The probability mass function of the geometric distribution is:

$$P\left(X = j\right) = \ \left(1 - p\right)^{j-1}p$$

This can be read that as "the probability of something occurring on the jth trial, but no earlier, is given by."

This probability distribution is discrete because all the possible answers can be listed. If, as in the previous example, the question is "what is the probability of a system failing to turn on after we've turned 10 different systems on successfully," then the answer is $P\left(10\right) = 0.017$, or a 1.7% chance.

The expected value of the Geometric distribution is $E\left(X\right) = \frac{1}{p}$, and the variance is given by $\text{var}\left(x\right) = \frac{1-p}{p^2}$.

5.5.3   *The Binomial Distribution*

While the Geometric distribution asks "when is the first success" the Binomial distribution asks "what is the probability of j successes in n trials?" For example, if a coin is flipped n times, what is the probability that j of them are heads? Or if 50 computers are turned on, what is the probability that one fails?

The probability mass function of the Binomial distribution is:

$$P\left(X = j\right) = \binom{n}{k}p^j\left(1 - p\right)^{n-j}$$

The symbol $\binom{n}{k}$ is read "from n elements, choose k" and is equivalent to $\frac{n!}{k!(n-k)!}$. In this case, the value of n is fixed, which means before the distribution is computed, it is known how many trials will be attempted. The number of successes is what can vary over the n trials.

Using the earlier example, if 50 computers are turned on, then the probability that one fails is $P\left(X = 1\right) = 0.37$, or a 37% chance that one computer will fail to turn on.

The expected value for the distribution is $E(X) = np$, and the variance is $var = np(1-p)$. If a coin is flipped 10 times, then it's expected that 10*0.5, or 5 of them, to be heads. This doesn't mean that every time a coin is flipped 10 times that five heads will results, it means that if we take lots of sets of 10 flips, on average that will happen.

Returning to the computer example, then turning on 100 computers has an expectation that two will fail to turn on. Sometimes all will turn on, sometimes more will fail. Two is an average.

5.6 Continuous Distributions

We saw continuous data in our examples earlier in this chapter. We can also create continuous probability distributions which we can use to model our experimental data. These distributions also can take any value which means we can't list out the possible values for the distribution. There are many continuous distributions available. In this chapter we'll only talk about two that are commonly seen in cybersecurity research, the normal and Pareto distributions.

5.6.1 *The Normal Distribution*

The normal distribution is one of the most common distributions and one of the first recorded uses was by the mathematician Gauss in the study of astronomy, which is why it is sometimes called the Gaussian distribution.

The distribution is symmetric, with a peak where the mean of the distribution is located. The shape of the curve is defined by the variance of the distribution. This means that if the the mass and variance are known, then the shape of the distribution is also known. It's common to use the Greek letter μ ("mu") to denote the mean and the letter σ ("sigma") for the variance. The normal distribution is often referenced as $N(\mu, \sigma)$ because the two values determine the shape of the distribution. It is an important distribution because it is often used as a basis for models.

5.6.2 *The Pareto Distribution*

An economist in the early twentieth century named Vilfredo Pareto noticed that the number of people whose income exceeded a certain level could be modeled by the equation $\frac{C}{x^\alpha}$ where C and α are values determined by the data. This distribution is also known as the *power law distribution* or the *long tail distribution*. Fig. 5.11 illustrates it.

The power law distribution is common in cybersecurity data. For example, the number of peers that each AS has in BGP has been modeled by a

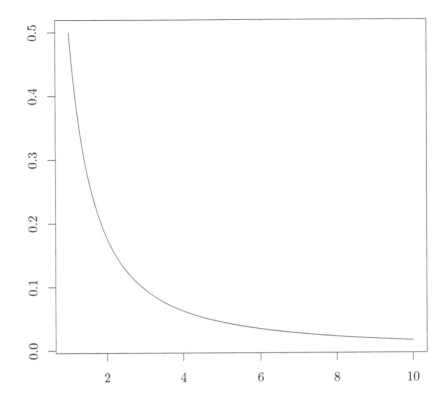

Fig. 5.11   The Power Law Distribution

power law distribution. Similarly, the amount of traffic to a web server has also been modeled by a power law distribution. This means that in general, most connections have a small amount of traffic whereas a few connections are extremely large.

The expected value of the power law distribution depends on the value of α. If $\alpha \leq 1$, then the expected value is infinity. This is a shorthand method of saying it grows so large with the computation, it trends to infinity. If $\alpha \geq 1$, then $E(X) = \frac{\alpha x}{\alpha - 1}$.

The standard deviation is dependent on the value of α as well. For $\alpha \leq 2$, then the standard deviation is infinity. This is the same as the expected value for $\alpha \leq 1$, it keeps growing no matter what and it's common to say the limit of that value is infinity. For $\alpha \geq 2$, then $\sigma = \left(\frac{x}{\alpha - 1}\right)^2 \frac{\alpha}{\alpha - 2}$.

5.7 Data Outliers

Suppose a researcher performs an experiment, collects the data, and determines that it precisely fits the normal distribution. The researcher can take the average of the data, the standard deviation, and generate a function that lets them predict future behavior. Everything is perfect; there's nothing more to do.

Unfortunately, real life is rarely like that. An *outlier* in a data set is a variable that is far removed from distribution used as a model. It's the anomaly in the data set, perhaps the weird thing that happened that makes it interesting. For example, in network traffic, an anomaly could be that IP address that is beaconing to the malware domain, looking for instructions. In general, anomalies are not security violations. But it is often useful to improve your understanding of "normal" behavior by understanding what causes anomalies and whether they are security violations. To find an anomaly in the millions of flows in a busy network we need a way to quantify outliers.

Outliers can also mean that there's a problem with the data set. Suppose a researcher is collecting passive DNS data through a sensor on their network. Every day, they collect 4 gigabytes of data, except for that odd Tuesday when only 1 gigabyte of data is collected. That's an anomaly in the data collection and should be studied. That could also be an experimental error, because the sensor failed that day. Either way, the outlier should be identified and studied. Experimental errors are sometimes removed from the data set as they would affect the outcome of the study, but because they are incorrect data points, they should be removed.

5.7.1 *Finding Outliers*

In the normal distribution, 95% of the values are within two standard deviations of the mean. If the data are far away from the mean, then they aren't like the majority of the data. But that doesn't automatically make them unexpected. We expect 5% of the values to be at least that far away, since that is what defines a normal distribution.

It's common to use three standard deviations as a guess for what data points are outliers. The method starts at the mean and any point that's greater than the mean plus three standard deviations or less than the mean minus three standard deviations is considered an outlier. The shaded area in Fig. 5.12 illustrates potential outliers found in a normal distribution.

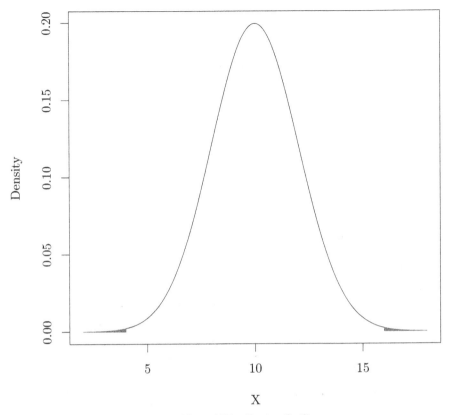

Fig. 5.12   Normal Distribution Outliers

If any of the data falls within that shaded area, then they are considered anomalies. Anomalies are not necessarily outliers, but they are often "weird" and worth investigating. For example, suppose a researcher is studying the length of domain names that are used by malware. The anomalous domains would be the very short or the very long ones.

Another method for finding anomalies uses the quartiles. Where standard deviations are based around the mean, quartiles are understood in relation to the median. The median is the middle data point, but half of all the data points fall in the spread between Q1 and Q3. The spread is the difference between the third quartile and the first quartile, or $Q3 - Q1$. The outliers are often considered to be be anything more than 1.5 times as far away from this central grouping as the ends of the spread are from each

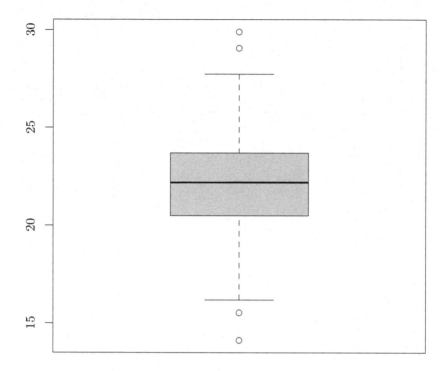

Domain Length

Fig. 5.13   Box Plot Outliers

other. That is, anything less than $Q1 - 1.5 * (Q3 - Q1)$ or greater than $Q3 + 1.5 * (Q3 - Q1)$.

A box plot can illustrate anomalies. In Fig. 5.13, the spread is shaded gray, and the line at 16.5 is $Q1 - 1.5 * (Q3 - Q1)$ and the line at 28 is $Q3 + 1.5 * (Q3 - Q1)$. The circles at the top and the bottom of the plot denote the outliers in this plot of domain length. Those are the domains that are either much shorter than the rest or much longer.

5.8   Log Transformations

Suppose a researcher has decided to study and plot network traffic. Some of their traffic, for example, the traffic to a name server, is very small. On the other hand, a mail session can generate a lot of traffic, especially if users are sending large attachments. Fig. 5.14 is an example.

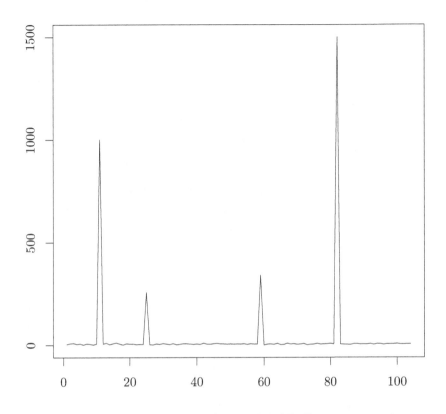

Fig. 5.14   Distribution of Mail Traffic

Most of the data are very small, but they are obfuscated on the plot because the large spikes dominate it. It's not possible to determine anything other than "there are four very large spikes" in the data.

The natural log of a number x is the number y where $e^y = x$. For example, $\ln 1 = 0$. while $\ln 2000 = 7.6$. If the data is plotted between 1 and 2,000, then Fig. 5.14 is created. If data are plotted between 0 and 7.6, it's easier to view on a graph. To do this, the natural log is applied to every variable in the data set. This is a *log transformation*. Fig. 5.15 is the log transformation of Fig. 5.14.

The spikes no longer dominate the entire plot. It's possible to get a better idea of what is happening with the smaller numbers.

The log transformation can also de-emphasize outliers. We discussed earlier how the outliers lie outside the normal distribution and how the log can take a very wide spread and narrow it down. If the the natural log

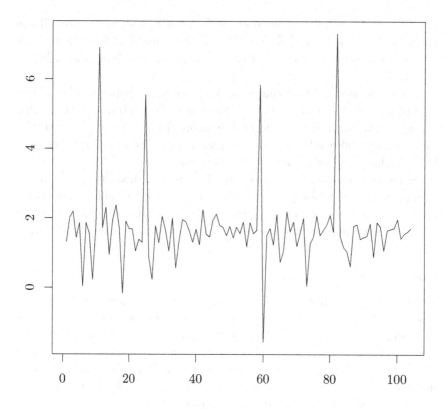

Fig. 5.15   Log Transformation of Mail Traffic Distribution

function is applied, then the outliers aren't going to stand out as much. If the end goal is to remove outliers from a distribution then a log transformation might be useful. It certainly won't help to highlight anomalies though.

5.9   Data Classification

It would be nice if a method could be created that automatically sorts data into two categories, good and bad. Then finding bad traffic would be very easy. This method is known as a *classifier*. It's the creation of a model that will apply labels to data. Unfortunately, cybersecurity data isn't that easy to sort.

Suppose a researcher is creating a model that looks for exfiltration of data, that is, when data is sent outside of the organization that shouldn't be. A user could have a valid reason for sending a large file for a customer, but that could look like exfiltration of data when analyzing traffic. If the analysis classifies this behavior as "bad," then that is a *false positive*. A false positive means it appears that bad behavior has been found, but it hasn't.

DNS has been used for command and control by botnets. This means that what looks like a standard DNS query is malicious traffic. If this traffic is classified as good, since it has all the hallmarks of being standard traffic, then we've found a *false negative*. A *false negative* means it appears good behavior has been found, but it's actually bad.

Suppose a researcher creates a method to find maliciousness. In an operational sense, a false positive means the researcher is telling the security analysts that something is wrong when it isn't. A false negative means the opposite —the researcher missing the malicious result. Either way, that is incorrect information to give a security analyst.

5.10   Bivariate Analysis

The discussion in this chapter so far has been one measurement per variable, also known as *univariate analysis*. We found a domain, we took a measurement, we analyzed the results. On the other hand, what if we want to be more complex and take more than one measurement? That's called *multivariate analysis*. In this section, we'll discuss one version of multivariate analysis called *bivariate analysis*. That's where we take two measurements of a unit and analyze the results.

Suppose there is a theory that the longer a domain name is, the fewer times it is resolved. The first thing needed is the domain, in order to measure its length, the second is the resolutions of the domain. The number of resolutions is dependent upon the initial measurement of the length. The domain length is the *exploratory variable* or *independent variable,* and the variable that is dependent on that measurement is the *response variable* or *dependent variable.*

5.10.1   *Visualizing Bipartite Data*

The visualizations created for bipartite data depend on the types of variables that are explored.

It is possible to have categorical data for both the exploratory variable and the response variable, categorical data for one of the variables, or quantitative variables for both. If the variables are both categorical, the best solution is a *contingency table*. This isn't a plot like the bar plot or box plot; rather, it is a table that shows the relationships between the two

Table 5.3   A Contingency Table

	Javascript	PDF	PE	Totals
Adware	100	54	16	170
Spyware	9	23	66	98
Rootkit	26	33	44	103
Totals	135	110	126	371

variables. The exploratory variable is on the horizontal while the response variable is on the vertical. Table 5.3 illustrates this.

The exploratory variable is the type of file, either javascript, Portable Document Format (PDF), or Portable Executable (PE), while the response variable is the kind of malware. It's possible to analyze to analyze the correlation between the two variables by examining the table.

If exploratory variable is a categorical variable, such as the top level domain, and the response variable to be quantitative, such as length of a domain, then they can be combined into a side-by-side box plot. Fig. 5.16 illustrates this.

The four most common gTLDs were used and a sample was taken of each set of domains. Next the length of each domain was measured and plotted in the box plot for each top level domain. Examining the plot, it's clear that .com has the longest average domain and has the biggest spread, including outliers. The gTLD for .mobi has the smallest spread.

If both variables are quantitative, then they can be combined into a *scatterplot*. In a scatterplot, the x-axis is the exploratory (or independent) variable and the y-axis is the response (or dependent) variable.

Fig. 5.17 illustrates the scatterplot that examines the bivariate analysis of domain length and number of resolutions. The theory earlier was that the shorter the domain, the more resolutions were associated with it. The visualization can be used to make a guess at the answer, but without further statistical analysis, that's only a guess.

5.10.2   *Data Correlation and Regression*

Suppose a researcher wants to know if there is a relationship between the size of malware and the number of files it drops. They also want to prove the relationship using statistics. The *correlation* is a measure of the relationship between two quantitative variables. The variables can be strongly related, that is, have a high correlation, or weakly related, which is a low correlation.

The formula for computing the correlation is known as the *correlation coefficient, Pearson's correlation coefficient,* or the *linear correlation coef-*

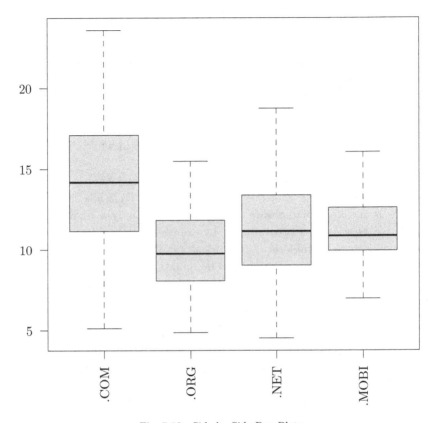

Fig. 5.16   Side by Side Box Plots

ficient. All three names refer to the same formula. The formula computes a number between −1 and 1. If the number is greater than 0, that means there's a positive correlation. A positive correlation means that both values increase. A negative correlation, or a result less than 0, means that as one variable increases, the other decreases.

For a positive correlation, the larger the value of the correlation, the stronger it is. There are various rules of thumb, all dependent upon the area in question. For example, in some areas, a value between 0.75 and 1 is considered a strong correlation.

Univariate data is studied by measuring how close the data was to the middle by using the mean, median, and mode. In bivariate data, *regression analysis* is used. Like the univariate measures, this is a measurement of the tendency of the bivariate data to move towards the middle. There are

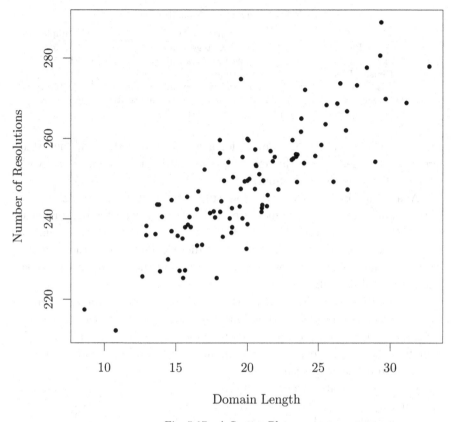

Fig. 5.17   A Scatter Plot

multiple methods for computing regression; almost all of them are very complicated. Ironically, one of the methods for bivariate data is called simple regression analysis, but it isn't a very simple process at all.

The point of the correlation and regression analysis is to consider the relationships between the variables. If one variable can influence another, that is an interesting result. Suppose a certain strain of malware is highly correlated to a set of domains that are owned by one individual. That's not saying that individual is the creator of the malware but it does indicate that the relationship should be investigated closer.

5.10.3   *Time Series*

A special form of bivariate analysis is *time series* analysis. In this case, the exploratory variable is time, and the response variable is the event. For

Table 5.4   Summary of Visualizations

Visualization	Variable Types	Example
Bar Plot	Categorical	Fig. 5.2
Histogram	Discrete Quantitative	Fig. 5.3
Density Plot	Continuous, Time Series	Fig. 5.7
Box Plot	Alternative to Histogram and Density	Fig. 5.8
Side by Side Box Plot	Bipartite Categorical and Quantitative	Fig. 5.16
Scatterplot	Bipartite Quantitative and Quantitative	Fig. 5.17

example, if the queries per minute for a domain are measured, then that creates a time series. Another example is measuring the amount of network traffic collected every five minutes.

Analyzing time series data allows predictions to be made about the future. For example, if the amount of malware daily collected daily is measured and accurate records are kept of that amount, then the amount of malware collected in the future can be predicted. That allows the administrator to make plans for storing the malware and the researchers to make plans for analyzing it.

For another example, consider that a blocklist that is updated hourly was collected for months. That blocklist contains IP addresses that are originating scans, so if the number of unique IP addresses in each blocklist is counted, that gives a baseline for the number of IP addresses that scanned. Fig. 5.18 illustrates this time series.

From the plot, it's clear that during January and February, the number of scanning hosts grew. However, it peaked in March and seems to be declining in the months following.

Plotting the time series, where the horizontal axis is time and the vertical axis is the response variable, is a useful way to start analysis.

5.11   Lessons Learned

This introduction to data analysis focused on the visualization of the data. A good first step is to create a visualization of your measurement and let the visualization guide your next steps. Table 5.4 lists the visualizations discussed in this chapter along with the type of variable it is used for.

We also discussed random distributions and modeling. We can use known properties of random distributions to model our data if we can show that our data are close to the random distribution. There are many statistics books that cover such in depth analysis of the data; this section provided a taste of how to use your eyes as your first analytic engine.

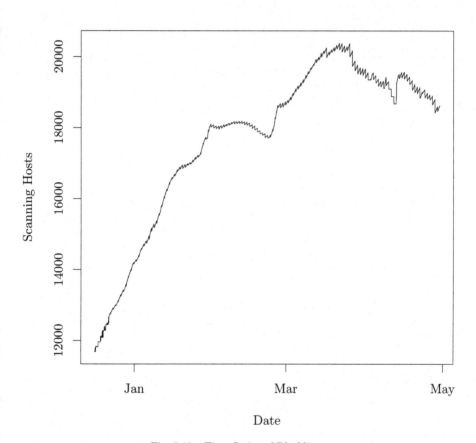

Fig. 5.18 Time Series of Blacklists

Chapter 6

Sampling in Cybersecurity

In cybersecurity, research often starts with a collection of data to analyze. Terabytes of data are collected in network traffic, in DNS as well as malicious software (malware). Log files can be huge. Incident reports can be large as well. Vulnerability reports, BGP, all of this data can be enormous. Analyzing this data all at once can take many hours, or even be impossible, so the goal is to make use of statistics in order to reduce the workload and at the same time, achieve results that are useful.

As we discussed in Chapter 5, statistics lets us take a smaller subset of our entire set of data and make inferences about the larger set. This chapter is about the various methods that can create the samples. It's important to understand how to create a good sample and what the problems can be in sampling.

Different sampling methods have different goals in mind. It's important to determine the goal of the research at hand when deciding what sampling method to use. For example, we discussed generalizability in Chapter 4. Sample methods effect generalizability of results.

6.1 Populations

In Chapter 5 we defined populations. In research we can take the population and perform a study on it to find patterns of behavior or anomalies.

Sometimes, we start by considering a study and then trying to determine the best population on which to perform the study. Both ways work in trying to find the adversaries.

If we start with a study design, then the first question is, "What is the population for the study?". If we are studying domain names, our population could be the set of all possible domains. This would include everything that is registered and everything that is not registered. We could enumerate every possible domain by systematically creating every possible combination of characters that could be a domain. This is a very large set and has been estimated to contain approximately a googol of domains (Spring, 2014). That is, a one followed by a hundred zeros. This means there are more possible domains than IPv4 addresses and IPv6 addresses combined.

Another possible population is the set of all registered domains. Unfortunately, enumerating this set is nearly impossible. Not every registrar allows access by researchers to the data. The registrars for the new TLDs must allow researchers access to the data (ICANN, 2013) but there is no requirement that the registrars of ccTLDs do the same. So while the population can be defined, it cannot be listed. Studying this population becomes difficult because we do not know exactly what is in the population and what is not.

Another example is malware. We have no idea how much different malware is out in the wild. We just know that at least 350,000 new pieces of malware are detected every day. (Genç *et al.*, 2019). That doesn't say anything about how much new malware isn't detected, just that we find that many in a day. Over a year, that's 127,750,000 pieces of malware, and that's only the ones we know about. Trying to enumerate all of the possible malware is an impossible proposition.

Vulnerability reports are often used in cybersecurity analysis, but it's dependent on who made the report. Not every vulnerability will be reported; companies keep some hidden for business reasons, and adversaries won't announce the new method they've found for accessing systems. There is no database of all vulnerabilities; we just "happen" to know some because someone reported them. If the population is, "all vulnerabilities in all software," we don't have any way of enumerating it. We can make guesses on the number of vulnerabilities because people have made estimates on the number of bugs per line of code, but that assumes we know how many lines of code are in each piece of software. Also, guessing the number of vulnerabilities doesn't let us list them, it just allows us to get an estimate of how many vulnerabilities are out there. It also assumes that every bug is a vulnerability.

The previous discussion has highlighted that we must define the population appropriately, and it is possible that the entire population is not accessible. Also, it is possible that the population is incredibly large. If we can't access the entire population, or it is too large to deal with, we need another method for dealing with the data in order to perform a study on it to learn something relevant.

That's where taking samples comes in.

6.2 The Sample

It is not always feasible to study the entire population, as much as we would like to. For example, if our population is all of the domain names that could possibly be registered, then as we said earlier, that is almost a googol of domains. From a quick estimate, a file containing these domains would take up about 1×10^{89} terabytes of space. This is an impossible amount of data to study.

If we change our domain population to be the set of registered domains, the number of domains drops dramatically. However, as discussed in the previous section, we cannot list every registered domain.

For another example, suppose we're capturing the network traffic for a large organization. This can generate up to a terabyte of data a day, at a minimum. If we are using full packet capture, this can grow geometrically larger depending on the number of users and their web surfing habits. Analyzing this data set as a whole soon becomes intractable.

In short, studying an entire population can be difficult, if not impossible. So instead of doing that, we will study a subset, known as a *sample*. If we choose our sample in a reasonable way, then we can make inferences about the population at large based on the sample. This means that we can take the results from a study and apply them to the population at large. The important part is that we must choose the sample in a reasonable way. If we don't, then anything we derive from the sample can not necessarily be applied to the population itself.

The sample chosen should be *representative* of the population. This means that it looks like a the population at large but on a smaller scale. It doesn't focus on one part of the population at all but is spread across the entire population.

To illustrate further, suppose we take every IP address and count how many domains point to it. We can average that number and get a result that we will call Ω. Now, suppose we choose a sample of IP addresses. We need to choose this sample so that if we count the number of domains that point to each IP address in this sample, then that average is close to Ω.

If our population is IP addresses, then choosing a sample from a single /8 is not reasonable. Suppose our study is the routing associated with IP addresses. If we choose all of the IP addresses from 234.0.0.0/8, then the study would fail. This network is reserved for multi-cast, and should not show up in any routing table. If we are studying "networks that shouldn't show up in the routing table," then this is still a bad selection. It focuses on one collection of IP addresses, and ignores the other networks that should not be routed.

All of these examples demonstrate that we can't focus on just one subsection of the population if we want the sample to be representative. We have to consider the entire population. Otherwise, we're not going to be able to apply the results from the study to the entire population.

No matter how the sample is taken, keep that in mind. Be careful about when and what the results apply. Be aware of errors and remember statistics shows us what could reasonably apply, but it isn't a panacea.

6.3 Probabilistic Sampling

In the previous section, we talked about how a sample should be representative of the population, and should not focus on one subset. A good method to accomplish this is by using randomness. Pick a subset of the population at random and that will be the sample.

An easy way to think of this is, suppose a list of 100 domain names is written on slips of paper, then dropped into a hat. A sample of size ten means to pull ten pieces of paper out of the hat and that is the sample. This is also known as *sampling without replacement*.

An alternative is called *sampling with replacement*. Each time a piece of paper is pulled out of the hat, the domain name on it is recorded, and the paper put back. Sampling with replacement means that it's possible to get the same item twice and record it both times.

If sampling is done with replacement, then the probability of choosing each element is 1 in 100. This is because each time a piece of paper is pulled out, there are 100 pieces of paper in the bag. Sampling without replacement means the first time a piece of paper is chosen, the probability of choosing each element is also 1 in 100. The probability of choosing the second piece of paper changes to 1 in 99 because there are now 99 pieces of paper in the bag. The third piece of paper now has a probability of 1 in 98. The tenth time a piece of paper is pulled out, the probability of getting any piece of paper in the bag has dropped to 1 in 90.

Sampling with replacement means that the probability of choosing each element changes each time a piece of paper is chosen. This means that the samples are *dependent*, since the elements chosen on each successive choice are affected by the previous choices. The samples with probability and without replacement are *independent* because when an element chosen, the successive choices aren't affected by that choice.

Statistically speaking, these methods are known as *probabilistic sampling*. Assumptions are made when either of these methods are used. For one thing, we assume that it is equally probable to choose any unique item in the population. That means if the population is a collection of IP addresses, it is as likely to get 8.8.8.8 as it is to get 127.0.0.1. If the population is a collection of malware, each piece is equally likely to be chosen. This is also what enables the sample to get a good view of the population at large.

It is considered the best method of sampling to gain a representative sample, but it can be costly and as we will discuss in the following examples, difficult to do.

Example 1.

Suppose the population is the set of all strings that could be domain names, and the goal is to make a probabilistic sample of it. The first attempt is a random string generator that creates strings that look like string1.string2, for example, fdjdfddf.dfjd or eabadrea.cod. This is not quite what is needed since there is a set of top level domains used on the Internet. The second string (string2) cannot be a random string, as shown in the example; it must be one of the top level domains. To be fair, it actually must be one of the top effective TLDs. There are some TLDs, such as .uk, which have subdomains that they treat as top level domains, such as .co.uk. So if the generated domains are string1.randomTLD, then the effective TLDs (Mozilla, 2007) will be omitted.

The probabilistic sample of all strings that could be domain names would then be generated by first choosing a random string that has between three and sixty-three characters. Then a random effective TLD from the list of effective TLDs would be chosen. Some TLDs, however, allow strings that are shorter than three characters. For example, overstock.com uses o.co as a domain, so it is known the .co TLD allows domains with one character. In order to create the sample correctly, research into what domains are allowed by each TLD would be required.

Example 2.

Suppose the chosen population is the set of all valid IPv4 addresses. This is the set of all dotted quads w.x.y.z where each w, x, y, and z is an integer between 0 and 255. There are many ways to do this, but this example will discuss two methods. The first is to generate four random integers, each between 0 and 255, and create an IP address from them. This is the equivalent of putting all of the IPv4 addresses in a bag and choosing them with replacement, unless the method ensures the sample only contains a set of unique addresses.

For the second method, an IP address is a way to represent a number between 0 and 2^{32}. It is much easier to write 127.0.0.1 rather than to write 2130706433, but there is a method to convert the IP address to an integer and vice versa. Making use of this, the method could generate random integers between 0 and 2^{32} and then convert them to IP addresses.

If it is decided that the sample should only contain IPv4 addresses that are publicly routed, then the sample would have to restrict the random number ranges to those. This means, for example, that the set of IPv4 addresses should not contain any address in 127.0.0.0/8.

Example 3.
Network flow is a record of the traffic that passed through a network. It is not necessarily the packet capture, but rather it is the trace of the start time, end time, number of bytes, protocol, and ports involved in the traffic, as well as potentially more information. The study is designed to analyze network traffic and the population for the traffic is network flow.

If every flow has a unique identifier associated with it, then the random sample can be a set of random identifiers. It's possible to then find the the flow associated with this data and analyze it. If this does not exist, another method is needed.

For the second method, time will be used. The start and stop times for the data set are known, so it is possible to choose random times in that period. The problem is, what if there is no flow that starts on the random time chosen.

Another method to fix this issue is to create a set of start times of all flow and choosing randomly from that set. However, it is possible that multiple flows start at the same time. This means that the assumption made using probabilistic sampling doesn't work. The assumption was that each element in the set is equally likely but if there are two flows that start at the same time, that isn't true.

It's also important to remember that if the population is the network flow from one network, then any statistical analysis done yields results that are local to that one network.

Example 4.
Incident reports often have a number associated with them, known as either the ticket number or the incident number. If the goal is to take a random

sample of incident reports, then the starting point is a set of the incident numbers. The sample is then chosen from these numbers.

Similar to the network flow example, if the population is the set of incidents at a given organization, then the statistical analysis is relevant only to that organization.

6.4   Stratified Sampling

In Section 6.3 we discussed taking a random sample of our entire population. This doesn't work for every situation. Suppose our population is a family of malware with different versions. Unfortunately, the collection process has been somewhat skewed. Suppose the population has ten times more samples of version A than version B and five times more of version C than B. If strict random sampling is done, then version B is going to be underrepresented in the final sample. This can skew the results.

Instead of doing a probabilistic sample over the entire population, the population is separated into three groups, and samples are taken from each group. This way, the sample isn't overwhelmed by version A.

This method is called *stratified* sampling. It is very useful when the population isn't uniform, such as in the discussion of malware above. The sample should be representative, but if it's overwhelmed by one group in sample, that wouldn't be representative.

Example 5.
Suppose a network consists of a /26, a /24, and a /27, and these networks are not contiguous. The goal is to sample from IP addresses from the network in order to do a study on the network traffic originating from the IP addresses. The /26 contains 64 IP addresses, the /24 has 256, and the /27 has 32. In a probabilistic sample, the /27 will not be as well represented as the /24. To get around this, a stratified sample is used. Random IP addresses from each network are chosen. That way, the /24 doesn't overwhelm the /27 in the sample.

6.5   Purposive Sampling

When the sample is taken randomly, a nice view of the population is created. Nothing in particular is focused on in the random sample. Sometimes, however, a specific feature is chosen to study. The random selection can be done and the hope is enough samples with the chosen feature are found, or the alternative is to pick samples with that feature. If the samples are chosen deliberately, then that is called *purposive* sampling.

It is possible to combine random sampling with purposive sampling. A new population would be created by choosing only those elements of the population with the desired attribute. Then a random sample is taken of that. In this case, the random sample is a representative sample of the new population, not the original population.

Example 6.
Suppose the population for a study is the network traffic for a large organization over 24 hours. There's a lot of traffic to be examined, but the study is mostly interested in ICMP traffic. We could sample all of the traffic, but ICMP traffic could get lost in the massive amounts of other traffic. The research would be started by purposively sampling to only pull out ICMP traffic followed by a random sample of the ICMP traffic.

Example 7.
The population is the set of all incident reports but the study is only interested in those incidents where an advanced persistent threat (APT) was discovered. Rather than trying to take a random sample of those reports and hoping that we find some with APT mentioned, those reports will be pulled separately. This means that anything discovered in the study only applies to those reports about an APT represented in the data set.

6.6   Convenience Sample

One day, a researcher decides to look at the number of IP addresses a sample of domains point to. Instead of collecting domains in a rational manner, the researcher pull the logs of a random user and determines what domains they use and examines those. They just happened to find those domains in a location and used them. They aren't representative and they weren't collected nicely, the researcher just happened to find them.

Creating a sample by what someone happens to find is called a *convenience* sample. The data were used because it was convenient, not because it represented a good cross-section of the population. This means that a convenience sample is not necessarily representative of the population at large.

Convenience samples are common in cybersecurity. Malware is collected using various methods. For example, using a honeypot or letting people submit samples. Those samples are ones that just happen to show up. It would be nice if all the malware authors in the world submitted their samples to a central repository, but that isn't going to happen. Researchers have to work with what they have, which is a collection of samples they happened upon. That is a convenience sample of malware. This means that there is no way of making statements of the population of malware as a whole. All the researcher can do is make statements about the sample they have collected, which may or may not be representative of the population of malware. There is also no way of determining if it is representative.

Example 8.

The convenience sample can be combined with the purposive sample. The convenience sample is a collection of malware that we collected through various means. One kind of malware is known as a file dropper. This malware exists to download and drop files; usually malicious ones. It can be said say that a lot of malware drop files, but file droppers definitely drop files.

The purposive sample then becomes the subset of the convenience sample. The sample is found from all samples of the convenience sample that are file droppers, and the study uses those. What is derived from this purposive sample cannot be used to infer information about the population of file droppers at large or even the original convenience sample. It can only be used to talk about the subset of the convenience sample that is file droppers.

Example 9.

Passive DNS (Weimer, 2005) is a very useful tool in cybersecurity. It is a trace of the queries made in DNS but doesn't include who made them. A malicious domain can be found in it because someone queried that domain and received a response, but for privacy reasons the origin of the query isn't saved.

The problem is that it isn't known how the passive DNS was necessarily collected or where it was created. It is entirely possible that the collector is with one particular company's name server, so all that is seen the queries that that name server receives. This isn't a representative sample of the internet as a whole, rather, it is a representative sample of what that name server sees. Without the context of how the data was collected, the sample only reflects the population from the passive DNS data set and not the Internet as a whole.

Another thing to consider is that some countries can consider an IP address to be personally identifying information (Spring and Huth, 2012). This can affect results so be aware of the possibility.

Example 10.
Using a passive Domain Name System (pDNS) data source, a researcher has decided that they want to study name servers. To do this, the researcher needs to find a list of all domains that are being used as name servers. This means they look for all responses that contain NS records.

After much consideration, the researcher has decided that they want a sample of 10,000 of these domains that act as name servers. They are not considering the number of domains that each name server record is associated with, just the fact that the domain acted as a name server. Once this sample is taken, they discover that 47% of it is related to one domain, call it example.com. This means that 47% of the domains that act as name servers are of the form string.example.com, where string appears to be a random string of letters and numbers.

Clearly, this is a problem with the sample. It is representative of the pDNS data source, but it is skewed. Any results we find using this sample will be heavily represented by the domains that have the pattern string.example.com, which can make the results useless. It's possible to make a new sample of 10,0000 domains that act as name servers, but leave out any domain that looks like sample.example.com. By doing this, the influence of this domain on the results has been mitigated.

As an example of how this can skew results, suppose the researcher is counting the number of domains each name server supports. The domains string.example.com only support one domain. This means that 47% of those results is a 1. If we want the median of the results, then that's going to be close to 1. It also will skew the mean as well.

Example 11.
In BGP routing, periodic updates are sent to peers. These updates include route additions and route withdrawals. The routing table is never static; there are always changes being made to it. One interesting thing about BGP is there's no security built in to it. There is no way of being sure, based on the basic protocol, that the addition received is a valid route to the destination.

In fact, route injections and route leaks often occur. These are the routes that are received that aren't valid routes to the destination. Route leaks are when the invalid route is an accident and route injections are when the invalid route is malicious. Suppose a researcher would like to determine what percentage of routes that are received are either route injections or route leaks. As this can be quite a bit of data, they will start with a sample.

Since these updates arrive over time, the best thing to do is to choose a time period, such as an hour, and take a sample of the updates in that time period. BGP has a delay timer built into it, which means two updates from the same source for the same route at the same time shouldn't occur.

This becomes a convenience sample when the source of the data is considered. The choices for the data are routing repositories available on the web or an organization's data. Either way, the sample is seeing the routes it just "happen" to see. No one sees all the possible routes on the Internet, due to route filtering and local communities.

6.7 Sample Size

We've covered various sampling methods in this chapter. It's useful to know how to take a sample; it's even better to know how many units one should choose for the sample. The size of the sample can affect how well statistics model the population at large.

The results of surveys are usually "$x\%$ agreed with this, with a sampling error of $\pm y\%$". This means that if the population is considered as a whole, the actual number of people that agreed with the survey is between $(x-y)\%$ and $(x+y)\%$. Someone took a sample of the defined population and did the survey, and they project that the amount of the population that agrees with it is between those two numbers. This means they inferred from their sample the actions of the population and determined how close that result should be.

That sampling error is very important to figuring out the sample size. It's important to create a sample that's large enough that there isn't a huge sampling error, but small enough that the entire population isn't used.

Consider an example related to cybersecurity. Pretend that it's possible to take take a random sample of all domain names and measure the length of the second level domain. That is, the length of `google` in the `google.com` domain or the length of `example` in `example.net`. This yields a number associated with each domain, and it's possible to plot that result. One might assume (unwisely) that this result fits a normal distribution or bell curve, meaning the length of most domain names is close to the average length.

This fact about the normal distribution is what is used in order to find the sample size. The goal is for the sample to fit this, meaning that it is desired that the average of the sample taken of the population of domain names to be close to the average of everything, so it should be with the other values in that 95% range. That 95% is what is called the confidence level. The goal is to choose the sample size so that the average is within the 95% confidence level. If the goal is to be more precise, then the sample can be chosen so that it is within the 99% confidence level. For less precision, choose the 90% confidence level.

This means that the acceptable error between the sample's result and the population's result is 100% minus the confidence level. Let e be the shorthand way of saying error. Also let P denote the size of the population. There are several complex ways to estimate sample size, but for this book, a simpler method is used. (Israel, 1992). Let s denote the sample size, then the equation is:

$$s = \frac{P}{1 + P * e^2} \tag{6.1}$$

Returning to Example 10, suppose there is a population of 4.6 million domains that have been identified to act as name servers. The goal is to create a sample with a 95% confidence level, so the formula is:

$$s = \frac{4600000}{1 + 4600000 * 0.05^2} = \frac{4600000}{11501} = 400 \tag{6.2}$$

Which is a rather small number, but according to the math, that's all that is needed to assure that there's a 95% chance the average associated value of the sample will be close to the average of the entire population. Remember that this is a probability estimate. Assuming that the distribution of results is normal, there is a 95% chance the average value over the set will match the value over the entire population.

Now, this doesn't mean it's necessary to restrict the data set to a small number. It is just a guide for finding the minimum number that will ensure the average of the sample is reasonably close to the average of the population.

The formula in Equation 6.1 is really an estimate for the sample size; the real equations use the slope of the normal distribution. A simple estimate of that value will work for this book. It has been determined that this estimate is really close to the value computed using fancier math though. The actual computation makes use of calculus which is beyond the scope of this book.

6.8 Lessons Learned

The statistical methods discussed in Chapter 5 are only part of the tools needed for analysis. The ability to take a sample of a huge population is another. This chapter discussed those methods and some of the pitfalls associated with them.

If you take nothing else from this chapter, the fact that cybersecurity is mostly based on convenience samples is an important concept. We can't enumerate the populations for most of our data. Either those data doesn't exist or they aren't' available for us. Malware, domain names, and BGP routing are just three examples of the populations that we can't enumerate.

That shouldn't stop us from analyzing the data we can retrieve, but we should be aware of the limitations that exist. The gold standard is a random sample of the entire population, but that isn't always available. Describing the sampling method used in your analysis is important.

Chapter 7

Designing Structured Observations

This chapter is about how to go about learning about the cybersecurity world through structured observations. There are many kinds of structured observations, the most famous of which are probably experiments. The popular notion of a lab experiment is more precisely called an RCT. However, the cybersecurity practitioner should not be limited to experiments. Broad guidance for designing structured observations in cybersecurity is difficult because of the wide variety of topics and specialties that are relevant to cybersecurity. This chapter relies on the fundamentals covered in the preceding chapters. The following chapters will provide detailed examples of putting this chapter into practice.

Especially for studies with statistical tests, the jargon to describe the results of a study is a "positive" or "negative" result. "Positive" and "negative" results are equally valuable. Both mean that the researcher conducted the study well and reached an informative result that others can understand and use. Researchers, unfortunately including journal publishers, have a human tendency to think "positive" results are better (Open Science Collaboration, 2015). This effect seems to be related to the human tendency to think novel or exciting things are more true. The resulting publication bias is quite dangerous and interferes with researchers forming reliable collective knowledge. The outcome to avoid is a *non-result*, in which the study was designed badly, executed poorly, or the study population was too small or too skewed. No one can use a non-result, except perhaps as a cautionary tale about studies could be done differently. But if you have either a "positive" or "negative" result, your study has succeeded.

Section 7.1 will discuss some heuristics for selecting which study type is appropriate for which situations. Section 7.2 will cover the major types of structured observation, their strengths and weaknesses, and some guidance on how to learn to design adequate instances of each type. Strengths and weaknesses are largely in relation to the desirable study properties introduced in Chapter 4, but also depend on limitations and resources of available data on populations of interest (see Chapter 6). The types of structured observation we will cover are case studies, natural experiments and measurement studies, interventions, RCTs, and simulation or mathematical exploration. A designer usually needs to conduct some exploratory analysis (Chapter 5) before they have enough information to select a study type.

7.1 Choosing a Study Type

In most cases, to get a thorough model of a system of interest requires an interlocking set of studies drawn from all these study types. Each of the five types has different situations to which it is better at adapting. So choosing a study type has at least as much to do with what has already been done as it does with what the study designer wants to know.

No system of interest is completely new. So the first step in learning about it is really to do some reading about similar systems and what other people have found. Conducting a systematic review is its own kind of study, in a way. A systematic review need not cover academic literature; there are various practitioner communities that publish talks and proceedings as well. Like other studies, a systematic review should have a literature search method laid out ahead of time. The method includes search terms, search locations, and how the results will be evaluated for relevance. It is preferable that someone else has already done the literature review; you should search common computing sources of literature reviews before repeating the work, such as the IEEE S&P Systematization of Knowledge (SoK) papers and the *ACM Computing Surveys* journal. Talking to people who have experience with the system of interest is also a good start. After gathering information about the system of interest and what has been done, a study designer is much better positioned to know what aspects of the system could be better understood.

As a first heuristic, observational studies, such as case studies and measurement studies, are a prerequisite for designing adequate studies that involve an intervention. Without some basic knowledge of the important entities and activities in a system, a study designer will be hard-pressed to form a hypothesis about what to intervene on. This advice mirrors cybersecurity practice. An adequate inventory and asset management system are prerequisites for an incident management program. Asset management is similar to a series of measurement studies, whereas incident management is similar to a series of intervention studies.

Cybersecurity is the study and assurance of a sociotechnical system. Many studies are realized and designed differently if they will focus on the sociological or the technological aspects of cybersecurity. A measurement study of how users cope with complex password studies and a measurement study of the features of servers with open Secure Shell (SSH) ports may look quite different. They certainly use different research tools to achieve their aims. But they can both inform different aspects of our understanding of the authentication ecosystem.

This kind of discussion is uncommon in many fields because many academic fields are at least partially defined by their characteristic methods of study (Craver, 2007; Mitchell, 2003) and jargon built up around and about those methods (Galison, 2010). However, cybersecurity got rather large, rather fast. Both the norms and useful approaches within subfields are under development. This ongoing development means the designer must be more conscious of meeting the goals of consistency, generalizability, transparency, and containment (Chapter 4) than in more established fields.

As a second heuristic, study design should focus on much smaller questions than people often expect. It is important to break the problem into as many smaller problems as plausible. That is, decompose the problem (Bechtel and Richardson, 1993). "How did the attacker get in?" is not an actionable research question. "Were there any unauthorized access attempts to the file server between January 1 and January 14?" is approachable, but will need to be accompanied by other interleaving questions about other methods and times. The research program is then a description of these various interleaving questions and how they are related.

Another complementary way of choosing a study type is to try to find a similar study that would be applicable if it were repeated in a slightly different place, time, or with a small variation. This approach would provide two benefits: (1) a draft study design and (2) some related results with which to compare.

Study design, and choosing a study design, is a skill. As such, it can be developed with considered, effortful practice. Practice helps develop a sense of what an achievable study is, but it also develops skills in executing study types. A study designer is constrained by the kinds of studies with which they have experience. So practice a variety of study types to gain practice both in study type selection as well as to broaden your experience.

7.2 Types of Studies

This section introduces five broad categories of study. Often, a scientific field will grow up around a narrow interest, a combination of a phenomenon to study and a way to study it. For example, many fields in the life sciences study memory in mammals, but cellular physiology studies neurons with a few characteristic study types, whereas behavioral psychology studies whole animals with a different set of characteristic study types (Craver, 2007). Cybersecurity has not yet developed a clearly delineated set of sub-fields, so this chapter introduces different study types for a wide set of situations. This chapter is focused on providing enough information about the study types so that a designer can select which type is most suitable for their topic of interest, but not enough detail to provide a how-to guide on designing it. These five types are:

Case studies are scientific reports that detail a specific occurrence of interest as observed by the author. A case is a complex functional unit.

Natural experiments and measurement studies take as central the observation of the state of the world; natural experiments focus on special events of interest outside the study designer's control, whereas measurement studies isolate a few measures of interest in relevant populations.

Interventions are a pre-planned change to a live system and accompanied by observation before, during, and after the change.

RCTs test the effectiveness of an intervention by creating two groups that are statistically equivalent except for the intervention. The results measure the difference when only one group receives the intervention.

Simulation and mathematical exploration starts with a description of the system of interest and a model of how the system changes over time; the study is to evolve the start state, based on the model, and observe the outcome states.

7.2.1 *Case Studies*

A case study is a scientific report that details a specific occurrence of interest as observed by the author. Case studies can be active, including interviews or other questioning. They can be solely passive observation. Case studies can follow just one case in isolation or they might follow a series of related cases in similar ways for comparison. A *longitudinal study* is a specific kind of case study that follows one or more cases for an extended period of time (often years), repeating the same observations at multiple points in time. Case studies usually do not involve a planned intervention by the observer (see Section 7.2.3 for intervention studies). Case studies may track changes such as the result of interventions outside the observer's control, but we cover these studies under the name *natural experiments* (see Section 7.2.2).

Case studies are traditionally associated with the social sciences, but they are common in cybersecurity as well. Stake (1995) is the canonical reference for how to design and conduct a good case study. Most things that are called case studies in the cybersecurity literature are conducted by researchers with a social science background, but these do not make up the majority of case studies in cybersecurity. Most case studies in cybersecurity are vulnerability reports or papers documenting how to attack some specific system in a specific situation—a case.

A case study should have a rigorous research method. It is no different than any other study type in that regard. The research question should be clearly articulated at the beginning. It is a kind of structured observation, not haphazard observation of convenient surroundings. The most important aspect of a case study is the data gathering plan. Analysis and interpretation of results should be systematized with a plan ahead of time, separated from data collection, and any judgement of the data should wait until all the data are collected. To the extent possible, the analysis of the case should search for plausible explanations of the case and connect it to other established cases as well as relevant pieces of more general knowledge.

A case is a complex functional unit. To do a case study means to analyze it as a whole complex unit rather than to try to break it down. The crux of a case study method is to observe the case while (1) avoiding an unknown change in the case by the act of observing and (2) preserving an accurate description that is orderly and accessible.

Some changes due to observation are known and so can be accounted for. If the case is a potentially vulnerable piece of software, running it in a debugger provides more opportunities for observation but also may alter its behavior. The insights gained from observing the software need to be analyzed and usually codified as a crashing test case before the study is usefully complete.

A theme with all types of studies is taking good notes. But detailed observational notes—whether intentionally selected logging of a program

Attacks and vulnerabilities as case studies

Heartbleed is a vulnerability in OpenSSL that was found in 2014 (Durumeric *et al.*, 2014). An adequate description of the vulnerability is also a case study. In cybersecurity, that means there are enough details to verify the vulnerability is real and understand how the vulnerability works. This understanding allows defenders to test if they are vulnerable and deploy mitigations; it allows the software vendor to fix it and issue a patch. Heartbleed is an important case because OpenSSL is such a common library, and it is used for a security function. We do not need to generalize beyond this case for a vulnerability report—the case itself is important enough that it requires a thorough understanding.

Heartbleed took advantage of the OpenSSL Heartbeat extension and was able to download the OpenSSL certificate information as well as other information stored in the web server's memory. In the OpenSSL Heartbeat extension, the client would send the server regular packets to keep the connection alive. Otherwise, the client would have to renegotiate the connection periodically, which had its own dangers. The keepalive packet had three sections: a payload consisting of random strings, the size of the payload, and a request to the server to send an acknowledgement packet in return to keep this connection alive. The server then saves the packet's payload at a random place in its memory stack. The server's response was to take the payload size from the client stack, then look at the memory location where it stored the client's random string and return a string starting at that memory location of payload size.

The attacker would lie to the server about the size of the payload. Instead of, for example, 8 bytes (which was the true size of the payload), the attacker would claim it was 65,227 bytes and would receive back data of that size. The attacker would receive everything in the memory of the web server starting at the point where the packet was stored; if the attacker is mildly lucky, this data could include the private TLS key of the server. If they're unlucky, they can send another heartbeat and try a few times until they are lucky.

To provide a good vulnerability report, like a good case study, the analyst needs to present all these details, how they result in a situation of interest (leaking cryptographic keys, in this case), and connect the case to the Internet ecosystem and why it matters.

of interest, or handwritten notes of human behavior—are also part of the results of a case study. Data collection should be repeatable, so that if another researcher were to conduct the study, they would collect similar information. To meet this requirement, data collection should be intentional. While "collect everything" isn't the worst plan, storage and search can become impractical, and even the act of defining what falls under "everything" requires some intention.

The main strength of a case study is that it's connected to the real world and system of interest both immediately and thoroughly (see Section 4.2.1). If the study population is only a small fraction of the population of interest, the extent to which the results generalize beyond the case study is typically low. This situation is common in case studies of humans. However, if the population of interest is TLS libraries, then a study on just OpenSSL (population of one) may tell us rather a lot about the population of interest since OpenSSL is the mostly commonly used TLS library. When the population of interest is small, then as long as the study population is carefully selected, the extent of generalization from the study may be adequate.

Case studies tend to be weaker on insulation (see Section 4.1.1). The case is a complex whole embedded in its context in the world, which is the antithesis of an insulated study environment. Consistency across time and space are often not expected with a case study. This lack is not a failing of case studies but rather a result of the complex nature of cases. A good case study should seek to identify the ways in which the context of the case, including its temporal and spatial situation, contribute to the history and salient observations about the case. It is not that a case study on a similar subject replicated at a later time or reproduced at a different location would be wrong if it acquired different results. Those would just be studies of different cases—related cases, to be sure, but also importantly different ones. These sorts of minor variations on a case study can help to identify differences which might be good targets for more controlled studies.

7.2.2 *Natural Experiments and Measurement Studies*

The core of both natural experiments and measurement studies is to observe the state of the world. Observational studies involve observing the world without changing it as part of the study. A special kind of observational study is a "natural experiment," in which the researcher observes the world during some interesting change that occurs outside the researcher's control. When natural experiments are important is if the change during which we can observe is somehow larger than any researcher *could* make or control. These can be due to either physical or social processes. For example, how electrical equipment behaves during a solar flare is one kind of natural experiment; humans cannot create magnetic fields as strong as those created occasionally by the sun. But the coronavirus pandemic created various natural experiments because of changes in the human social world; for example, oceanographers could listen to quiet oceans without noisy cruise ship engines in Alaska (Mars, 2020). The word "natural" only means the researcher did not design the intervention. The change can be in nature (solar flare) or not (human vacation habits), and the observation of interest can be in nature (ocean and whale noise) or not (electrical equipment).

A measurement study and a case study are both observational studies. We differentiate them based on the system of interest and the study population. A case study focuses on the complex, situated nature of a case. A measurement study is focused on abstracting away some of the complexity of the case and measuring certain representative features. A measurement study also tends to focus on a larger study population, selected more intentionally to be representative of the population of interest (see Section 4.2.3).

The strengths and weaknesses of a natural experiment both revolve around its key feature: the most important aspect of the study is outside the control of the study designer. One important strength is related to containment. The kinds of interventions that might be found via natural experiments cannot be plausibly designed because, even if possible, the intervention would cause inordinate harm if planned as part of a more controlled study. Like case studies, natural experiments have a high degree of connection to the world and systems of interest because the experiment is simply part of the world itself. While the topic of interest in a natural experiment may be studied in other ways, the kinds of observations and study populations that are possible with natural experiments just are not possible any other way.

Due to that uniqueness, study designers are willing to tolerate imperfections and weaknesses in aspects that, in other situations, would not be acceptable. There is essentially no consistency across time or space with a natural experiment. However, unlike with case studies, this failure of replication and reproduction is not intentionally due to the complexity of the case. It's because the intervention is out of the study designer's control. This fact makes natural experiments fragile and difficult. There is no chance to try a pilot study to see what data should be collected, and there is no restarting and trying again if the researchers were to make a mistake. Sometimes, there is hardly time to prepare for an event that induces a natural experiment. These factors, combined with the expected lack of in-

General Data Protection Regulation (GDPR) as a natural experiment on WHOIS

The GDPR is a law in the European Union (EU) to regulate data protection and privacy. Enacted in 2015 and effected in 2018, the law applies to every member of the EU, without regard for the national laws already in place (Albrecht, 2016). It contains rules and regulations for processing personal data. For example, IP addresses and cookies are now considered personally identifying data (Tankard, 2016).

The effective date of big public policy changes is one classic source of natural experiments. Just before and just after the policy change, the EU and the world are approximately the same, except for the policy change. One aspect that is affected by the GDPR is access to the *whois* data. *whois* links a DNS name with the registrant to whom it is delegated and the registry that is responsible for maintaining the delegation.

As of 2020, we are still in the midst of a natural experiment about what happens if access to *whois* data suddenly disappears. This data had been a useful tool to cybersecurity researchers (Piscitello, 2018), and the GDPR changed its availability. ICANN has been slow to clarify the policy stance on registrant data, and that uncertainty has lead several *whois* providers to turn off or restrict the service.

Anti-abuse staff and law enforcement would not globally elect to have a favored data source taken away overnight. That's what makes this sort of intervention only possible via a natural experiment (apologies for stretching the term natural to include political actions). While such a study cannot be repeated (we cannot implement the GDPR again for the first time), it is a unique source of insight about how useful *whois* data for anti-abuse work. Seeking this sort of insight amidst a momentous event is the crux of a good natural experiment.

sulation that comes with situating a study in the world, make interpreting natural experiments rather fraught. Natural experiments provide important evidence about what sorts of sequences of events are possible. But it is not possible to declare, on the basis of a natural experiment alone, why it happened that way.

Measurement studies have a profile of strengths and weaknesses that can particularly complement case studies (see Section 7.2.1) and simulations (see Section 7.2.5). One reason for this is that a measurement study has the best chance of reaching a census of the population of interest (as defined in Section 4.2.3. The important result is to learn how the measured properties are distributed within the population of interest. Chapter 6 introduces some statistical techniques that are useful for this kind of assessment. Case studies need to be paired with these kinds of data because, while they provide a thorough description of the situated case, we need population data to learn to what extent those characteristics might be shared by others. Simulations need to be paired with these kinds of data because the data ground either the starting or ending point of the simulation in the real world. Such grounding is vital assurance the simulation is exploring plausible scenarios and explanations rather than wild fancies.

Insulation can be challenging in many ways for measurement studies. The act of measuring can influence the observed system. Even leaving Schrödinger and his cat aside, humans know when they are being watched, and they behave differently. Network or host measurements consume system resources that will change behavior on a resource-exhausted system. So whether it is psychology or packet throughput, measurement studies should measure the same property in multiple ways and cross-check the measures for consistency.

Measurements and information are also powerful. Both measuring and not measuring something can cause harms; a measurement is not value-free, and assessing containment is important for a measurement study just as anything else. For an example of how measurement choices can cause harms, see Noble (2018).

There are some things that cannot be measured almost by definition: for example, the security incidents undetected by defensive layers. This lack makes it tempting to measure the mirror of the unavailable values, in this case, security incidents detected. But take great care in measuring an item whose interpretation is heavily influenced by an unmeasurable item. Without knowing something about the base rate of occurrence, it is easy to mistake an increase in detected security incidents as a problem, for example. But without knowing how many total (detected and undetected) incidents there are, it is impossible to know whether detecting 99 incidents is 99% effective or 2% effective. While a strength of measurement studies is that they provide concrete values for the measured items, a weakness is that, by themselves, they provide no context for how the measured items are related to other aspects of the system of interest. Other study types need to provide that context.

Measurement and observation of cyber crime

Cyber crime costs billions of dollars each year. Measuring the amount that it costs is a tricky process. Anderson *et al.* (2012) describe that there are over a hundred different sources for cyber crime statistics, but they are fragmented and have issues with collection consistency, over-reporting, under-reporting, sampling bias, and more. However, the authors attempt to control for these issues and measure the amount of cyber crime in 2012.

We also know that different cyber crimes have different scales of operation. We can't lump all cyber crime into one category; instead, we must create different categories to measure more effectively.

It is also one thing to measure the amount of losses from crime, but another to measure the true cost. If a bank loses $10 million dollars to fraud, there are also the costs of investigating the fraud and fraud prevention. These are direct outlays of money, but then there is also indirect loss: the lack of trust consumers have in their bank, the lost business opportunities due to the fraud, and more.

The researchers also returned to repeat the study in 2019 (Anderson *et al.*, 2019). Mobile crime was not a large factor in 2012, yet it has grown in 2019. Both papers use estimates as their basis but also discuss the underpinnings of why the estimates are useful.

There is really only one global cyber crime ecosystem, so this kind of measurement study is both widely applicable and very specific. These accurate measurements and observations about the state of the world are tremendously valuable. They inform public policy and organizational risk policy by setting expectations and contextualizing the resources involved for all parties effected by cyber crime.

7.2.3   *Interventions*

A study in which an intervention on the system of interest is planned and executed by the researcher is common. Young children naturally explore the world with a naïve version of intervention studies. The archetypical vision of an experiment is an intervention, but usually, when lay people say "experiment" they actually mean an RCT. This section will cover studies where the intervention is planned by the study designer (distinguishing them from natural experiments) but lack the very specific controls expected of an RCT. RCTs are discussed in the following section.

There are various possible kinds of intervention studies. Cybersecurity inherits much of its received terminology from computer science, for better or worse (Spring *et al.*, 2017). In this case, it is probably for the worse, as there are a variety of conflicting views about the term "experiment" (Tedre and Moisseinen, 2014). The five interrelated views on experimentation in computing identified within the literature review are feasibility, trial, field, comparison, and controlled experiments (Tedre and Moisseinen, 2014, §3). A feasibility experiment is better judged for strengths and weaknesses by the terms of a case study since it is a proof of concept based on the specific case. Controlled experiment is a synonym for RCT, discussed later. This section will introduce the middle three as varying degrees of intervention.

A trial experiment "evaluates various aspects of the system using some predefined set of variables" (Tedre and Moisseinen, 2014, §3). The intervention in a trial experiment is quite light. Essentially, the intervention is introducing a new software system to an environment of interest and observing the interaction and how the system fares. A trial is appropriate if the software system performs a novel function or an established and useful function in a novel way. Such an intervention should probably be accompanied by a measurement study of how existing related systems perform on the same measures taken on the novel system.

Some kinds of trial experiment are better assessed by the criteria of a simulation. Program verification and fuzz testing might be seen as trials of the new system to measure certain features. But the main concerns with program verification and fuzzing are whether the results apply to the actual world, which is the main challenge in simulations. Therefore, we handle them in Section 7.2.5. Trial experiments that deploy a system into a novel environment have a very different set of concerns.

In some ways, trial experiments are the worst combination of study design properties. They provide all of the detail of a case study that makes insulation hard but without any of the connection that assures the observations apply to a genuine situation in the world. One valuable way to think about planning good trials is to think of the test environment(s) as the study population and the spectrum of current and potential future environments as the population of interest. The core question can then be phrased as how to select a meaningful study population to argue for an adequate extent of generalization from the trial.

Field experiments are the quintessential intervention in cybersecurity practice. The basic idea is to change a live system and observe it before, during, and after the change. The research question should be specified ahead of time; in practice, it is often a goal state such as discarding enough abusive packets to quell the DDoS.

Incident response as a study based on interventions

The entirety of computer security incident response (CSIR) could be viewed as a series of loosely controlled field experiments. Consider the classic case of Stoll (1989) hunting what would turn out to be Russian intelligence operatives on the Lawrence Berkeley National Laboratory (LBNL) computer system in the 1980s.

Don't know where a suspicious user account came from? Delete it and see if anyone or anything complains. Can't see what is happening when the suspicious user logs in overnight? Invent a wire-to-paper IDS logging system and see if their activity can be tracked with it. Not sure if the attacker is gaining access through a vulnerable emacs version? Upgrade the version and assess attack success. Not sure who the hacker is? Invent fictitious LBNL department documents and see if they will stay in the honeypot long enough to track them.

Stoll trained as an astrophysicist, and so his abilities to design suitable interventions and take thorough notes are no accident. They're an example of how scientific training can be adapted to a cybersecurity context. Stoll (1989) remains one of the de facto standard accounts of how an analyst should think in CSIR to this day (Spring and Illari, 2018b).

As with trial experiments, the main weaknesses of a field experiment are insulation and consistency. Field experiments often do not enable you to understand why an intervention works as expected or not. On the other hand, field experiments are more like case studies in that they capture a sequence of events embedded in the world and so connection is high. The results may have a low extent of generalizability, but if the population of interest is the same as the study population, that might be fine.

On the other hand, no attention to generalizability and lessons learned from field experiments leads to a vicious cycle of repeating nearly identical interventions without much improvement in efficiency. There are various names for this repetitive cycle of analyst effort: firefighting, playing whack-a-mole, etc. The purpose of viewing incident response and other cybersecurity practices as field experiments is to structure that knowledge as both interconnected to other field experiments as well as to identify the most critical gaps in general knowledge that would enable more efficient synthesis of the results and thus better planning, defense, and prevention. Incident management has advocated feeding lessons from response back into preparation and protection for decades (Alberts *et al.*, 2004), but advice on how exactly to do that has been absent (Spring and Illari, 2018b). Interlocking study types with complementary study properties provides a way forward if we view incident response operations as a kind of intervention study.

Comparison experiments are common in the academic literature; they refer to a comparison between two or more possible solutions to a problem. Although the concept of comparison is good, to meet the stated goals of a comparison paper, a study designer should conduct an RCT. Computer science is plagued by "horserace papers" that are merely biased comparisons of the author's favored solution against a study population selected to make the author's choice look good (Tedre and Moisseinen, 2014). Given the failure to hold comparison experiments to standard precautions and design norms, our professional opinion is to not conduct them and to avoid basing decisions on them. The exception would be any comparison experiment that is strict enough to be considered an RCT, but then it is no longer a comparison experiment. A comparison study should also not be confused with a set of case studies of possible solutions; however, a set of case studies should also avoid basing a comparison on a biased set of parameters, measurements, and tests. Standard benchmark sets might be adequate defenses against the abuse of comparison studies in some parts of computer science. Due to the highly contextual nature of cybersecurity solutions, as evidenced by the difficulty of comparing blocklist contents (Metcalf and Spring, 2015), it is unclear that security-related performance could reasonably have benchmarks in the same way.

7.2.4 *RCTs*

The term *randomized controlled trial* (RCT) has a specific meaning within the medical sciences to be a particular kind of clinical trial involving people; RCTs are also used in the social sciences to study humans. Specifically, an RCT tests the effectiveness of an intervention by creating two groups that are statistically equivalent except for the intervention and measuring the difference when only one group receives the intervention. The phrase "statistically equivalent" requires a lot of unpacking. Although the term RCT is specific to sociomedical studies, the concept of a study with statistically equivalent groups and different interventions goes by other names in fields adjacent to cybersecurity, such as "controlled experiment" (Tedre and Moisseinen, 2014) or "A/B testing" (Beyer *et al.*, 2018).

Discussion of how to design RCTs is the topic of several books (Kabisch *et al.*, 2011). When to use an RCT is also the topic of several books. When public policy makers should expect an RCT and how to integrate results into policy is even the topic of books (Parkkinen *et al.*, 2018). This section will orient this vast space, but we will not be able to do more than a brief introduction here.

Cybersecurity authors have generally endorsed the view that there is a hierarchy of evidence quality and that RCTs are unequivocally at the top of it; the only thing supposedly better than an RCT is a meta-analysis of multiple RCTs. Edgar and Manz (2017, ch. 1) explicitly do so, while Dykstra (2015, ch. 1) implicitly adopts this stance. However, there are well-documented problems with this simplistic evidence hierarchy (Parkkinen *et al.*, 2018). Perhaps the most important is that a researcher cannot decide which RCTs are important or helpful to conduct without understanding something about the real-world problem. That is, the topic of interest needs to already have a basic breakdown into entities and activities, how they are related or organized, the topic's history or how it comes about, and some important similarities and differences to other interesting topics (Spring and Illari, 2018a). This information is best gained through the other types of structured observation described in this chapter. RCTs certainly have an important role to play, but that role is not necessarily more or less important than other kinds of studies.

Cybersecurity practitioners often express a kind of dismay that they could never do proper science, and therefore become demoralized (Spring *et al.*, 2017). What these practitioners are often actually expressing is the very sensible observation that an RCT is not an appropriate study type given their topic of interest and the maturity of the community's understanding of that topic. However, they have mistakenly conflated "doing science" with the much more limited "conducting an RCT." This outlook is dangerous because it makes those practitioners closed off to advice on study design for other study types.

Compared to the biochemistry of pharmaceuticals, there are relatively few scenarios in cybersecurity where RCTs are an appropriate study type. But that's alright; astrophysics conducts exclusively observational studies and it is not somehow less worthy of scientific accolades than biochemistry because of it. Similarly, a cybersecurity researcher does not need to conduct an RCT to be a "real" scientist; they only need to select an appropriate

RCTs during release engineering

Outside the medical and social sciences, study designers may not use the term RCT; however, they still frequently conduct studies with controlled intervention on statistically equivalent groups. For example, these principles are used in "canarying" releases as a part of release engineering. Beyer *et al.* (2018, ch. 16) refer to this practice as a kind of A/B testing; that is, a study with two groups (A and B) that are statistically equivalent except for the test of interest.

Canarying in software releases is the act of choosing a random subset of systems to which to deploy a new software release (Beyer *et al.*, 2018, ch. 16). If the software is released all at once, then the failure of a release can take the entire installation offline. By using a randomly chosen subset, the potential errors can be discovered without requiring downtime for all of the systems.

The canaries are then measured for various properties, such as response time or error rate. These measurements are then compared against the control, that is, the systems that were not upgraded.

There are issues to be aware of; for example, an overloaded system in the control group could mimic a canary due to the load. Using canarying for software releases is a useful method to constantly deploy upgrades without affecting the entire population of systems. The use of different terminology—A/B testing versus RCT—hides a lot of deep similarities in how the two practices contribute to study design goals and desirable study design properties.

study design for their research question and conduct that study with the desirable properties described in Chapter 4. We are emphasizing this point so strongly because, in our experience, the biggest threat to conducting an RCT in cybersecurity is doing one because that's what the researcher assumes "doing science" means rather than actually understanding which study type should be used. Such an inappropriate RCT will fail no matter how well-designed it is. Before embarking on an RCT in cybersecurity, ensure the problem of interest is both relevant and well-studied by other research methods so that the place where the RCT will be informative is clear.

If an RCT is appropriate for the topic of interest, whether it is canarying during release engineering or analysis of human biometric performance for authentication, then the main work for the study designer is to truly understand how to create and maintain *statistically equivalent* groups. The

How an RCT can fail

Beckman *et al.* (2017) sets out a research question to understand where in the brain humans process representations of cryptography. This topic has the potential to be fascinating, but it has not been thoroughly studied. The authors might have been better off conducting some exploratory studies (Chapter 5) or case studies. But they endeavored to design an RCT on the basis of prior brain imaging studies. Unfortunately, the efforts highlight several ways an RCT can go wrong:

- WEIRD population taken as representative of all learners.

- Insufficient statistical power (Ellis, 2010).

- Not understanding the properties of the tool (when functional magnetic resonance imaging is misused, it leads "to a biased and inappropriately constrained characterisation of functional anatomy" (Friston *et al.*, 2006)).

- Inadequate blinding for an RCT: Chalmers *et al.* (1981) recommends quadruple blinding.

The result is not a negative result, but a non-result. A negative result means the study was conducted properly but the statistical analysis indicates the posterior belief should be that the intervention had no effect. A non-result means the study was conducted in such a way that we have no idea whether the intervention had an effect or not. A negative result contributes to knowledge about the system of interest. A non-result is a waste of time unless it is used as a case study on how to design better RCTs.

key step in any RCT is to divide the study population into two statistically equivalent groups, except for the intervention of interest, and maintain their statistical equivalence during the period of intervention and observation. This section introduces just two practices that assist that goal: appropriate blinding and pre-registering trial methodologies.

Appropriate blinding has at least four components (Chalmers *et al.*, 1981):

- The population selection process draws from a uniform distribution; the study designer cannot view nor influence the process.

- The study designer and research staff do not know which group is receiving the intervention.

- The study groups do not know which study group is receiving the information.

- The study designer and research staff do not know the partial progress or ongoing results of any study population group.

Each of these is important because there is ample evidence that without each blinding technique humans will consistently manipulate the results, whether consciously or subconsciously. To increase transparency and accountability, the study designer should pre-register an RCT method that ensures these kinds of blinding.

Pre-registering the trial has at least two positive effects, centered around ensuring the research staff maintain the statistical equivalence of the study groups: execution of the RCT and unbiased publication of results (Sterne *et al.*, 2011). Expecting the study designer to register the trial method incentivizes the designer to think through the method and that the execution abides by the plan. If the study designer cannot specify an RCT plan in enough detail ahead of time to register a methodology, then they should revisit whether an RCT is the most appropriate study type for the situation.

If the results of a study are buried or otherwise not published, it distorts the community's knowledge creation (Sterne *et al.*, 2011). There are various points at which publication of results can be influenced, such as by the researcher, by funding bodies, by program committees, and by publishers. For why this distortion is problematic, consider the release engineering example. Release engineering does not call its practice an RCT, but, for all intents and purposes, it is. Consider the results were filtered so that 100% of the successful release instances and between 20% to 50% of the failed release instances are returned to the engineers. Clearly this will prevent the engineer from building the best system, as failing cases definitely exist, but they are under-reported and therefore unfixed. It also makes the overall success of the release look (with these example numbers) between two to five times better than it really is. An analogous problem occurs if RCT results are not published because they are "uninteresting," "well-known," "unsurprising," or just not what the study designer hoped for.

The way to fix this publication problem is to register the trial method before it is conducted and commit to publishing the results, whatever they are. A designer does not need a journal or publisher to mediate this; a method signed with Pretty Good Privacy (PGP) including a timestamp, especially with the hash registered on some third-party store or even a block chain would accomplish the same non-repudiation of the study method. For release engineering, writing the code that conducts the canary tests is a way to register the method via the git commit, as long as the version of the code is strictly tied to the study.

7.2.5 *Simulation or Mathematical Exploration*

In a simulation, the study designer starts with a description of the system of interest and a model of how the system changes over time. The model is used to calculate (that is, simulate) future states of the system. If the system is a computer system, it is essentially a mathematical system itself, and so simulation and mathematical exploration collapse into nearly the same thing in computer science. In cybersecurity, where humans, security policies, economics, and cyber-physical systems are involved, there is an extra bit of care in ensuring the model represents the system of interest in the relevant ways. The goal of a simulation is often to test the plausibility of the model based on plausibility of the resulting outcomes. Many simulations may be conducted (in parallel) in order to compare the outcomes and select a preferred model.

Mathematical exploration and simulation play similar roles in building knowledge of the world. Whether the calculation is via pencil and paper or via a computer is the main difference between the two terms, and that is a distinction without a genuine difference, as far as learning about the world is concerned.

Simulation is more efficient than conducting all the studies. A simulation also has relatively low risk of harm, and so can be used as a strategy to improve containment. Simulation can be used to explore boundary conditions within which a more connected study might be needed. Simulation can be used to make predictions which can then be tested against future observations.

Simulation has a special place in cybersecurity because it has a special place in computing. The core problem for simulations in most fields is that they have to represent their system of interest on the computer. If there is a mistake or even just imprecision in that translation, then the simulation is likely useless if not misleading. But simulating behavior of other computers does not have this fundamental problem. Any computer can perfectly simulate any other computer; this was one of the first axioms of computer science (Turing, 1936). Of course, it will be impractical for a slow computer to simulate a fast computer, but this is a minor inconvenience rather than a core problem.

The strengths of simulation revolve around control. High insulation, high transparency, and high containment all stem from the fact that the simulation is entirely contained within the study designer's virtual environment.

The weaknesses of simulation revolve around its lack of connection. Strictly speaking, the subject of a simulation is the model itself, not the system of interest. So a simulation has no direct connection to the system that it simulates. Any connection is mediated by the model of the system. However, a primary thing a simulation tests is the consistency of that very model (see Section 4.1.5). This situation makes it unwise to trust the model being tested to carry the weight of a connection between a simulation and the system of interest.

The extent of generalizability of a simulation is a similarly tricky question. A simulation can be quite good at producing generalizable insights about models. But whether a truth about a class of models provides any insight into the situated system of interest which may be modeled by one element of that class is another, much foggier, question.

One way to reduce the bite of these weaknesses is formal modeling, such as logical modeling. Formal models, if constructed carefully, can provide structured guarantees about the relationship between the simulation and the studied model as well as the studied model and a real computer system (Pym *et al.*, 2018). For example, the specification and implementation of an important hashing function in OpenSSL has been verified using three such intermediate steps (Beringer *et al.*, 2015).

7.3   Recap

This chapter introduced six types of useful studies for cybersecurity science. In general, start out by observing via careful case studies and measurement studies. If those have already been completed adequately, consider simulations and interventions to help choose between competing models of the system of interest. After several iterations of observation and intervention, developing the model of the system of interest further may then require a carefully controlled RCT.

The strengths and weaknesses of the study types are loosely summarized in Table 7.1. RCTs have transparency in both the strengths and weaknesses because while a well-done RCT can provide a great deal of insight into

Simulating program inputs as a security test: Fuzzing

Fuzzing "is the execution of the program under test using input(s) sampled from an input space that *protrudes* [that is, extends] the expected input space of the program under test," usually to test the program for security policy violations (Manès *et al.*, 2019, p. 2). Each fuzz test is a trial or simulation of how the program under test behaves given a particular input. Fuzzing has proven quite successful in identifying flaws in programs and any production system should have fuzz testing as part of its development lifecycle.

In important ways, each round of fuzzing is automating the study design process. The model the simulation is probing is the mapping between input files and security policy. The desired behavior is that no input causes an exploitable crash. A fuzzer repeats many fuzz tests to explore that mapping and searches for exploitable crashes. The model of the program under test is updated based on the prior fuzz test's results. Those results are used to inform the selection of the next test input. A fuzzer contains a systematic method for checking whether the results support or trouble the model (that is, security policy) of the system of interest. And the next fuzz test considers the past two results, and the process continues. Fuzzing results will not be exhaustive, but the more evidence gathered without a crashing test case, the stronger the assertion that the program under test does not have exploitable input processing errors.

the whole process, any small lapse in transparency or study planning can introduce biases that undermine the results.

Table 7.1   Loose Summary of Strengths and Weaknesses of Six Broad Types of Study.

Type	Strengths	Weaknesses
Case study	Connection, documenting complexity	Insulation, consistency across space and time
Natural experiment	Containment: opens up possibilities otherwise unavailable	Consistency, fragility of execution, extent of generalization
Measurement study	Potential for conducting census, extent of generalization, replicability	Insulation, transparency of data collection is costly
Intervention study	Connection, application of designer's tools	Insulation, extent of generalization
RCT	Insulation, extent of generalization, transparency	Connection, transparency
Simulation	Insulation, transparency, containment	Connection

Chapter 8

Data Analysis for Cybersecurity: Goals and Pitfalls

When we begin research, we generally have a goal in mind. It may be to prove a new threat exists, to analyze a current one, to examine patterns of behavior, or another goal. Adversaries have asymmetric advantages in cybersecurity; the job of defenders is to mitigate that advantage.

To achieve the best results, researchers need to avoid pitfalls that can compromise their goal. A pitfall can compromise the validity of results and negate the work. Careful work is needed to create the best research. People want to learn from research and to use it for themselves but if the work falls into one of the common pitfalls, it isn't usable.

It's a careful path to take. The end goal is to do the best research, but the dangers of negating work are real. This chapter covers the goals and pitfalls from a cybersecurity point of view.

This is not an in-depth look on this topic; instead it is an introduction to the obvious pitfalls and goals in cybersecurity research. We want the results to be meaningful and useful and these are the first steps to look for or avoid.

8.1 Goals

Research is a process. At the end of the process, the goal is to move the field forward in some way. In cybersecurity research, this can be considered as two main goals.

One goal is to observe events and provide good explanations of security events. Participating in the events can introduce bias and change the results, so it is best to be an outside observer. This is often called *structured observation*. The collection should be done in a structured manner, which means there is a plan to collect data, and it is followed exactly. It also means if the plan is handed to someone else, they can follow it and also collect the same kind of data. For example, a program that collects passive DNS data is an unbiased observer. A program that queries the local name server for domains collected by asking random friends isn't.

In cybersecurity, this can include case studies as well as studies. In a study, the entire population or ecosystem is considered. Samples are taken and analyzed. Results are generated. For a case study, a single item or event can be analyzed. Case studies can illuminate the origins of an event, the changes over time, or even suggest solutions. They can suggest research directions or highlight previously unknown events and are important to comprehensive research.

A second goal is to create clear and comprehensible explanations for security events. Collecting data through structured observation allows researchers to achieve this goal. For example, explaining a malware's command and control system via DNS can be clear and comprehensible, and it can be useful for stopping the malware. Leaving out the channel for command and control when describing the malware or explaining that the malware is Internet-controlled isn't clear and comprehensible or useful.

Results should be replicable and reproducible. Those are actually two different things even though they sound like synonyms (Broman *et al.*, 2017). A study is reproducible if someone else can take the data and methods and create the same result. A study is replicable if someone can take the methods used in the study and repeat it. They won't start with the data used in the original study, but if the researcher defines their methods appropriately, the other researcher can take the methods, the process for collecting data, and replicate the results.

All research should be both. The results should be consistent if someone else tries to do the same study.

Researchers want their research to be used. If the results are so unique and not replicable by anyone else, then they're not useful to anyone else. Cybersecurity is, at its heart, a practical field. Results that are usable and applicable to more than a single person are important.

Another goal is to encourage corroboration. Corroborating evidence only strengthens research conclusions. If someone else can use their own methods to recreate results, that only adds to their usefulness.

8.2 Pitfalls in Statistical Analysis

In Chapter 5, we discussed methods that could be used to analyze data. In this section, we cover problems that can arise from those methods.

Table 8.1 Mean of the Three
Distributions

Distribution	Mean
normal	100.2
poisson	100
skewed normal	100.2

Statistics is an integral tool to research. It allows us to make inferences about a population based on a sample. Not every population can be studied in its entirety; the ability to take a random sample of that population and restrict the study to that sample is important and integral to research, not just in cybersecurity.

It is just that, though, a tool, and it can be misused. Just because something is proven statistically doesn't mean it is a truth, and unfortunately, people and researchers (Amrhein *et al.*, 2019) often conflate the two. Statistics just means the probability of something occurring is known, not that it must occur.

This section will discuss various pitfalls in statistical analysis and how to avoid them. It doesn't cover every possible pitfall, but does highlight the more common issues.

8.2.1   *Summary Statistics*

Mean, median, mode, and standard deviation are all summary statistics. That means that they take the measurements of a data set and distill it down to a single number. It's possible to say things like, "The average length of a domain in this set is 7.6," or "The median length of a domain in this data set is 6." A single summary statistic can be misleading, especially when comparing different sets.

Fig. 8.1 displays three distributions that are distinctly different, but all have the same mean. Table 8.1 has the means in question.

If consideration is only the mean, then the three very different distributions are conflated. Two of them appear visually similar, but the third, the Poisson distribution, is different; it is flatter. The visualization illustrates the difference, but the single statistic claims similarity.

The summary statistic can also mask variation. During the study of a botnet and its traffic, the amount of traffic every five minutes was measured every five minutes. Fig. 8.2 illustrates this, where the straight line is the average of the sample, 2111.94. If the analysis relied only on the average, then the spikes that occur in the data would be missed.

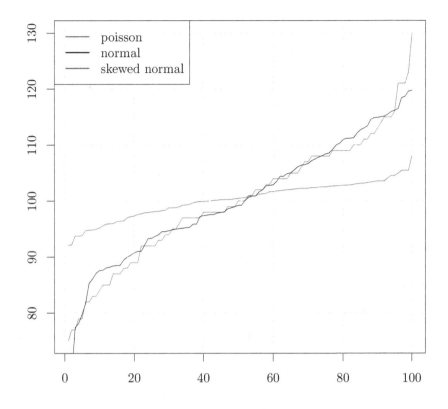

Fig. 8.1   Three Distributions with the Same Mean

Those two examples highlight the dangers of relying on a single statistic. Variation is missed, and data sets can be conflated as being similar when they clearly aren't. Describing a data set requires more than a single summary statistic.

Suppose there are two sets of domain names collected using different collection methods. Each set has 100 domains. The length of the domain names has been used as an indicator for maliciousness (Bilge *et al.*, 2011) so that is the measurement in question. The average length from Data Set 1 is 9.52, and the average length from Data Set 2 is 9.49. Using just that single statistic about the two sets, it would appear the sets are similar.

However, the median for Data Set 1 is 9 while the median for Data Set 2 is 10. The sets are looking a bit different now. The standard deviation for each set is 1.05 for the first and 1.22 for the second.

Finally, the two distributions are plotted in Fig. 8.3.

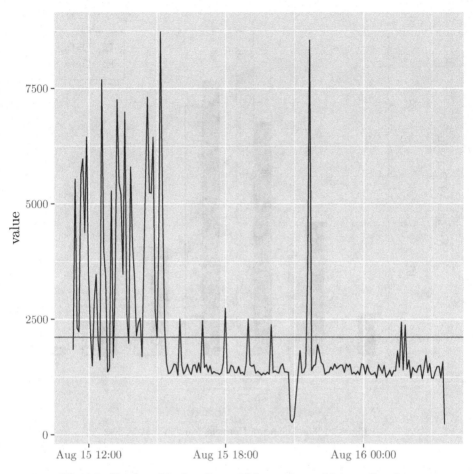

Fig. 8.2   Number of Packets Every 5 Minutes from a Malware Sample

Relying only on the mean misses the actual variances of the data. The average of both sets is close to 9.5 but if the median and the standard deviation are also considered, then the sets are different. Relying on one summary statistic to describe a set is a bad idea.

8.2.2   *Bad Visualizations Hinder Analysis, Not Help*

A visualization allows the human brain to find patterns and draw conclusions. Falling back onto the old adage that a picture is worth a thousand words, it can tell a story about the data. A good visualization can illumi-

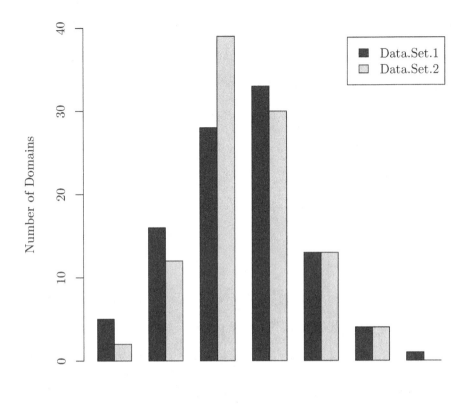

Length

Fig. 8.3   The Length of Domains from Two Data Sets

nate the data; a bad visualization can disguise patterns or lead to spurious conclusions.

In the discussion on summary statistics in the previous section, if it had started with Fig. 8.3, it would have been immediately apparent that the distributions are different, thus short-circuiting the discussion. Summary statistics wouldn't have been needed to compare the distributions.

Let's start with creating some bad visualizations and discussing their issues.

A networked computer has 65,535 ports. When a connection is made between two computers, one of those ports is used on both the source computer and the destination computer. It's not necessarily the same port on both computers. Some ports have been designated to belong to certain services. For example, port 80 is customarily for `http` and port 443 is for `https`. Mail uses port 25 whereas DNS uses port 53.

The destination port of a connection can potentially give an indication of which service that connection is using. Taking the network traffic from a botnet (Garcia *et al.*, 2014) and visualizing just the source and destination ports, we get Fig. 8.4.

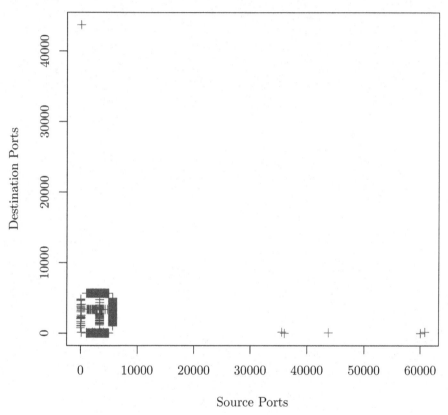

Fig. 8.4   Source Ports vs. Destination Ports

While there is a pattern in the lower left corner, the visualization is lacking context. The lack of IP addresses means there is no context from where these connections originated. It's just a pretty picture of how ports talk to each other.

Instead, make the *x*-axis the source IP addresses and the *y*-axis the destination ports, as in Fig. 8.5.

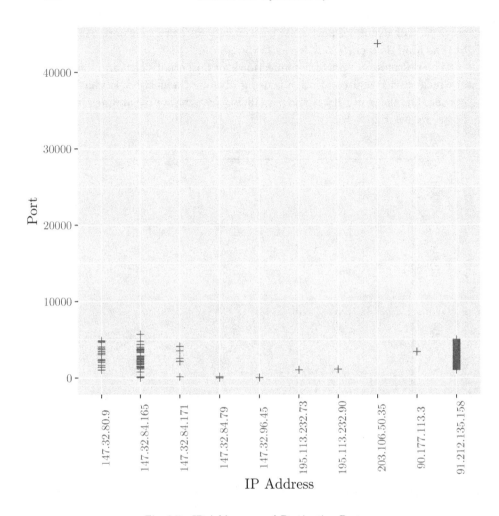

Fig. 8.5   IP Addresses and Destination Ports

This still lacks necessary context. This shows a list of ports to which each IP address connected, but it lacks the time factor as well as how often the IP addresses connected to the port. An IP address that just happens to connect to port 80 on another IP address once isn't interesting, but one that does it every 10 minutes for 24 hours is.

The two figures are interesting, but they don't aid in analysis.

For a different example, consider the traffic from two botnets, Virut and Donbot. The goal is to determine how similar the two sets are. Start by looking at the top 10 ports to which each one connects during a test run of the botnet client. Fig. 8.6 shows the plots of the frequencies of the top ten ports. They look very similar, and in fact, if the correlation of the two is computed, it's 0.99. That means they're linearly related (Gorunescu, 2011). Section 5.10.2 in Chapter 5 has more information on correlation.

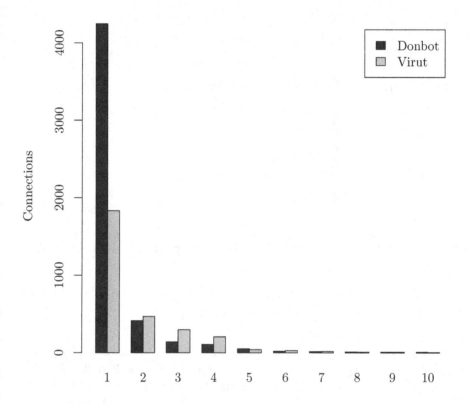

Fig. 8.6   Comparing Botnets by Traffic Pattern

There's something very important left out of those plots, though. The x-axis is the position of the count in the list of the top 10 ports. It isn't the port itself at all. Botnets can exhibit similar behavior if the frequency at which they connect to their command and control servers is considered. To examine this, Fig. 8.7 has the actual ports as the x-axis.

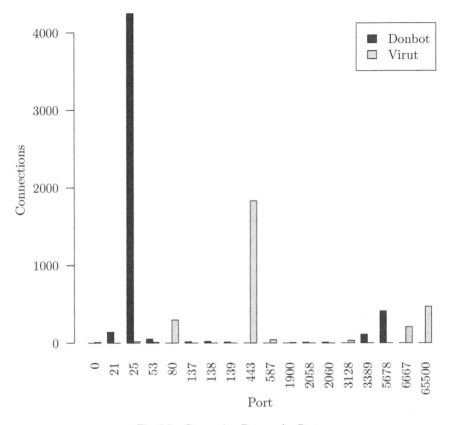

Fig. 8.7   Comparing Botnets by Port

The ports are different. In particular, the most common port for the Danbot botnet is 25 whereas the most common for the Fast flux is 443. Using only the first visualization omits the ports. It's possible that the botnets have similar behavior but without the knowledge of the different ports, it is possible to say they are the same.

A visualization lets the eyes assist in analysis, but a bad visualization can confuse the issue or obscure results. Be careful when creating the visualization to be sure it tells a reasonable story. The visualization of ports versus ports isn't interesting because computers talk to each other using ports —it's anticipated to see connections. But if it is known which port is most common, or which IP address talks to the most varied destinations, that can be an interesting figure.

8.2.3   Correlation Doesn't Mean Causation

It's tempting, when similar outcomes occur, to assume that the same event caused both. It's a logical fallacy; the belief is that because two events occurred together, then the cause was the same for both. Returning to Fig. 8.6, it appeared that the two botnets were correlated. However, there were different underlying causes for them. The Donbot (Etengoff, 2009) botnet was known for sending URL-shortened spam whereas the Virut (Polska, 2013) botnet was an all-purpose cybercrime botnet. They had different underlying code and functions.

For another example, consider two lists of domains. One is from the Malware Domain List https://malwaredomainlist.com and the other is from Cisco's Top Million Domains (Hubbard, 2016). Fig. 8.8 compares the distribution of the letters and numbers in the second level domains of the two sets.

The correlation between the two distributions is 0.98. This means that the two distributions are close to having a perfect linear relationship.

This doesn't mean the two domain lists are related. Turning to the TLDs in both sets, the Cisco data set has 1,950 TLDs and the Malware Domain List has 78. In a more important distinction, the malware domain list is community-reported malicious domains whereas the Cisco list is high use domains that are assumed to be non-malicious.

While it appears that the two lists are similar using one simple measure, in truth, they are very different once we look at them in their entirety.

This is an example of how a correlation can be spurious. It appears to mean something, yet it is actually uninteresting or misleading. Finding a correlation doesn't mean the research is finished, it means the source of the correlation should be investigated. Keep an open mind that it could be meaningless.

8.2.4   Assumptions — What Are They?

An assumption is something that is accepted as true, or at the very least, plausible. It is assumed that the Internet is a global network. This is a plausible assumption, and can be proven it's a valid assumption by studying the allocations of IP addresses, using GeoIP data, or any number of other methods. The point is it is possible to show that the assumption, "the Internet is a global network," is a valid assumption.

There are assumptions often made in data, in data collection, in methods, and in analyzing the results. Assumptions must have a strong base,

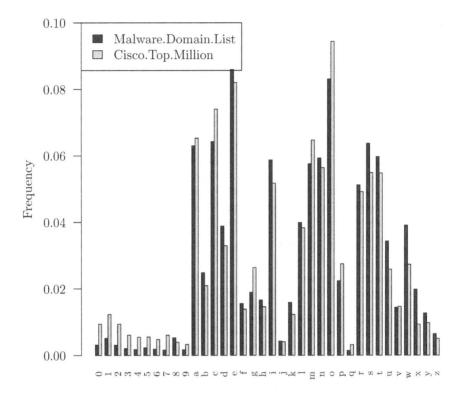

Fig. 8.8 Comparing Letter Distributions

meaning we can show that the assumptions are valid. It's not good research to just pull assumptions from thin air and expect them to be true.

Suppose a research goal is to measure the efficacy of attacks made on an organization. This is started by cataloging all of the attacks made. The assumption in that case is that it is possible to catalog all the attacks. Not every attack leaves a noticeable trace. A DDoS is an obvious attack, a spearphishing attack may not be. Basing research on the assumption that all attacks are countable is a bad assumption.

However, if the analysis is on DDoS attacks, then it is possible to start by making the assumption that a service that is interrupted should be investigated. Not every interruption is the result of a DDoS, but it is a good starting point.

It's very easy to make bad assumptions in cybersecurity. Context is lacking for most events, mainly because they occur outside the sphere to which a researcher would have access. Every organization and study designer has their particular view of the Internet. Assuming that what a single researcher sees is applicable to the entire Internet is a mistake study designers often make. Remember, a convenience sample is not a representative sample. It's not possible to make inferences from a convenience sample and imply that they apply to the entire population because that isn't necessarily true.

It's also important to catalog the assumptions made. Suppose a researcher has a collection of domains they think are from a DGA. The assumption is that they're from a Conficker campaign. Research has shown that the distribution of letters in Conficker domains looks like Fig. 8.9.

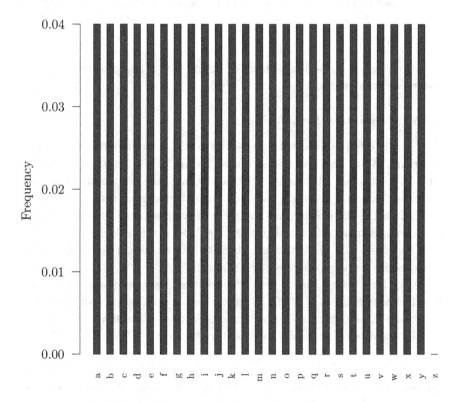

Fig. 8.9 Distribution of Letters in Conficker Domains

Let's list the assumptions made so far:

(1) The domains collected were malicious. There must be a reason the domains were collected and the assumption was made they were malicious.

(2) The domains collected were all created by the same DGA. Determining if a set of domains was all generated by the same DGA is a very difficult problem. If the set of domains is contained in a known set, that would nullify this entire discussion. It wouldn't be necessary to analyze if the domains are part of a botnet because it would already be known.

(3) All Conficker domains look like Fig. 8.9. Conficker has variants. In fact it has even changed the DGA algorithm (Porras *et al.*, 2009b). Fig. 8.9 doesn't state which version of the algorithm to which it appears.

Acknowledging the assumptions is important. They can influence the results and the analysis.

8.2.5 *Estimating Probabilities*

Research is often started with a discussion of the probability of an event occurring. With the broad, distributed nature of the Internet, it can be difficult to estimate. A meteorologist can estimate the probability of rainfall occurring based on historical data and current events for a single location, but estimating the chance that the piece of software that was downloaded is malware is more difficult. If everything a person downloads is malware, then their personal bias will make them believe there is a high probability of a random piece of software being malware.

Don't let personal biases skew probabilities. Let the data be the guide. In cybersecurity, most of the IP addresses seen are malicious, so it's possible to assume that holds true for a great percentage of IPs available. There are 2^{32} IPv4 addresses available, so let's start by looking at a set of malicious IPs.

Suppose a researcher found a data set online that claimed to be IP addresses with malicious reputations. Taking a year of this data and counting the number of unique IP addresses in the set yields 655,322 IP addresses. While that sounds like a lot, it is only 0.0152% of the entire set of IP addresses. Not every IP address should be routed, so restricting the count to those that should be routed, it's 0.0177%. This means if an IP address is chosen at random, there is a negligible chance that it is in this set.

There are two things to take away from this. One, the probability of choosing a malicious IP address at random is negligible, assuming maliciousness is defined as, "Part of this malicious reputation IP set." Two, this set was generated based on the view the creators had into the Internet and potentially by people reporting the IP addresses. It's a convenience sample and it's not possible to say it represents all of the malicious IP addresses on the Internet.

Estimating probabilities is difficult, especially since cybersecurity research often deals with convenience samples.

Various reports (Security, 2019; Householder *et al.*, 2020) find that 5% of all CVEs have exploits. That can be used to estimate the probability of a CVE having an exploit as 0.05. This is an estimate based on data and it is a good estimate.

However, it is necessary to be careful using this estimate. This isn't an estimate over all vulnerabilities; it's an estimate on a curated subset. Not every vulnerability is assigned a CVE. In fact, estimating the number of vulnerabilities available in the world is a very difficult, if not impossible, problem. Even if that number was known, this probability still couldn't be used. It only applies to those vulnerabilities with CVEs.

Estimating probabilities is difficult and always requires context to be safe. Remember, a lot of cybersecurity research uses convenience samples, so any probability estimating on that sample may or may not apply to the population as a whole.

8.3   The Data

Cybersecurity analysis depends on data. Data collected through direct observation or studies is called *empirical* data. We can categorize that into two types, based on the method used to collect the data. *Qualitative* data are observed data, things that can't be measured. *Quantitative* data are collected through measurement.

How data are collected and how they are used is an essential part of research in cybersecurity. This section discusses the pitfalls to avoid in working with data in this field.

8.3.1   *Anecdotes Aren't Data*

A single IP address doesn't explain IP addresses in general. It's just that, a single IP address. It's possible to build a case study around why that IP address is in the set, and it can suggest future areas of research, but it isn't a data set that can be statistically analyzed.

Little determined in a case study built on the single IP address can be used to make inferences about the set in general. It isn't a sample of sufficient size; it's just a data point in the set.

For another example, suppose a researcher collects all of the spam sent to them and uses it to study spam. They can't say much about spam in general; they only have the single point of data, or anecdote, about how spam affected them.

This case study does constrain the story about spam generally because it documents a single case that happened. But if the researcher wants to know what other cases are likely or even possible, it does not help at all.

In order to use a sample to make inferences about a larger set, the sample has to be the right size and selected in specific ways. If it's too small, then it's impossible to make those inferences. Taking a single IP address or a single domain and expecting its behavior to explain anything about the larger population is impossible.

8.3.2 *Obtaining and Collecting*

Suppose a study is focused on security incidents. The researcher has a hypothesis about the pattern of them in general, so they want to collect all the incidents seen at several companies in the same industry. Then, they can determine if the theory is correct.

This is clearly a worthy goal, but it might not be achievable. The companies will have to be convinced to share proprietary data, and not only that, to also allow a researcher to publish based on it. Proprietary data are often the organization's intellectual property and sharing isn't an option.

In short, data aren't always obtainable. Take, for example, routing data. BGP is an external routing protocol. It controls the routing between organizational units. There are open data sources available for BGP. However, this is outside the organizational unit. An outside observer won't know the routing protocol used in the organizational unit at all and they won't have a view into that unless that organization shares information.

Suppose a researcher wants to measure all of the attacks made against their organization. This is impossible to determine. If the organization's monitoring is good, then they will find a subset of these attacks, but the researcher won't know which attacks they missed.

If data can't always be obtained, then it's reasonable to assume that what can be found can be collected. Unfortunately, that's not always the case. Sometimes, it's an overwhelming amount of data.

Packet capture data is a complete record of a network connection. For example, if a connection is made to a website, the packet capture would have that request as well as everything the website returned. As discussed in Chapter 2, that data can be 7.2Tb in an hour, assuming a saturated connection. Not only is this untenable for storing, but searching it also becomes unwieldy.

It's not always possible to obtain the needed data and when it is possible, it isn't always tenable to collect it.

For a further issue with obtaining data, consider at network traffic. It is very useful to study for patterns and anomalies. However, it isn't always easy to collect from outside sources. A researcher can study their own environment, but that's a convenience sample and not something they can generalize.

Luckily, some organizations make their data available. Unluckily, this data isn't always usable. In order to remove personally identifying information, anonymization is often used. Anonymizing the data isn't always a perfect technique. It has been reversed at times. It is possible to anonymize data to the point that it isn't usable any longer.

Collecting, storing, and using data isn't always possible in cybersecurity research. Be aware of the possible problems when a study is started, and be aware that not everything is either available or collectable. If it isn't, don't force your research —the results won't be useful.

8.3.3   *Data is Always Consistent*

Data in cybersecurity are influenced by humans. What is reported, what is saved from the reporting, and how that data is presented are all questions that a human will ask and answer when deciding to create a data set. The data needed may be collected by different sources. However, the collectors aren't necessarily consistent.

Companies buy blocklists to shore up their security infrastructure. A blocklist can contain domain names, IP addresses, or other strings. This example is going to use domain names used in spam.

A company that is blocklisting spam domains usually has an infrastructure to collect these names. For example, an email honeypot (Morey, 2019) is a technique used to harvest spam. The spam is then parsed and new domains are added to the list.

If another company with a different infrastructure also collects spam to create their own list, then they aren't necessarily going to get the same domains. In fact, it has been demonstrated that these lists are generally disjoint (Metcalf and Spring, 2013b). There's limited consistency between the lists. Each one is specific to the company's infrastructure and collection methods.

Data bought from various companies can have the same problem. A feature that is important to one company may be omitted from another company's data. If a researcher is creating a data source from multiple companies, it is necessary to keep this in mind.

IP addresses are assigned by IANA to regional routing registries which are then responsible for assigning them in their region. The whois protocol exists to allow people to query the databases for ownership of the IP addresses, which sounds very useful for research.

On the other hand, the output from a query to each of the registries isn't consistent. This is an example for a query to `whois.arin.net`:

```
NetRange:        64.94.0.0 - 64.95.255.255
CIDR:            64.94.0.0/15
NetName:         PNAP-05-2000
NetHandle:       NET-64-94-0-0-1
Parent:          NET64 (NET-64-0-0-0-0)
NetType:         Direct Allocation
OriginAS:
Organization:    Internap Corporation (IC-1425)
RegDate:         2000-06-05
Updated:         2019-03-06
Ref:             https://rdap.arin.net/registry/ip/64.94.0.0
```

And this is an example of a query to RIPE:

```
inetnum:         217.244.0.0 - 217.244.0.7
netname:         BAUER-UMWELT-WERK-HIRSCHFELD-NET
descr:           BAUER Umwelt GmbH
country:         DE
admin-c:         RS23769-RIPE
tech-c:          RS23769-RIPE
status:          ASSIGNED PA
mnt-by:          DTAG-NIC
created:         2015-08-11T06:38:50Z
```

```
last-modified:   2019-06-05T11:44:35Z
source:          RIPE # Filtered
```

There is similar information in each. Each one contains the network and the owner, but it is presented slightly differently. While there is similarity, there isn't consistency of reporting. In general, with these data, we can create consistent data, but it is important to keep track of how.

This example also illustrates another point. The ARIN data and the RIPE data are inconsistent on precision. RIPE considers the exact date and time of the creation to be important whereas ARIN only reports the date. RIPE reports a range of IP addresses whereas ARIN reports the cidr. If data are collected from multiple sources, then the precision can vary from source to source.

8.3.4 *Measure the Right Thing*

Suppose a researcher has a hypothesis that domain names with the letter z in them are more likely to be malicious than those without. If the researcher measures the letter q instead of the letter z, then they are measuring the wrong thing for their hypothesis. This is a simple and egregious example, but the principle remains. Be sure to measure the right variable for the research.

An attacker can (mis)use a *gadget* in an application they are attacking to gain access. A gadget is a short sequence of machine codes that ends in one of three things: a return, an indirect jump, or an indirect call instruction (Brown and Pande, 2019).

It is tempting to count the number of gadgets in software and use that as a measure. This implies that each gadget is equally exploitable. It's like counting the number of leaks in a dam. Just counting them without considering how big they are equates the small leak that lets through a tiny trickle of water with the giant hole in the middle that threatens to collapse the dam.

Frequency has been used in this book as good measure, but it depends on what it is counting. If it's equally likely for any of the events to happen, then it can be useful. For gadgets, some are dangerous, and some aren't. Counting them equally equates the non-dangerous with the dangerous and confuses the issue. Fig. 8.5 illustrated a similar problem: the count was IP address's connections to ports without taking into account the context of the data, such as length and frequency of connection.

Always consider context and goal before deciding to measure, and ensure the measurement is useful and reasonable.

8.4   The Analysis

Data often have idiosyncrasies; little oddities that are particular to the sample but not in the population at large. Sometimes, a researcher focuses on those oddities. The problem with that is it isn't present in the population nor is it present in other people's data. The analysis should be applicable beyond the particular data set.

Oddities can be interesting, and it is tempting to focus on them. However, research should be applicable to data sets beyond the current sample.

Specifying analysis to the weirdness in a data set is called overfitting (Babyak, 2004). Things found in an overfitted sample don't usually appear in the population. Good research should be applicable to other samples or other people's data that's similar to the current data set. The goal should be to find a model that talks about more than just the data set in question.

In this section, we'll talk about how to *avoid overfitting*.

8.4.1   *Researcher Degrees of Freedom*

If research can't be verified, then it can be considered false. The methods that cause overfitting have been discussed as those that cause that very problem (Dwork *et al.*, 2015).

We're going to discuss what to avoid to make research replicable and to avoid overfitting. These are often called *researcher degrees of freedom* or *p-hacking*. We'll start with an example of how an analysis could be done.

Suppose a researcher has 1,000 malicious domains. Every month, for three months on the first day of the month, they determine how many IP addresses to which each domain points. This is a data set created by structured observation and measurement.

In Fig. 8.10, the three means are graphed as a bar plot. Month 1 and Month 2 have similar means, but there's a jump between Month 2 and Month 3.

Month 1 seems to be a repeat of Month 2, at least looking at the average, so the researcher decides to just drop that one. They're looking for changes, and based on the average, there weren't any.

Consider Fig. 8.11. The first 398 domains don't have any IP addresses, so the researcher decides to drop those too. They're interested in domains with IP addresses, not domains without them.

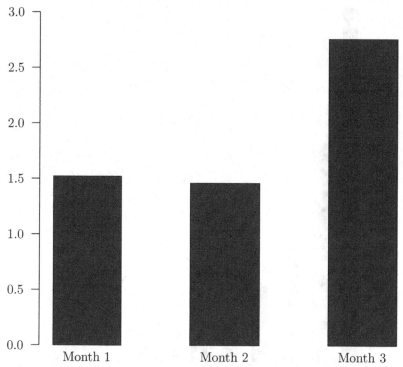

Fig. 8.10   Average Number of IPs per Domain in Each Month

Fig. 8.12 shows the distributions of Month 2 and 3 after removing the domains with 0 IP addresses from Month 2. To do this correctly, they had to take the domains with 0 IP addresses in Month 2, and then remove them in Month 3. They could have removed the domains with 0 IP addresses in both months, but those aren't the same IP addresses in each month.

If the researcher did, the distributions would look like Fig. 8.13, which is different from Fig. 8.12.

Now, the researcher can compare the distribution of IP addresses of the malicious domains over time and can say something about those sets and how they changed. This data set is fabricated, so the results are actually meaningless in cybersecurity terms, but it does illustrate the choices made during the analysis. These are incorrect choices because the researcher modified the data and the results aren't relevant to the original set.

Those choices are the *researcher degrees of freedom*. They altered the data set as they did the analysis. Researcher degrees of freedom include:

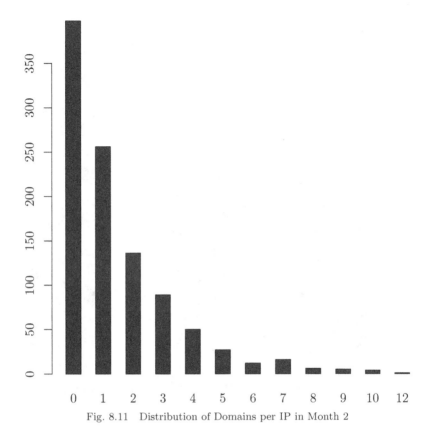

Fig. 8.11　Distribution of Domains per IP in Month 2

- Screening the data for unusual anomalous data
- Re-scaling variables
- Graphs and tables to identify patterns
- Fitting models to the data
- Measuring a variable using different methods
- Manipulating data
- Including additional data after the analysis has begun
- Discarding data
- Arbitrary decisions on outliers and anomalies
- Changing the method of analysis

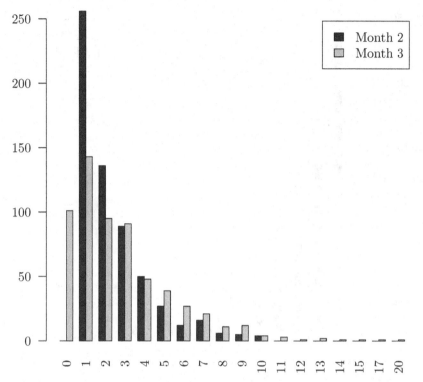

Fig. 8.12   Revised Distributions for Month 2 and 3

This isn't an exhaustive list and it is rather specific. Let's step back and examine what the researcher did to generalize it into categories that should be avoided.

In the first step, the researcher decided to drop one third of the data. That decision was made based on something they saw in the data.

Observed results shouldn't be used to alter the analysis. It is important to start with a plan and stick to it. When the researcher decided to drop some of the results from the data sets, the focus of the research changed.

The final analysis wasn't based on the original data but on choices made as the data were analyzed. It's entirely possible that due to these choices, the results won't generalize and won't be repeatable.

From this discussion, several steps can be given (Cruz, 2017) to avoid overfitting:

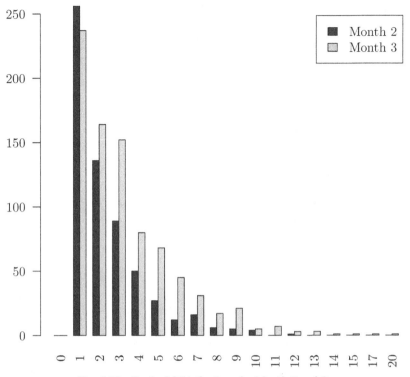

Fig. 8.13   Revised Distributions for Month 2 and 3

- Before analyzing data, make study design decisions. Don't change the plan based on the data.

- Use subject matter knowledge to inform data aggregation. Aggregating domain names alphabetically doesn't make much sense, but aggregating them by TLD could.

- Limit exclusion of data. For example, data can be unusable if it can't be parsed, but it should be made clear why it is being dropped.

- Validate results. Take another sample from the population and see if the result can be replicated.

Validation of results is very important. It allows a researcher to step back and make sure that the result they found in the original analysis holds true for the data in the data set. It allows them to double-check that they didn't do any steps that forced overfitting in the first analysis. Always validate if possible.

Avoid researcher degrees of freedom in research to avoid overfitting. Research should be replicable and reproducible by others, and fitting results to the oddities in the data won't allow that to happen.

8.4.2 Marrying an Idea

Often when research is started, the researcher has an idea of what they'd like to find. For example, suppose they would like to prove that all domains with a q in them are more likely to be malicious than those without q's. They believe it's true, so they're going to go design a study to prove it.

They start with a sample of malicious domains, a sample of domains deemed not malicious, and start counting the presence of q's. Unfortunately, at the end of the study, they haven't proved their hypothesis. The presence of q's is about equal in either the malicious domain set or in the non-malicious domain set.

However, this researcher is sure it's true. Maybe the set is wrong, and they need to remove certain domains because of reasons they define that are completely arbitrary. They repeat the study and this time, they get the results they wanted.

Unfortunately, they're still wrong. They were so sure that their idea was true they were willing to modify the data in order to show that it was true.

The point is to accept the results of the research. Don't be so sure that the hypothesis is correct that it seems reasonable to change the data or even cherry-pick the correct samples to the hypothesis. Doing this may seem to produce good results but they're wrong. Someone can't come along and validate the research because of the steps taken.

If the researcher had taken the malicious domain data set and picked out all the domains with q's in them just to prove themselves right, they would definitely be wrong.

Random sampling is the goal, not picking the data that will prove the point. Hypotheses are often wrong. That's the point of research: to determine if they are valid or not.

This behavior is also called *data dredging*, the act of repeatedly searching through a data set to validate a predetermined result. The example in Section 8.2.3 was created using this method. We took multiple sets of domains and considered the correlation between the distribution of letters in each until one matched what we were looking for. Domains from multiple lists, both good and bad, were examined to create distributions of letters until one gave us the results we wanted.

It was done to create an example, but if we had done that as part of research, we would be wrong.

Data dredging is wrong in research. Repeatedly going back to a data set to find something isn't the right thing to do and has often been discussed as the reason some research isn't repeatable. Don't cherry-pick samples or comb over the data to find any possible result. If the result you want isn't there, don't force it.

8.5   The Results

Assumptions are made in results, not only when the research is finished but also when it is started. As we discussed in Section 8.4.2, it's possible to determine the result before starting the research. This can affect the analysis as well as the results.

In this section we'll discuss common assumptions made in research results. It's important to avoid these assumptions in order to keep research as repeatable and replicable as possible.

8.5.1   *Every Problem Has a Solution*

Every researcher would like to solve every problem in cybersecurity. It's a worthy goal, to make a system completely secure. Unfortunately, not every problem has a solution. Some problems only have approximate solutions, and some have no solution at all.

For an arbitrary computer program, there's no general method of determining the behavior of it (Kfoury, 1982). That's known as the *halting problem*. It also implies that given any arbitrary program, it's impossible to develop a general method to determine if it's malware. Malware is defined by its behavior, so if it's not possible to determine all behavior of the software, it's impossible to use that to decide if it is malware.

Research can create approximations and heuristics, but there's no way to create a direct solution to this problem.

The same is true for a program that would determine all vulnerabilities present in a piece of software. Vulnerabilities are related to the behavior as well, so to enumerate all the vulnerabilities, it would be necessary to determine all possible behaviors of the software.

Another example of an unsolvable problem in cybersecurity is enumerating all attacks that have occurred. If there is no evidence that a cybersecurity event occurred, that doesn't mean it didn't occur. The lack of evidence is not evidence that the attack didn't happen. It's possible to approximate a list of attacks, but there's no way to create a definitive list.

These problems are examples of unsolvable problems in cybersecurity. They're used to illustrate the fact that not every problem has a solution. Approximations of solutions are possible, but there's no direct method to solve them.

Not every problem has a solution or an effective approximation of a solution.

8.5.2 Negative Results Are Still Results

It is a common thought process that if the study didn't prove the hypothesis correct, then time has been wasted. The only good and useful results are positive results.

This is not true. A *negative result*, to be clear, is when a study is performed correctly, yet the hypothesis isn't proven. A negative result is useful information that reliably communicates that something didn't work. It is often confused with a *non result*, which is where the study was not performed correctly and so is not useful at all (except perhaps as a lesson about how to better design studies).

For example, suppose it is known that all malware of a particular family, call it the UFI family, has a particular sequence in the binary that's precisely 64 characters long. It is in this family only and no other. It's possible to use this sequence as a signature and be sure that are only that malware is found.

After some time, a researcher decides to go back and analyze a collection of malware that will include samples from the UFI family. Their hypothesis is that this sequence is still true, and they will continue to find that malware family due to that string.

Unfortunately, they prove themselves wrong. When they analyzed the new data set, they couldn't find a single piece of malware with that sequence. The family has changed slightly, so the entire sequence is no longer present in all the UFI family malware.

It's a negative result, but it's an important one. It demonstrates the need to change how to look for that family as the malware has changed over time. Cybersecurity is rarely, if ever, static.

Negative results fill in gaps in research. Publishing negative results doesn't just fill in that gap, but it also helps other designers by showing them areas that have been studied (Fanelli, 2012).

Science isn't just the positive results; it's everything. Explaining that a given behavior is no longer malicious is important in cybersecurity because it allows practitioners to focus resources on more important problems. Negative results are critical – but the important difference between a negative result and a non result is the study design and execution. Reliably knowing that something is not true is much more useful than not knowing whether something is true or false.

8.6   Common Logical Fallacies in Cybersecurity

A logical fallacy is a flaw in reasoning. Either the structure of the argument is flawed, or the content of the argument is flawed (Van Vleet, 2012). Either way, there is a flaw in the logic of the argument.

For example, Section 8.4.2 is a logical fallacy. Confirming results that were decided beforehand is known as confirmation bias (Pohl and Pohl, 2004). This is rejecting any possibility that the hypothesis could be false, based on feeling or remembering of past events.

In this section, we'll discuss some common logical fallacies that occur in cybersecurity research. We don't discuss how to avoid them, but to determine when you're falling prey to them. Each study is unique and has its own issues that could cause you to fall prey to the fallacies.

8.6.1   *Base Rate Fallacy*

The Base Rate Fallacy is a common fallacy in cybersecurity research. An easy way to explain this is to start with an example (Axelsson, 2000). Suppose after some work, a researcher has a method that will test for malicious domains. Out of every 100 they identify, 99 are actually malicious, so they're correct 99% of the time.

But malicious domains in a set are rare. To keep the math nice, pretend that in a random set of 10,000 domains, only one of them is malicious. Using the aforementioned math, there's an obvious question, "Given a domain that our method called malicious, what's the probability that it actually is malicious?" From the method created by the researcher, they expect it to be 99 out of 100 because that's how effective their method is.

However, the calculation shows the answer is 1%. If this method produces an alert about a malicious domain, then there's only a 1% chance that it's actually malicious. In other words, the method is going to be unreliable 99% of the time. An analyst will not be happy using this method.

That's a contradiction of the statement that 99% of the time, the method will be right. The problem is the number of malicious domains in the set is so small compared to the set at large. The base-rate of occurrence, that 0.01% of the huge set, is what drives this result.

This is a common problem in cybersecurity called the *Base Rate Fallacy*. For a similar example, suppose there is an organization that creates 100Tb of network traffic a day. Only a very tiny amount of that is actually malicious. If only one gigabyte of that is malicious, and a researcher devises a method that is 99.9% effective, they're still going to be wrong more than they're right.

Researchers want their research to be used and be meaningful. A method that is wrong more than it is right because of the base-rate of the occurrence in the data set isn't usable. The Base Rate Fallacy occurs often in cybersecurity because there are enormous data sets with a low rate of maliciousness.

8.6.2 *Absence of Evidence is Not Evidence of Absence*

If there is no evidence of attacks made against a network, that doesn't mean that there were no attacks. It's wrong to assume that if there is no evidence, none exists. Even if an organization has the best IDS available, there's still a chance that one will slip by without notice.

Not finding something is not evidence that it doesn't exist. That lack of evidence doesn't imply that the result the research is looking for doesn't exist. It just implies that using current methods, it can't be found.

The statement, "This system has no malware," is another example of this fallacy. It's only reasonable to say, "This system has no malware that we have found." The definitive statement can't be made because there's no way of knowing if it is true or not.

In a similar way of thinking, the *argument from ignorance* fallacy is the assertion that something is true because it hasn't been proven false (Schreuder, 2014). This means asserting something is true due to a lack of contrary evidence is committing this fallacy.

For example, the assertion that, "My network has the same properties as the Internet at large" without any evidence proving that is wrong. It's tempting because it allows a researcher to continue research assuming they're modeling the Internet, but they're not. They're examining their network, which is their local convenience sample. Assuming a convenience sample is representative of the entire population without other evidence commits this fallacy.

It's tempting to think this because it allows the analysis to continue. However, it's incorrect analysis.

8.6.3 *Sampling Bias*

The gold standard in research is the random sample. It allows researchers to infer results about the population at large. The amount of data in cybersecurity can be overwhelming, which means sampling is necessary. In Chapter 6, we talked about the various methods to sample that aren't the gold standard but often occur in cybersecurity research. If the sample is taken repeatedly using the same method and the mean is computed each time, then the means are averaged, that is called the *expected mean*.

The difference between the expected mean and the actual mean of the population is the *sampling bias*. If the expected mean is the same as the actual mean, there is no bias in the sample. The random sample is the gold standard because there is limited bias in the sample.

The two components of sampling bias are *selection bias* and *estimation bias*.

In selection bias, not every member of the population has the same chance of being selected. For example, suppose a researcher is collecting domain names from multiple sources, putting it in a big data set, and then selecting from it. If they aren't careful to only keep unique domains, then some domains have more of a chance of being selected than others. Refer to Section 6.4 in Chapter 6 for another example of an attempt to avoid bias.

Suppose a researcher wants to know the value of their favorite statistic, let's call it Γ ("gamma"). It's hard to compute that, so the researcher is going to use a different method to estimate Γ, which will give them $\hat{\Gamma}$. The value of $\hat{\Gamma}$ is an *estimator* for Γ. The difference between the estimation and the real value is the bias.

For a statistical example, the median is an estimator for the mean in that it is looking for the center of the data. Researchers often compute median because outliers can affect the actual mean, but bias is introduced when this is done.

Suppose a researcher is examining IP addresses they find in a botnet network traffic. Fig. 8.14 illustrates the distribution of the counts on a per IP address basis. They decide to use median as an estimate for mean because the data is skewed.

The actual mean of this distribution is 3.16 whereas the median is 1. That means the estimation bias for this sample is 2.16. Sampling bias is about the sampling method; estimation bias affects the results.

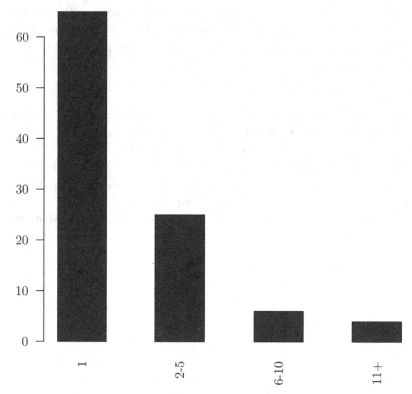

Fig. 8.14   Distribution of IP Address Counts

8.6.4   *Fallacies of Anomalies*

Cybersecurity research is often the search for anomalies. The anomalous behavior of malware, the anomalous network traffic, and anomalous domains are just a few of the possibilities. Researchers look for the anomalies and assume that's where the maliciousness lies.

It's tempting to see anomalous behavior and immediately it's malicious if there isn't a good reason surrounding it. Doing this is called an *argument of anomaly* (Dunning, 2010).

Without verification, it isn't known if the anomalous behavior is malicious. Not every anomaly is. New traffic on a network might be a new app that someone tried out. A new domain could be a new company. Anomalous software could be anything from a new app to an app with a bug. Not all of it is malicious and verification is necessary.

On the converse, not all malicious behavior is anomalous. Botnets have used DNS for command and control (Dietrich *et al.*, 2011). Assuming the network doesn't have a dedicated DNS server, seeing traffic to a DNS server isn't necessarily anomalous.

8.7   Lessons Learned

One underlying goal of research is for it to be usable by others. You want your research to contribute to the field, to bring new methods or results to the attention of others so they can use it and build it.

To achieve this goal, we must be careful of the pitfalls in research. Be careful of your data, your analysis, and your results to ensure that whatever you do or find, your research is repeatable and reproducible. That means avoiding the pitfalls discussed in this chapter as well as other events that can preclude this.

Chapter 9

DNS Study

DNS is a powerful tool, both for adversaries and the defenders. Associating domain names with IP addresses at its core, it's a phone directory for the Internet. Before it existed, a computer had to have a file that contained all the hostnames and IP addresses it wanted to contact, which is a very static situation. DNS allowed for a more dynamic solution making it very easy to change the IP addresses of domains quickly.

Domains are a mixed bag of malicious versus non-malicious. Some domains are malicious, some are used for malicious purposes but aren't definitively malicious, and some aren't malicious at all. There isn't necessarily a simple measure of maliciousness but a spectrum.

We want to examine the domains used by adversaries and hopefully determine common properties of them, so we can predict the maliciousness of domains. Since both adversaries and defenders of domains use domains, then the ability to discriminate between the two is important.

To start, domains need name servers to function, registrars to register them, and IP addresses to work. This is true of all domains. The domains themselves have properties, such as distribution of the letters, length, TLD and more. We can leverage this information to examine a domain name and look for adversarial behavior.

A standard goal of research is to start with a population and take a sample of it. We can't create a list of all domains. Not every registrar will share the list of domains they have registered. Not only that, but creating a population of malicious domains is impossible as well. First, as noted earlier, maliciousness is a spectrum, so it is required to define what is malicious. Second, we don't know what all the malicious domains are. We can create a sublist, but we have no idea what is missing from that list. We can't even guess how much of the list we actually have.

In this chapter, we discuss a measurement study on domain names. Given a set of malicious domains and a set of non-malicious domains, we'd like to be able to delineate between the two. We'll take one property of domains and discuss the differences between malicious domains and non-malicoius domains.

This chapter begins with a discussion of DNS and possible maliciousness. If you already have a background in the field, you'd be best served by skipping to Section 9.2.

9.1   Discussion

If a new domain is suddenly being resolved, we want to determine if it is a malicious domain or just a new destination. This requires us to be able to determine properties of a domain that can indicate maliciousness in order to determine what to do with the domain. It could be a new company related to the web page the system is visiting, it could be a new domain set up by an old company, or it could be a domain owned by a botnet. Just the fact that the domain was new and resolved is interesting, but not necessarily concerning.

This leads us to a different discussion. That is, the behavior of a domain required to denote it as malicious. It could be hosting malware, a command and control server for a botnet, delivering spam, related to spyware or other malicious behavior. It's also possible that the domain isn't malicious at all but due to the way it is being used, it appears malicious.

For example, suppose `example-bad-domain.com` is labeled as being malicious. After careful analysis, it is determined that it hosts a botnet command and control server which is eventually taken down. If the domain is resold by a registrar to a new owner, it would possibly be no longer malicious. This adds a temporal element to the situation. Maliciousness is context-dependent. Just because someone used a domain maliciously today doesn't mean it's going to happen tomorrow.

Botnets have used `twitter.com` for command and control (Kartaltepe *et al.*, 2010). Twitter has also been used by terrorist groups for communication (Klausen, 2015). Those two actions don't mean that `twitter.com` is necessarily a malicious domain. It just means that malicious actors have used it.

The domain machine.cu.ma is on a list of domains used by Zeus (abuse.ch, 2018). This domain was taken over and blackholed due to its malicious behavior, so it's reasonable to tag it as malicious.

Is a domain as malicious if it has been used maliciously, or is a domain tagged as malicious if it is registered specifically for malicious purposes? That is an underlying question that must be answered when trying to determine the status of a domain.

Unwanted email is called *spam*. (The name comes from a Monty Python skit.) Spammers (i.e., the people who send spam) send it to steal information, steal money, or install malicious software. Spammers uses domains to send the email as well as domains for the URLs within the email. In the beginning of the Internet, email could be sent from any email address without verification. For example, it was easy to send email from `santaclaus@northpole.com`. The advent of spammers meant verification was put in place. This verification included checking that the domain has an IP address. If email is sent from `thisdomaindoesntexist.com` and the mail server looked that up and found that it didn't exist, then the mail server wouldn't accept the email. Spammers know this and now register domains to get around this. In order for the URLs contained in spam to function, those domains must be registered as well.

Botnets and their command and control servers also use domains. Rather than hard-coding the IP address into the malware, the botnet has a domain it uses. This way, the botnet owner can move the domain to different IP addresses and keep one step ahead of the defenders.

Adversaries like domains because they make hiding themselves much easier than not using domains. If they don't use domains, then they have to hard-code into their mailware the IP address they're using going into their malware or where they're coming from into their spam and they wouldn't have any flexibility or ability to hide. They're cheap, disposable, and an integral part of their infrastructure.

9.1.1 *Common Bad Behaviors That Might Not Be Bad*

A record poisoning starts when a query for an A record returns an IP address that is incorrect. The name server will cache the bad response until it times out. Until that bad response times out of the name server's cache, the name server has been poisoned. This is called *cache poisoning*.

To see how this can enable malicious behavior, consider the process a mail server uses to send e-mail. The first step is to query the MX record of the destination domain to determine where to send it. It then follows by looking for the A record of the domain in the MX response. If the A record is wrong, then the email is sent to an intermediary location where the owner of that server can read it. This would occur without the sender of the email knowing that their email has been potentially read by someone other than the intended recipient.

Clearly, this is unwanted behavior and can be malicious. However, a misconfigured name server can also have the same effect. Some name server software (Liu, 2002) allows for a default value to be sent to all queries. Generally, administrators set this up for particular domains, but a misconfigured name server could send a response to all queries. If a query asks it for something to which it doesn't immediately know the answer, it would send the default.

The presence of *A* record poisoning should be investigated, but without other information the assumption that it is malicious behavior is incorrect. Some malware will point infected systems to its name server rather than using the default so that it can control resolutions. For example, the browser hijacker `fwdservice.com` (Metcalf, 2018a) does this. If this is the case, then the response could be malicious.

If a collection of domains cycles through multiple IP addresses that are announced by multiple ASes, it is a *fast flux network* (Caglayan *et al.*, 2009). The detection method for a fast flux network is to look at the number of IP addresses used by the domains. If this is more than 5, then we consider the number of ASes that announce the IP addresses. If this is more than five, then it is a fast flux network (Stoner, 2010). Malicious actors often use fast flux networks to attempt to hide their behavior. The domain `superdrugtesting.com` (Cooney, 2012) was on a fast flux network and used in a botnet. It is, or was at the time of its detection, a malicious domain.

A *Content Distribution Network* will look like a fast flux network. It has domains with IP addresses that seemingly change rapidly in multiple ASes, so it fits the definition of a fast flux network. However, these aren't malicious. They're merely used to transport information in the most efficient method possible. While it is possible to use the method to find fast flux networks, Content Distribution Networks will skew the results.

Without additional context, like the owner of the ASes and the IP addresses, the results are meaningless. Tagging everyone who has a fast flux network as malicious will find incorrect results.

For a specific example of fast flux, consider the name server. If the nameserver is part of a fast flux network, then it changes IP addresses rapidly. The domains attached to these name servers have been shown to be involved with pharma campaigns. The behavior of these name servers is of concern, but again, it isn't unique. The name servers of Content

Distribution Networks behave in a similar fashion. They have multiple IP addresses and seem to change over time, but their domains are not necessarily malicious.

A botnet's command and control server signals to its clients and responds to signals from the clients. A botnet has used DNS as its communication channel (Dietrich *et al.*, 2011) since it is a form of traffic that is commonly allowed through firewalls. The response given to the DNS query would be the signal to the bot for the required behavior, such spam or DDoS. Another use of this signal is software activation. A software company would have a name server that responds to particular queries with activation codes. A new installation of the software would query the name server with the software-defined domain and use the signal from the software company's name server to perform an action, just as a command and control server would do.

Domain parking actually has two meanings. One meaning is where registrars attempt to monetize domains by setting them up with a webpage (Vissers *et al.*, 2015), inviting visitors to contact them to buy the domain. That definition of parking can be annoying, but it isn't necessarily malicious.

The other meaning of domain parking is when a domain is pointed, or parked, to an IP address (Metcalf *et al.*, 2017). This isn't the IP address that the domain owner wants to use. It's a temporary location that lets the domain resolve but isn't the active destination. When the owner of the domain is ready to activate the domain, they change the IP to which it points.

At its core, this form of parking is moving from one IP address to another, after which the domain is either moved back or discarded. The case of domains using private IP addresses has been studied, and it was shown that a very small amount of those domains are malicious.

Domains can appear to be parking, when the cause is actually incorrectly configured name servers. An organization using an internal name server might point domains to IP addresses that are private and shouldn't be routed. The external name server should be giving a different result. These domains, in a short term, would look like they are parking when they aren't.

While parking for the non-routable case has been shown to have limited value as a malicious indicator, it is still a feature of domains that should be investigated.

To summarize these examples, what appears at first to be malicious behavior could be behavior that is not malicious. More information is always required to determine if that is the case. In the case of A record poisoning, it could be malicious behavior, or it could be a misconfiguration. Just having the syntactic result doesn't have the semantics, that is, explain why it happened. Sometimes it's not possible to determine why the action occurred, and there is no way to say that the domains under study are malicious. It's only possible to say that they seem malicious. That happens often in cybersecurity research because context is lacking.

9.1.2 *Features of Domains*

To study domains effectively, a measurement is needed. The variables chosen could be categorical or ordinal due to the nature of domains. In this, section we'll talk about various features we can measure and what kind of variables they are. These are features that can be determined about all domains, not necessarily only malicious domains.

Of course, since domains are essentially strings, we can measure the length, the presence of non-ASCII characters, or the distribution of letters and numbers in the string. The properties in the following list are specific to domains.

- Number of IP addresses

    If an adversary is using a domain for malicious activities, they want to make sure that it is available for use which means it should have at least one IP address. The more IP addresses it has, the more likely it is that it can be reached.

    The number of IP addresses a domain uses is a factor in analyzing a domain for malicious intent. The malicious domains are most likely hijacking the IP addresses from legitimate owners, so the IP addresses would be announced by multiple ASes. As discussed in the section on fast flux analysis, this is also a feature of domains that use a Content Distribution System.

    If a list of the owners of the ASes is available, then it is possible to control for this issue. The number of IP addresses and the number of ASes that are owned by multiple organizations is a feature of domains that can point to malicious behavior. The ownership must be examined carefully; the records are not always updated when organizations are acquired.

It is also possible to consider the number of countries in which the IP addresses are located. This is similar to the check for multiple owners of the ASes. Instead, it is a validation of the location of the IP addresses. Unfortunately, this is dependent on the origin of the geographical Internet Protocol (GeoIP) data that is used, which may or may not be correct.

The counts of each are ordinal data. They can be averaged across domains.

- Domain Generation Algorithms

  DGAs are algorithms used by malware to create domain names. This way, malware doesn't have to contain the actual domain name. Instead, the malware contains an algorithm used to create the domain name. It's another way for malware authors to hide themselves. If they only use a few domains, then it is easy to shut them down by taking over the domains. However, using DGAs gives them one place further to hide. Instead of figuring out which domain the malware is using, the defenders are inundated with possibilities.

  For example, the malware called Conficker is one the first malware known to use a DGA for its domains. Conficker would generate 250 possible names and attempt to resolve them all. If it could resolve a name, then that was the domain it communicated with. In analyzing the malware, researchers were able to reverse-engineer the DGA and were then able to sinkhole the domains used by the malware (Porras *et al.*, 2009a)

  Botnets commonly use DGAs, and luckily, some (Gavrilut *et al.*, 2016) of the algorithms have been reverse engineered. This work allows us to create a list of domains used by that botnet and either detect their usage or block them. Unfortunately, this means a defender can only block the ones they know about. Determining if a random domain is generated by a DGA is a very difficult problem.

  It's important to note that not every domain that is a DGA domain is malicious. Companies have been known to have their own generation algorithms for domains and for host names.

If a researcher has a method they believe will detect the use of a DGA, then the question of whether or not it is becomes a categorical question.

- Number of name servers

Domains need two things to work. Something to point to, whether an IP address or another domain, and something to do the pointing, or the name server. The name server is the point of contact for the domain, the entity that associates the domain with its IP address.

A domain that changes name servers often can be moving from hosting provider to hosting provider quickly, which can be a bad sign. The name servers changing IP address often is also a bad sign, assuming that the domain isn't hosted by a Content Distribution Network.

The number of name servers is an ordinal.

- TLD/effective TLD of the domain

A domain is read as labels from right to left. For example, with `www.google.com`, the first label is the `com`, then the `google`, and finally `www`. The `com` is the TLD and the `google` is the second-level domain (SLD).

There are ccTLDs and gTLDs. Generic TLDs are regulated by ICANN, and ccTLDs are regulated by the country registrar.

Some countries have restricted their ccTLDs. This means they have predefined a set of labels for their ccTLD and only sell domains of the form label.country_label.TLD. An example of this is the ccTLD `.uk` for the United Kingdom. All domains in the `.uk` ccTLD must look like label.country_label.uk, where the country labels include ac (academic), co (company), and gov (government). The SLDs `co.uk` and `ac.uk` effectively act as independent TLDs. Mozilla started an initiative to keep a list of such effective TLDs (Mozilla, 2007).

Using this list, it is possible to determine if a set of domains don't follow the rules. For example, `example.uk` is a domain that shouldn't exist, due to the rules of the registrar of the `.uk` domains. It shouldn't resolve at all because the name server for the ccTLD

.uk should fail to resolve the domain. If an adversary is using the domain, then perhaps they have their own name server. If they are controlling that, then they can resolve anything they want. These domains should be considered suspicious.

There are some ccTLDs that have been known to harbor malicious domains. It's not their aim to be malicious, but the amount of money that a small country can make selling a ccTLD may be a significant portion of their country's gross domestic product (GDP) (Metcalf and Spring, 2013a). So the registry's incentive is to maximize registrations, not remove them for abusive or malicious behavior. While not all domains in these ccTLDs are malicious, it's still a significant amount.

The TLD is a categorical variable. The TLDs of domains can be counted but no other operations apply.

- Domain lifespan

  A domain used for legitimate purposes will have a long lifespan. Google wants people to access `google.com`, Microsoft wants people to access `microsoft.com`, and business owners want people to access their websites.

  However, malicious domains don't generally have long lifespans. A spammer will register a domain, use it for a few hours, then dump it. They know that the defenders will be blocking the domains as soon as they can find them, so they drop the domain before that happens. If the first resolution of a domain is determined and the last time it was resolved is also found, the short time period is an indicator of a potentially malicious domain. On the other hand, some companies use temporary domains, such as `temporary-string.example.com`. The domain `example.com` has a long lifespan, but the fully qualified domain `temporary-string.example.com` does not.

  Lifespan is an ordinal variable.

This isn't everything that can be measured on a domain, just a short list of examples. The time to live (TTL) of the domain, the length of the domain, the number of subdomains, the distribution of letters, and more can be measured. The point of this list is that there is both categorical and ordinal values that can be measured.

9.2   Study Design

The traits of domains can change over time. A simple example is to consider TLDs. In 2011, ICANN announced that they would accept applications for new gTLDs (ICANN, 2011). Domains before 2011 were restricted to only a few gTLDs, whereas domains today can vary quite a bit. If someone analyzed malicious domains in 2010 and made inferences about the TLDs of the domains, this wouldn't hold today. For example, the TLD .baseball is a new TLD that wouldn't have existed in 2010.

In 2011, a paper (Lasota and Kozakiewicz, 2011) defined a list of lexical features about domain names that they considered malicious traits. They compared their blocklist domains to a list of top websites in 2011, so we're going to pick one of malicious lexical traits they defined in 2011 and see if it still holds true in the current data.

The features they considered include:

- Domain name length

- Number of dots in the fully qualified domain name (FQDN)

- Occurrence of a keyword

- Probability of occurrence of specific characters

- Number of different characters

This paper has research that can be examined as it only uses the domain names as its basis, not external data that may not be available. The study for this chapter will focus on domain length.

For this study, the data used should be defined and described. Without that, the study makes no sense. The worst case is to say the domains are malicious without context as to why. The reason that the domains are tagged as malicious should be recorded or an important step is lacking for anyone who wants to repeat the work.

9.2.1   *First Data Set*

A data set can be created by collecting spam for a period of time. The spam would then be examined for all email addresses, sending domains, and URLs, thus creating a list of potentially malicious domains. This has been done before using honey pots, and the usual opinion is that this collection must span millions of messages to be useful. In 2011, there were at least half a billion(m3aawg, 2011) mailboxes worldwide. From this report, each mailbox received on average 5,200 pieces of spam email in a quarter. A single spam collection isn't enough to create a representative sample of spam.

However, one email address that collected spam was tagged by Vade (VadeSecure, 2019), and a second email address was set up to only receive spam and no legitimate email. This is the basis for the spam collection used in this chapter.

The collection period spanned ten months, and then the domain names were parsed out of every spam message, examining both the message header and the body. Collating this into one set, 15,414 domain names were collected.

There's a problem with this method. Some of the domains are used to send spam, and some of them are used in URLs to deliver malware, steal information, or other malicious activities. By aggregating the two lists, the issue has been confused. A list that contains both spam domains and domains used by the Zeus botnet isn't very clear, and in fact, can confuse the issue.

The domains that were found in the URLs in the spam may or may not be malicious. For example, marketing email is often tagged as spam. The aim of those URLs is to get users to come to the website to learn about the latest offer from the company, not to download malicious software to their computers. Without accessing every URL in that list, there's no way to know for sure. It's also impossible to know if they are malicious now compared to when the spam was sent.

Returning to the spam samples, it was re-analyzed and determined that there are 8,896 domains that sent the spam and 7,780 domains contained within URLs found in the body of the messages. From those numbers, we know there's some intersection between the two sets. It turns out that 1,262 domains appear in both lists.

This is truly a convenience sample. The emails just happened to be sent to the two email addresses, and in one case, they happened to be tagged as spam. Suppose it is determined that 95% of the domains in the sender of the spam are in the .example TLD. That doesn't mean 95% of all spam is sent from domains in that TLD. That just means that in this sample, 95% of the domains came from that TLD.

Starting with a little exploratory data analysis on this set is a good idea and the focus of the analysis is the distribution of domain length.

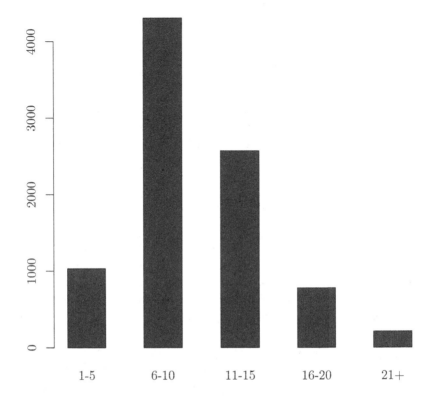

Fig. 9.1   Length Distribution for Domains that Sent Spam

Figure 9.1 has the distribution of lengths from domains that sent spam whereas 9.2 has the distribution of lengths from domains found in the message of the spam.

9.2.2   *Second Data Set*

A community project to collect malware domains is the Malware Domain List `https://malwaredomainlist.com`. It is available for anyone to download, so a collection was started to download the data for several months. Choosing a day at random, 1,154 domains were on the downloaded list. Since the list only contained domain names, there's no context as to why these domains were on the list. It's just known that someone reported the domain to the owners of the website as having malicious intent.

This is another convenience sample. Someone happened to share with the website that they found this domain malicious. It's possible that an

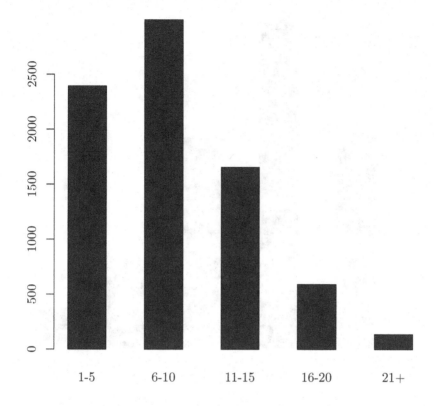

Fig. 9.2   Length Distribution for Domains Found in Spam

adversary could feed incorrect data to the website, which means that we have no way of knowing how good or bad this site is. Another file available at the website lists why the domain was reported. For example, the domain `adversarylikesphishing.example.com` could be on the list and have been reported for phishing, or the domain `adversarydelivery.example.com` could be on the list as a website that delivers malicious content.

The assumption is that the people reporting these domains have done verification on the domains to verify that they are malicious, but without context, there's no way to be sure. There's also nothing that demonstrates the domains are still malicious at the time the list was downloaded. It's just know that at some point, someone declared that the domains were malicious.

Continuing the exploratory data analysis from the first data set, Fig. 9.3 has the distribution of the lengths of domains found in the set. Most of

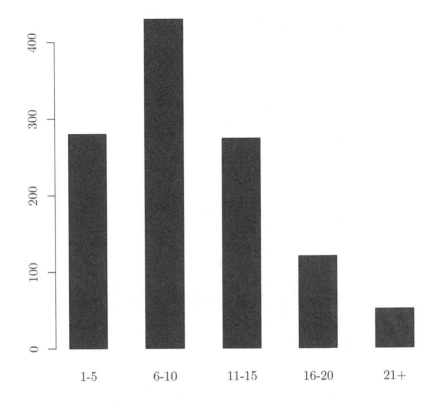

Fig. 9.3   Length Distribution for the Malware Domain List

the domains were between 6 and 10 characters long, like the domains from spam, but the shape of the distribution is different.

9.2.3   *Third Data Set*

In the discussion of DGAs, it was mentioned that several of the algorithms have been reverse engineered. Using these algorithms, it's possible to generate all domains for the malware, depending on how the algorithm was seeded. If the algorithm relies upon the day, then for each day, it is possible to generate a population of domains for the day. This is the entire population of DGA domains for that malware for that day. An example of this is the Cryptolocker Flashback malware.

Some of the DGAs are not seeded by day, so it's possible to generate all of the domains for that malware or a population of DGA domains for that malware. An example of this is the Banjori malware.

Bambenek Consulting (2017) has created the domains from the algorithms, so that researchers can download them there rather than using the algorithm. The site says that they do their best to avoid errant data, but there are no guarantees. In other words, it's possible that non-DGA domains have been added to the lists, but they aren't sure.

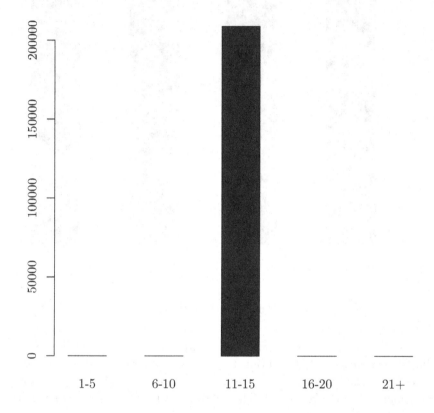

Fig. 9.4   Length Distribution for Cryptolocker Domains

Looking at the data on a randomly chosen date, there are 439,228 domains listed for the Banjori malware and 1,000 listed for Cryptolocker–Flashback. Fig. 9.4 has a plot of the domain lengths for Cryptolocker. All of the domains for Cryptolocker are between 11 and 15 characters long. Looking deeper into the data in Fig. 9.5, the number of domains of each length seems almost equal.

This is a completely different distribution than shown in the previous data sets. The focus is on one length of domain.

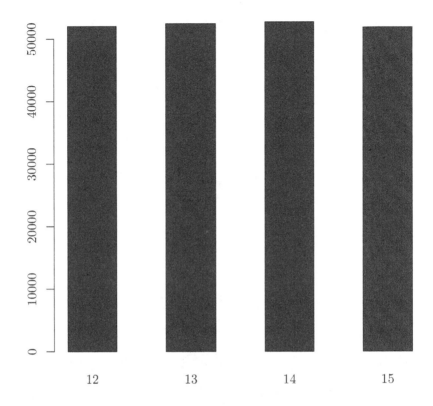

Fig. 9.5   Length Distribution for Cryptolocker Domains Revisited

Turning to the Banjori domain list, Fig. 9.6 has the distribution of domain lengths. This distribution is completely different in shape from the others examined so far. There are no short domains and a large number of domains are longer than 21 characters, which is unlike the other four distributions examined so far.

9.2.4   *Fourth Data Set*

The paper this case study is following compared malicious and non-malicious domains. To replicate their research, a list of non-malicious domains is needed.

As said before, some popular domains like twitter can be used for malicious activities. However, the assumption that will be used in this example is that most popular domains do their best to keep malicious activity to a minimum. It's not possible to assume that they're perfectly good, but

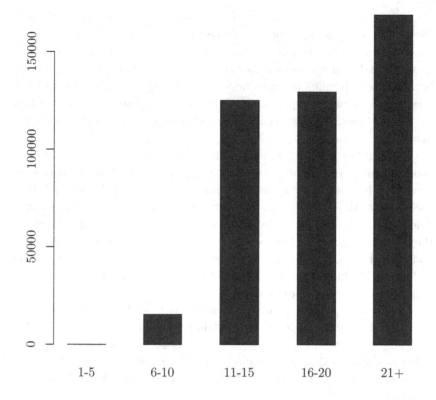

Fig. 9.6   Length Distribution for Banjori Domains

finding perfectly good domains is tough. Just because malicious behavior of a domain isn't known doesn't mean that the domain has none.

An example of a top list is a top one million list created by Quantcast. This is a list of sites based on the number of visitors from a given country during a month. According to the website, they measure this by a Quantcast specific tag on each website. This implies that only those domains with websites and tags were measured, omitting all domains that don't fit that requirement. It is possible that there are websites without the tags since there is no context to describe which sites got tags. If this site is used as a list of good domains, it's assuming any site with a tag is, by default, not malicious.

Cisco announced their own list (Hubbard, 2016). The domains in this list are from DNS queries, and it also uses a popularity algorithm to determine domain popularity. This algorithm isn't published, so domains are added to the list but researchers don't know how or why. However, it is free to the public and can be used in research.

A third list is the Majestic Million (Majestic, 2016). Domains are added to that list based on the number of referring subnets. It claims to use backlinks to determine the presence of the domain on the list. However, it doesn't tell us how it populates its database that it uses to create the list.

Each list method of creation is different and each claims to contain good domains.

This highlights a problem with both the data for malicious domains and good domains. In general, there's no knowledge about how the lists were created. The criteria for adding a domain to the list might be published, such as the Majestic Million, but that would be the only thing known. There is a lack of criteria that these domains are popular and therefore, they should be good. Remember, `twitter.com` has been used as command and control for botnets before. It's reasonable to assume that Twitter could end up on blocklists for its behavior. However, it is also prevalent on top domain lists due to its popularity.

An interesting analogy to this situation is three biologists studying a lake. Each biologist gives us their definition of a fish and a collection of examples. Whether or not each sample is actually a fish is unknown. What is known is that they defined a fish to fit their criteria. This is the same situation with these three sets. Each has their own definition of good domains.

Let's turn to exploratory data analysis on the three sets of potentially good domains. First, the Quantcast set isn't a million domains. Instead, it contains 532,053 domains. In this case, the name of the set is misleading. Data should always be verified.

Now, let's look at the distribution in each case. Fig. 9.7 covers the distribution in Cisco, Fig. 9.8 is the Majestic Million, and Fig. 9.9 is the Quantcast data set.

The Cisco and Majestic Million distributions appear similar whereas Quantcast distribution appears completely different visually. Statistical methods are needed to say for sure that that is true.

9.2.5 *Hypothesis*

The variable in the study is domain length but now a hypothesis is needed. Let's start with something a bit too broad:

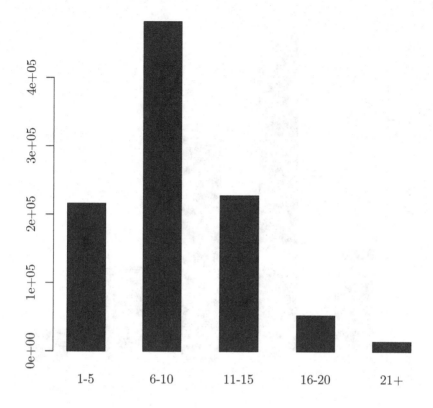

Fig. 9.7   Length Distribution for Cisco Top Million

Malicious domain names change over time.   As discussed, that's clearly true. First, the TLDs could change due to the creation of new TLDs. Narrowing this down is required.

The length of malicious domain names changes over time.   This is a good hypothesis, but the current data available doesn't allow this hypothesis to be tested. The 2011 paper states that, on average, malicious domains are shorter than non-malicious domains, but it doesn't give any precise data for 2011. That leads to better, testable hypothesis.

On average, a malicious domain is longer than a non-malicious domain.   This would be opposed to the conclusion of the 2011 paper. Or rather, the hypothesis is that this property of domains changed since 2011.

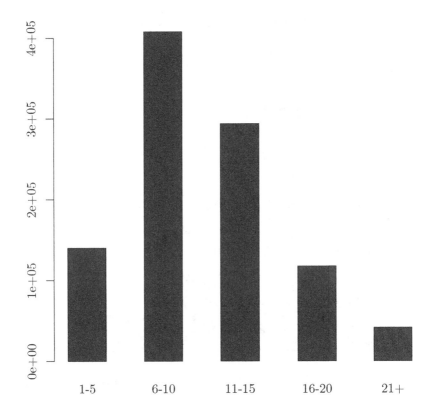

Fig. 9.8   Length Distribution for the Majestic Million

9.2.6 *Brainstorm Methods*

Now that there is a hypothesis, the next step is to test it. The first step is to toss out ideas for methods, then the next step will be to refine them.

- Malicious domains and non-malicious domains are needed for the study population.

- The paper used a single source of malicious names, so the population should follow the same trend.

- Is a sample size required?

- The effective TLD of the domains is needed.

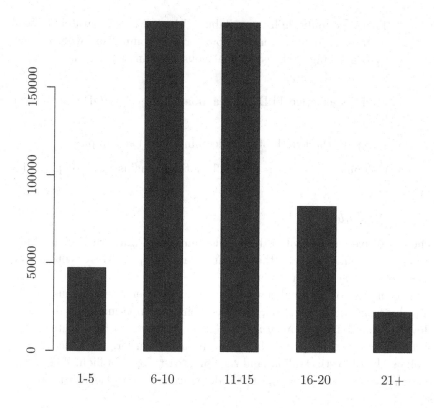

Fig. 9.9   Length Distribution for Quantcast

The paper says that their first step is to parse the domains to pull out the real domains and real TLDs. From the paper, the real domain is the highest-level second-level domain that can be registered. In other words, for `example.com`, the real domain is example and the TLD is `com`. It also says that it uses the Mozilla list to find effective TLDs, so this case study should follow that.

9.2.7   *Actual Method*

Let's boil down those ideas listed in the previous section into the actual method.

1. Determine populations.

2. Determine sample size, if necessary.

3. There are multiple lists available. Using all lists separately is necessary to follow the paper, however, the comparison will be done by comparing each list of malicious domains to each list of non-malicious domains.

4. Find the effective TLD and real domain for each FQDN in the two lists.

5. Compute the length of each domain in the two samples.

6. Compute the average over all of the domains and compare the results.

9.2.8 *Assembly*

There are five samples of malicious domains, the Malware Domain List, the domains found in spam, the domains that sent spam, the CryptoLocker domains and the Banjori domains.

For the list of non-malicious domains, the paper references using the domains from Alexa (Amazon, 1997) as their list of non-malicious domains. However, this list is no longer available to researchers for free. Instead, the study is going to use three data sets discussed earlier, the Cisco Top 1 Million, the Majestic Million, and the Quantcast Top 1 Million. The paper referenced using a sample of 40,000 domains from the Alexa list, so this study will create a sample as well.

The first step is to pick a day and download the lists from all three websites on that day.

9.3 The Measurement Study

In the previous section, we discussed the parts of the study and talked about how to assemble it. We can put that together and create our study. We want to replicate the method the paper used, so our steps will follow that.

1. Determine sample size.

   a. For the malicious domains, the entire set will be used. This replicates the method used in the paper.

2. Create the two data sets.

3. Now, find the real domain for each domain the domain lists.

Table 9.1 Average Domain Length of Malicious Domains

Data Set	Average Domain Length
Domains Sending Spam	10.228
Domains in Spam	9.00
Malware Domain List	9.95
Cryptolocker	13.434
Banjori	18.16

Table 9.2 Average Domain Length of Non-malicious Domains

Data Set	Average Domain Length
Cisco Top 1 Million	8.775
Majestic Million	10.63
Quantcast	11.59

4. Finally, compute the average domain length.

Let's begin by tabulating the results for each set of malicious domains as seen in Table 9.1.

Now, create the same average for the samples of domains from the three lists of non-malicious domains in Table 9.2.

The hypothesis is that the malicious domains are longer, on average, than the non-malicious domains. The next step is to create a table to determine for which data sets this is true.

Table 9.3 summarizes the results for all of the hypotheses. If the data set for malicious domains was restricted to the two DGA data sets, Cryptolocker and Banjori, then the hypothesis is true for all three of the non-malicious data sets. However, considering the other three malicious data sets, the hypothesis is true only for the Cisco Top 1 Million data set and not for the other two non-malicious data sets.

This demonstrates how the data source is important to the results. The results of the study completely depend on which data set chosen. It is possible to skew the results by choosing the data set that gives us the desired result, but that would be wrong. It would be data dredging, the act of looking through the data to find the desired result.

There is one thing neglected here: the sampling bias. A single sample was created from the samples of non-malicious domains. The entire pop-

Table 9.3   Malicious Domains Hypothesis

Malicious Domains

	Data Set	Hypothesis
Domains Sending Spam	Cisco	Y
	Majestic Million	N
	Quantcast	N
Domains in Spam	Cisco	Y
	Majestic Million	N
	Quantcast	N
Malware Domains list	Cisco	Y
	Majestic Million	N
	Quantcast	N
Cryptolocker	Cisco	Y
	Majestic Million	Y
	Quantcast	Y
Banjori	Cisco	Y
	Majestic Million	Y
	Quantcast	Y

Table 9.4   Average Domain Length Sample vs. Population

Data Set	Sample	Population
Cisco Top 1 Million	8.775	8.771
Majestic Million	10.63	10.64
Quantcast	11.59	11.61

ulation of that data is available so it is possible to determine if there is a difference in using that instead.

Sampling bias is the difference between the actual value in the population and the value from the sample. In this case, only one sample was created, but the best method is to take multiple samples and average that. Table 9.4 shows the difference in the two values. There is a difference, but not enough to change the results.

9.4   Lessons Learned

In our discussion of data sets, we discovered that there is no universal way of defining a set of non-malicious domains. This is true in most fields of cybersecurity —there is no universal method of defining non-malicious behavior aside from "not malicious." In other words, non-malicious behavior is any behavior that isn't being studied as malicious. Just because it seems the domain is not malicious does not mean it hasn't engaged in malicious behavior in the past or won't in the future. It also doesn't mean that it doesn't engage in malicious behavior now, just that as far as we know, it doesn't.

This is a common problem in cybersecurity, not just for DNS. Mistakes happen all the time that appear to be malicious, but aren't. Categorizing data as malicious and non-malicious is a difficult problem because maliciousness is usually a spectrum.

We also discovered that the data set influences the results of the study. The average length of a domain in the three non-malicious data sets ranged from 8.775 to 11.59. This is quite the range, considering all three are labeled as non-malicious data sets. The result of our study depended on the malicious data set we chose and the non-malicious data set.

This is true in cybersecurity, not just in this study. If we're comparing malicious data to non-malicious data, the method used to define either will affect the outcome.

Chapter 10

Network Traffic Study

Network traffic is a common data set in cybersecurity research. Malware installed on a system often talks to external sources for commands, to exfiltrate data, or to spread itself to new victims. Almost all malicious behavior can be found in network traffic. Finding the malicious behavior allows researchers to learn the methods used by the adversary, to find malicious traffic on a network, and perform a longitudinal study on network behavior to see how maliciousness has changed over time.

In this chapter, we're going to discuss the pros and cons of network traffic for research. We'll consider the kinds of behavior that could exist and how examining network traffic can and cannot help in the study. We'll then turn our attention to botnet behavior.

It's impossible to create a data set that contains the population of network traffic on the Internet. There's no view into all the traffic everywhere at any given time, not to mention, there's just too much data to collect.

Section 10.1 begins the chapter with a discussion of the details of network traffic analysis. If you are conversant with this field, you should skip to the next section.

10.1 Discussion

Full packet capture is the exact record of everything that happened on a network. As its name suggests, it is the capture of every network packet sent on an interface. This includes the source IP address, the destination IP address, the source port, destination port, TCP flags, protocol type, and the full packet of information sent on the link.

Finding malicious traffic is easier when there is a record of everything that happens. The traffic can be examined to find the exfiltration of data, the beaconing of a command and control botnet server, and the sending of spam. It does require that the researcher must know what they're looking for to to find it, but it is a good data set for finding malicious actions.

We saw in Chapter 2 that full packet capture over 72 hours can take up over 24.3Tbs of space. Sampling has been used to attack this problem in the past, (Zhang *et al.*, 2011) but it's not an easy problem.

Another type of data is network flow. These are the traces left behind on the network, not the full record of the traffic. It doesn't include the full packet but includes information such as source IP address, the destination IP address, the source port, destination port, TCP flags, protocol type, the amount of data sent, the start time for the transaction, and the end time for the transaction.

As this data is much smaller than the full packet capture, it is easy to store long term, so historical analysis is possible. An estimate for the System for Internet-level Knowledge (SiLK) Network Flow tool (CERT/NetSA Security Suite, 2019) is that to store a 1Gb link for one year is 3,152.82Gb, or 3.15Tb. Clearly, this is several orders of magnitude less than the full packet capture storage requirements.

In full packet capture, the exfiltration of data is visible whereas network flow shows only that a large amount of data left the system. Usually, the context of what the flow contained is needed to definitively determine the maliciousness of the act.

However, long spans of historical data, which is only really possible with network flow, allow researchers to study different questions.

The features of the Internet change over time, even in network traffic. For example, in 1993, the gopher protocol was common for file transfers (Anklesaria *et al.*, 1993). Today, gopher is nearly non-existent. Another example is uucp (Ravin *et al.*, 1996). Uucp is another file transfer protocol that occasionally appears in legacy code but is not nearly as common as it used to be.

It can be difficult to determine malicious network traffic versus benign traffic, even with full packet capture. The WannaCry ransomware attack (Mackenzie, 2019) attempted to resolve a domain. During the time that the domain failed to resolve, the ransomware was active. As soon as a researcher registered the domain, WannaCry turned itself off. A system infected with WannaCry would periodically attempt to resolve this domain, which full packet capture would capture, but this isn't necessarily a sign of maliciousness. People attempt and fail to resolve domains all the time. The sign of interest was the domain name itself combined with the ransomware attack.

In network flow, it would look like a connection was made on port 53 to a name server, which isn't anomalous at all. Domain resolutions aren't necessarily an odd thing, so finding them in network flow wouldn't have been a sign of malicious traffic. This is true for both full packet capture and network flow. Determining that the domain was the key to the ransomware involved not only finding the domain resolution in network traffic but also knowing that it originated from a system infected with the WannaCry ransomware.

Similarly, botnets have been known to use Twitter as a means of command and control (Pantic and Husain, 2015). DNS has been used as well (Dietrich *et al.*, 2011). DNS queries and twitter access are common activities and wouldn't raise suspicion.

Botnets want to hide their activity, so they also use traffic to and from standard web ports (Eslahi *et al.*, 2017) to mask themselves. This traffic doesn't look bad, unless the context associated with it is also available. Full packet capture may help with this as it can contain context, but network flow won't.

10.2 Data

Repositories of network traffic data can be found online. Most of these are illustrative of one variety of traffic such as botnets, malware, or other traffic anomalies. They're useful for studying what the traffic looks like in the given situation but only for that situation.

One example of a good data set is the Information security and object technology (ISOT) data set (University of Victoria, 2016). It contains multiple botnets as well as simulated traffic.

This leads us to another problem with network traffic data. Simulated traffic is traffic that a computer program created to mimic humans. This includes attempting to simulate the mix of applications used by a site, the protocols, and the levels of congestion. Strategies (Floyd and Paxson, 2001) have been suggested over the years for mimicking network traffic, but the inherent problem is that it is unnatural and does not necessarily include the random actions of users. This means it isn't exactly like what users do, but an idealized simulation of users.

Another problem with network data, especially from outside sources, is that it is often anonymized. Researchers don't want to share the structure of their internal networks, so they use schemes to translate the IP addresses of the capture data to private, unrouted networks. Anonymization schemes have been reversed in the past (Zhang *et al.*, 2007), so the structure of the anonymized data is probably completely unrelated to the structure of the network from which it originated. For example, an anonymized set might put all the webservers on one network whereas they're on different networks for redundancy. Another problem with anonymized data is that the ports can often be anonymized. The destination ports should remain from the original data set because otherwise, the context of which ports the traffic is attempting to use is missing. Source ports are a useful data source, as well, though not as useful as destination ports. If both sets of ports are anonymized, the data is no longer useful.

In summary, if the goal is anonymization, researchers have to be careful that the data aren't anonymized so much that they become unusable. The patterns found in anonymized data should be present in the original data. If traces are found of unusual traffic that occur in the anonymized data but not in the original, then that process created patterns instead of preserving them.

10.2.1 *Anomalous Behavior in Network Traffic*

A researcher has decided to study network traffic to find malicious behavior. They want to find the anomaly that is malicious or the underlying pattern of malicious behavior.

Consider a simple example. Suppose the administrator of a network has decided that everyone should use a central server for every DNS resolution. This means that the only traffic that's related to DNS should be to this central server. One system, however, suddenly starts using an outside server for its DNS queries. Either the owner of this system has decided on their own to change their server for DNS resolutions, or someone decided it for them. Malware has been known to change the DNS server used by a system it has infected (Meng *et al.*, 2013). This is anomalous behavior for the system and should be investigated, but without examining the traffic and the system, context is lacking.

Another example of anomalous behavior is a denial of service attack. Suppose an organization has a web server that suddenly is showing a large spike in traffic. The first thought is an outside attack; someone is attempting to knock the web server offline. On the other hand, someone may have posted the website, as an interesting site, to a popular forum. The users of that forum all decide within a short time of the posting to access the web site, which looks like a denial of service attack. Considering the forum users can be located around the world, this could look like a distributed denial of service attack, which it isn't. Determining the difference isn't always detectable just from the network traffic.

Given these two examples, outside validation is required to be sure that the network traffic is related to malicious behavior. Otherwise, the researcher would just know they something different than they expected.

Botnets are the workhorses of adversaries in cybersecurity. Botnets send spam, attack with a DDoS, are used with ransomware, are used for bitcoin mining and theft, and so much more. Finding botnet behavior in a set of traffic depends on the botnet, as each has their own way of doing things. A classic botnet is generally talking to a centralized command and control server, either a keepalive or receiving commands, for their next act. As the botnets have evolved over time, the command and control as evolved as well. Lately, some have started using peer to peer (P2P) protocols as their base (Khattak *et al.*, 2013).

Finding the beaconing (Hu *et al.*, 2016) and the actual conversation with the command and control of the botnet is an important part of characterizing the botnet as well as removing it from use. Determining if the botnet isn't using a centralized command and control, but rather a distributed communications system like P2P is another characterization. Unfortunately, as of this writing, there is currently no easy method for finding P2P traffic.

An APT is malware that has lodged itself into a network for a long-term attempt at stealing as much as it can from the network. These can ex-filtrate organizational secrets, so profiling their behavior and learning how to detect an APT on a network is a worthy goal.

These behaviors aren't the only adversarial behaviors possible, rather, it's a small subset. The adversary also changes their methods constantly. There are as many types of malicious traffic as there are threats from adversaries.

10.2.2 *Botnets Aren't Always Bad*

Let's turn our attention to botnets. Botnets are seemingly always bad. If a computer is part of a botnet then someone else is using its computing power and network to accomplish a task. One example of something that looks like a botnet was SETI@HOME (Korpela *et al.*, 2001), the search for alien life. SETI@HOME used home computers in a giant network to analyze radio telescope data looking for extraterrestrial intelligence. GPUGRID is a distributed computing project for biomedical research (Wiki, 2017). On the human side, there is Amazon Mechanical Turk. Turk allows tasks to be farmed out to a wide range of people. One person is the command in that scenario, and she sends out tasks to a wide range of IP addresses. In all three of these examples, the behavior of a botnet is demonstrated, but the outcome is not malicious.

Remember, a botnet can communicate with a central server, and commands are sent from this central server. In all three examples, systems communicate with a central server and receive commands from the server. In the case of GPUGRID and SETI@HOME, the commands are sent to the computers to execute tasks. The Amazon Mechanical Turk sends commands to addresses so that humans can execute commands.

Cybersecurity researchers have used botnets to their advantage as well. The Federal Bureau of Investigation (FBI) took over the GameOver Zeus botnet, turning off a malicious botnet off. (Franceschi-Bicchierai, 2015) That botnet was designed to be impossible to take down, so the FBI had to get creative. They managed to take over the network and not only turn it off but jail the creators.

The term botnet has connotations of maliciousness, but that clearly isn't necessarily true. Most people assume that a botnet is always bad, but it's the botnet's owners that use it maliciously.

10.2.3 *Adding Context*

This leads us to our next step. Suppose a researcher thinks they've found a botnet and they've even managed to locate the IP address used by the command and control server. They might think that they're finished with the analysis, but unfortunately, they aren't.

There needs to be some verification that a botnet is actually a botnet. For example, suppose an organization has many geographically diverse locations and uses a centralized network management system to manage them. The remote locations might contact the centralized system periodically as a keepalive or to receive instructions, which appear to be botnet behavior. Without context, this could appear to be a botnet. There's no maliciousness associated with the behavior though, so just finding it in network flow isn't enough.

Instead, if the research looked in full packet capture and found the same behavior, it is tempting to call it malicious. It appears that a central system is receiving messages from a distributed set of systems. Depending on the network management system, these messages could be obfuscated. This can look like a botnet. If it is known that all the IP addresses are owned by one organization, it's possible to assume it isn't a botnet, but we can't be positive.

Just looking at network flow isn't enough context. Using full packet capture can help, but that's not necessarily the complete solution. Also, due to the amount of disk space needed to store full packet capture, it isn't always available. What is needed is outside validation. This validation can come in various forms, from analyzing a system directly to correlation with other researchers. In the WannaCry case, the researcher had an infected system and observed traffic from it. He then decided to register the domain the system was attempting to resolve. The authors of WannaCry didn't register it, so he wanted to see what would happen. Rather than registering it, a researcher could also set up a mock DNS server that would return a valid response for the domain. This is a much more contained analysis rather than registering the domain.

10.2.4 *Botnet History and Behavior*

The original botnets were created for chatrooms in the Internet Relay Chat (IRC) network (Silva *et al.*, 2013). They could understand simple commands that helped out the chatroom administrators, played simple games, and other services. The original design wasn't malicious. However, other programmers took these simple creations and used them to attack IRC users or servers. It wasn't long after that that someone figured out how to weaponize the IRC bots to create a botnet for malicious purposes.

At the core of the botnet software is its origins, the IRC network commands. Botnets work together to attack in the form of DDoS or spam, so a central server can use the same commands from the IRC network to direct the bots.

This illuminates several things about the botnets. One is that in the original designs, there was a central server that directs the remote servers' actions. This means there is a single IP address to which all the clients connect. This is described as a one-to-many relationship. This feature alone doesn't necessarily mean a botnet is present. A similar one-to-many relationship can be found in DNS. When resolving a domain, many IP addresses connect to the name server for the domain.

The second is that the IRC protocol is often used by botnets. It isn't as pervasive as it used to be, but IRC is still used often. The presence of IRC traffic in a network doesn't necessarily mean that a botnet is present. The presence of IRC traffic that doesn't use traditional ports for IRC is an anomaly though. The assigned ports for IRC include 194, 529, and 994; however, IRC often uses port 6667.

Another feature of botnets is that once an infected server receives a command from the central botnet system, it acts. A command such as "DDoS *ipaddress*" would be sent from the central server, and the client would immediately attack the IP address. Similarly, the infected system could be directed to send spam. Botnets have been used for other malicious behaviors, like infecting additional servers, manipulating online polls or games, Google AdSense abuse, and more.

By acting immediately when it receives a command, a botnet is synchronized across the clients. This means that they all act at the same time. It wouldn't be very effective for a distributed denial of service attack if first, one client attacked, then the next, and then the next. For an effective DDoS, all the infected systems must attack at once.

The method the botnet uses to connect to the central server is another feature. It can't be by a hard-coded IP address, that would be easy to block. Instead, originally, the botnets had a domain name coded within the malware. It would resolve the name to retrieve the IP address and connect to the central server that way. Botnets have been taken down because the domain names the botnet used were discovered and then blackholed. The botnet designers found a way around this by using a DGA (Antonakakis *et al.*, 2012). The first botnets known to use a DGA were Conficker and Kraken. For Conficker, the botnet client would periodically generate a list of 250 domains. It would attempt to resolve all 250, and the one that did resolve was used as the botnet server. To block the botnet, the network defender would have to block all 250 domains whereas the attacker only had to get lucky once.

Botnets have evolved from the one-to-many approach, and some use P2P (Dittrich and Dietrich, 2008). P2P is a distributed network without a central server and is very difficult to detect.

In summary, botnets can use a many-to-one connection ratio where the clients connect to the servers for instructions. They can also use the P2P protocol where the connections are distributed and there is no centralized server. The IRC protocol is often used by botnets to send commands, and these commands are synchronized. A fourth feature are the domains the botnet uses, whether they are DGA domains or hard-coded domains.

10.3   Study Design

Botnets are going to be the focus for this study. There exists data that can be used for the study and features that can be measured. Akiyama *et al.* (2007) list three features of botnets. The centralized server that all botnets connect to, the immediate response, and the synchronized response are all listed in the paper as features of botnets in 2007.

We're going to design a measurement study to see if one of the features of botnets mentioned in that paper is still true today.

10.3.1   *The Data*

For our study, we've got two possible data sets. Each contains botnet and non-botnet traffic.

The first data set obtained is the (Garcia *et al.*, 2014) CTU-13 data set. It is botnet traffic that researchers at the Czech Technical University collected in 2011. Their goal was to capture botnet traffic and at the same time, regular background traffic. Thirteen different kinds of malware were executed, and the resulting traffic was captured. The only traffic released with this data set is the traffic generated by the botnet. This gives us thirteen different botnets to examine.

The second data set is the (Saad *et al.*, 2011) ISOT data set previously mentioned. This is a manufactured data set. They combined publicly available malicious and non-malicious traffic to create it. They included botnets, such as the Storm and Waledac botnets, collected by the French chapter of the honeynet project. For non-malicious traffic, they combined the LBNL data set (Lawrence Berkeley National Laboratory, 2007) and traffic from the Traffic Lab at Ericsson Research in Hungary.

The first data set is separated by botnet, and the second data set combines botnet and regular traffic into one comprehensive set. Both data sets are network capture files, saved in the packet capture (PCAP) format. Network flow can be generated from the traffic using the SiLK toolset (CERT/NetSA at Carnegie Mellon University, 2002–2016) as well.

The study will start with some basic exploratory data analysis to get a feel for what the data looks like. Start by choosing one of the CTU data sets at random and examining the number of IP addresses in it. There are 1,558 unique IP addresses in sample 6. Of those, 10 are sources of traffic, and this can be easily visualize that as a bar graph by counting the number of unique destinations each source has.

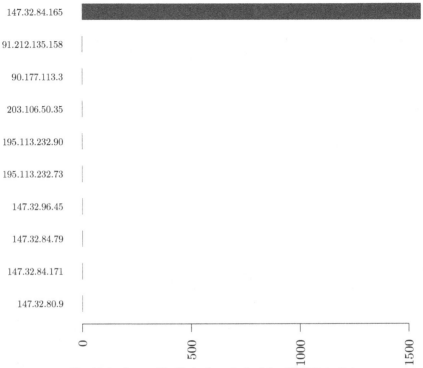

Fig. 10.1   Source Traffic in Sample 6 of the CTU Data Set

From Fig. 10.1, it's clear that the source IP address 147.32.84.165 has the most destinations. Turning to the destination IP addresses, there are 1,558 in the data set. The frequencies in this case are that all the IP addresses only have 1 connection, with the exception of 147.32.84.165, which has 9. That IP address is also the IP address in the source address set that has the most outgoing connections.

This seems like an anomalous result. An address with a large amount of connections isn't in the set as expected for a centralized command and control server. It's possible that this botnet uses P2P and distributed connections, but there's no easy way to look for P2P in network traffic.

Turning to another sample, consider sample 10 from the CTU data set. In this one, there are 65 IP addresses that are unique sources and 65 that are unique destinations. The plots of these are in Figs. 10.2 and 10.3.

Interestingly, the distribution of the two figures look similar. More work is required to determine if they are similar. Appearing to be similar and ac-

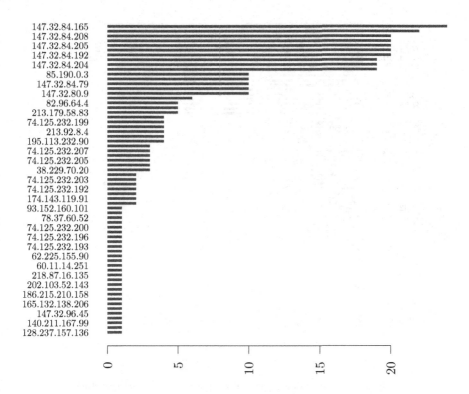

Fig. 10.2   Source Traffic in Sample 10 of the CTU Data Set

tually being similar are two different situations. One requires visualization and the other requires deeper statistics.

This initial exploratory data analysis has us looking for IP addresses that are either common sources or common destinations. A common source was found in the first sample, but not in the second sample. This analysis is restricted to IP addresses, the secondary feature of ports hasn't been examined yet.

Now, consider the ISOT data set. There are over 8,000 IP addresses in the set. Visualizing this isn't helpful. However, it's possible to count the number of IP addresses by number of connections and bin the results as shown in Fig. 10.4.

The ISOT data is also difficult to interpret. That is possibly because the data set contains multiple botnets.

It's apparent that most of the IP addresses have 1–10 connections, but it's impossible to determine how many have greater than 1,000 connections,

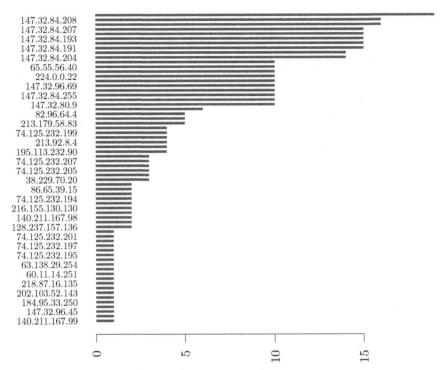

Fig. 10.3   Destination Traffic in Sample 10 of the CTU Data Set

other than it is fewer than 1,000 and close to 0. Returning to the data and ignoring the visualization, there are 7 IP addresses with more than 1,000 connections. This is plotted in Fig. 10.5.

There isn't a single IP address with the most connections as in the previous example. However, that can be explained by the nature of the ISOT data. It is a collection of botnets, and assuming they all used the same command and control server is wrong.

These two data sets both contain botnets but aren't necessarily applicable to the same study. For example, if the research is focused on the traits of botnets, then the CTU set is better. If the research is focused on trying to find a botnet in regular traffic, then the ISOT data set is more useful.

10.3.2   *Hypothesis*

We need a hypothesis to study, so let's start by brainstorming some.

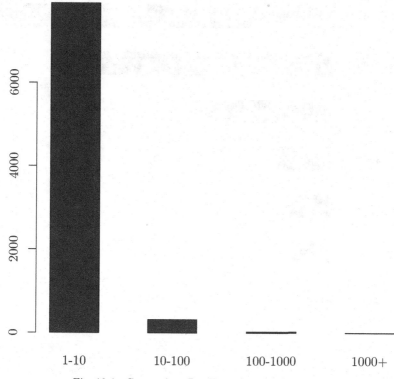

Fig. 10.4   Connections Per IP in the ISOT Data Set

Botnets haven't changed over time.   That's a bit broad and known that it isn't true. Botnets have evolved to use P2P connections as well as the standard one-to-many connection. Let's try again.

Botnets can still use centralized command and control.   That is still a bit broad since it assumes it is possible to test all botnets. A sample is available to test, but it's a convenience sample and it's not possible to make inferences on all botnets based on it. Let's try again.

Some botnets still use centralized command and control.   That's still a little broad. Let's try something we can test directly and is more specific.

The IP address and port combination with the most connections is the command and control server in the data set.   The data is

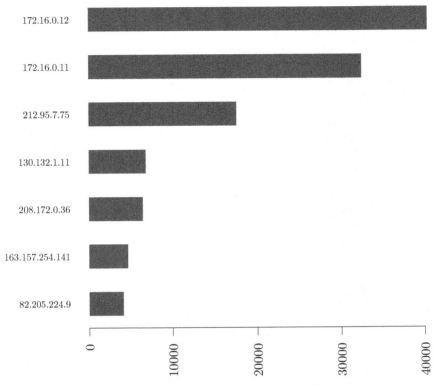

Fig. 10.5   ISOT Addresses with more than 1000 Connections

available to test this hypothesis. The hypothesis is that the botnets still use centralized command and control and that it's possible to find them by looking for the most connections in the data set.

10.3.3   *Brainstorm Methods*

We have a hypothesis, so let's brainstorm methods we can test it. The first step is to consider the tools and data required.

- Network traffic with botnets.

- A method to read the data.

- Is a sample required?

- It is necessary to consider IP address and port. The results of the exploratory data analysis imply that we need more than just the IP address.

- The data set should contain a single botnet because the hypothesis is about the current state of the art for botnets, not for finding botnets.

- A tool is needed to find the IP address and port combination with the most connections.

- Once the IP and port with the most connections is found, it's still not known if this is the command and control server. To determine this, context is required. Context will be found by examining the network traffic and determining the kinds of connections made. This method will only work for full packet capture since the context needed is not present in network flow.

10.3.4 *Actual Method*

Now, it's necessary take the ideas from the previous section and turn them into an actual method.

1. Determine sample size, if needed. The sample size will be based on the number of transactions, that is, connections between IP addresses. Consider the output from tcpdump (Jacobson *et al.*, 2003):

   ```
   04:47:32.419074 IP 147.32.84.165.137 >
   147.32.84.255.137:  NBT UDP PACKET(137):  QUERY;
   REQUEST; BROADCAST
   ```

   That's a transaction, and it's possible to count the number of transactions in each data set.

2. Use tcpdump to read pcap data.

3. Create a destination IP address and port combination frequency table.

4. Look for an IP address and port combination that is the most common destination.

5. Look into the pcap data to see if the connections have any further information that we can use, using the command line tshark from the wireshark (Combs *et al.*, 2008) package to verify that the connection is the botnet command and control server. Since IRC is a common botnet command and control protocol, the goal is to

Table 10.1   Number of Transactions in Each Set

Data Set	Number of Transactions
CTU-1	27,393
CTU-2	37,080
CTU-3	57,591
CTU-4	488
CTU-5	2,935
CTU-6	5,007
CTU-7	113
CTU-8	14,353
CTU-9	200,109
CTU-10	2,615,095
CTU-11	131,760
CTU-12	13,441
CTU-13	155,392

look for that. If it isn't found, it isn't an assumption that there isn't a botnet in the data because of the source of the data. However, it is a common method for communication in botnets and something that can be found.

10.3.5   *Assembly*

The two data sets have been discussed; the 13 samples of botnets from CTU, and the ISOT data set. The CTU data appears to be the best set for this study as it's designed. It's separate botnets in each sample, allowing the hypothesis to be tested. The ISOT sample contains multiple botnets as well as other traffic and won't fit within the study design.

10.4   The Measurement Study

Start by determining the size of the population, which means the number of transactions in each set as seen in Table 10.1. Sampling is used when the population is too big to study. In this data set, none of the populations are too large to use so sampling isn't required.

Now, create a table with the number of destination IP address and port combinations in each set in Table 10.2.

Next, expand that table and add the IP address and port combination with the most connections in Table 10.3.

These are the most common connections, but we need more context. To find this context, the tool `wireshark` will be used. It allows the close examination of the full packet capture data to see what is in the traffic.

Table 10.2   Count of Most Common
IP and Port Combinations

Data Set	IP and Port Count
CTU-1	5,907
CTU-2	4,881
CTU-3	33,959
CTU-4	199
CTU-5	909
CTU-6	1,853
CTU-7	59
CTU-8	3,091
CTU-9	45,453
CTU-10	69,074
CTU-11	65,867
CTU-12	5,597
CTU-13	22,759

Table 10.3   Most Common IP and Port in Botnet
Samples

Data Set	Count	IP	Port
CTU-1	5,907	147.32.84.165	2077
CTU-2	4,881	174.37.196.55	80
CTU-3	33,959	147.32.84.165	3389
CTU-4	199	147.32.84.165	8080
CTU-5	909	46.4.36.120	443
CTU-6	1,853	91.212.135.158	5678
CTU-7	59	123.126.51.33	80
CTU-8	3,091	222.189.228.111	3389
CTU-9	45,453	147.32.80.9	53
CTU-10	69,074	147.32.96.69	161
CTU-11	65,867	147.32.84.165	8080
CTU-12	5,597	147.32.84.165	32234
CTU-13	22,759	184.173.217.40	443

The goal is to look for traffic with both the source and destination address of our IP. This is because it's not enough to see what the destination IP address was sent, the the response is required as well. Table 10.4 has that for each data set.

For an example of what an analyst might pull off the wire during analysis such as this, see the box on **wireshark** packet capture results.

Samples 3 and 11 show evidence of IRC communication. If it is known that there is no possibility of IRC used on that network, then it is possible to

Table 10.4   Data Set and Traffic Description

Data Set	Traffic
CTU-1	DNS Query Response for Domain Lookups
CTU-2	GET requests, no response
CTU-3	IRC communication
CTU-4	TCP connections
CTU-5	TCP connections
CTU-6	TCP connections
CTU-7	HTTP communication
CTU-8	TCP connections
CTU-9	DNS Query Response for Domain Lookups
CTU-10	Obfuscated data in the same network
CTU-11	IRC communication
CTU-12	Obfuscated data
CTU-13	TCP connections

infer those to be the command and control centers for the botnet. Samples 1, 2, 5, 6, 9, 10, 12, and 13 lack any context to decide one way or the other. It's possible 7 and 8 could be command and control, 7 is using port 80 and 8 is using port 3389. Port 3389 is commonly used for Microsoft Terminal Server, not web servers. It's not possible to say that the hypothesis is true for all of the botnets in the current data set. It's only possible to say that it is true for three and potentially for two more.

It's also important that the hypothesis isn't revised due to the results. That's letting the data guide the results rather than the original results and can create irreproducible results.

Negative results are still results and should still be reported. In this case, the method has shown that the hypothesis that the IP and port in the data set isn't necessarily the command and control server. If a researcher expects botnets to behave as they always have, then they would expect that the busy IP and port combination would be the command and control server. It is possible that they have evolved to use the P2P method. Cybersecurity is an ever-changing field. Showing that it has changed in a methodical way is a good thing.

10.5   Lessons Learned

In this chapter, we saw that the data format can affect the results. If our data were network flow, then we wouldn't have been able to complete the study. The step that would have failed is the validation of the results since we would lack context.

Wireshark packet capture results

For example, CTU-3 uses TCP connections. However, the `wireshark` PCAP analysis found:

```
03:00:01:96:02:f0:80:7f:65:82:01:8a:04:01:01:04:01:01:
01:01:ff:30:20:02:02:00:22:02:02:00:02:02:02:00:00:02:
02:00:01:02:02:00:00:02:02:00:01:02:02:ff:ff:02:02:00:
02:30:20:02:02:00:01:02:02:00:01:02:02:00:01:02:02:00:
01:02:02:00:00:02:02:00:01:02:02:04:20:02:02:00:02:30:
20:02:02:ff:ff:02:02:fc:17:02:02:ff:ff:02:02:00:01:02:
02:00:00:02:02:00:01:02:02:ff:ff:02:02:00:02:04:82:01:
17:00:05:00:14:7c:00:01:81:0e:00:08:00:10:00:01:c0:00:
44:75:63:61:81:00:01:c0:d4:00:04:00:08:00:0a:00:6b:00:
01:ca:03:aa:09:04:00:00:28:0a:00:00:61:00:00:00:00:00:
00:00:00:00:00:00:00:00:00:00:00:00:00:00:00:00:00:00:
00:00:00:00:00:00:00:00:04:00:00:00:00:00:00:00:0c:00:
00:00:00:00:00:00:00:00:00:00:00:00:00:00:00:00:00:00:
00:00:00:00:00:00:00:00:00:00:00:00:00:00:00:00:00:00:
00:00:00:00:00:00:00:00:00:00:00:00:00:00:00:00:00:00:
00:00:00:00:00:00:00:00:00:00:00:00:01:ca:01:00:00:00:
00:00:08:00:07:00:01:00:00:00:00:00:00:00:00:00:00:00:
00:00:00:00:00:00:00:00:00:00:00:00:00:00:00:00:00:00:
00:00:00:00:00:00:00:00:00:00:00:00:00:00:00:00:00:00:
00:00:00:00:00:00:00:00:00:00:00:00:00:00:00:00:00:00:
00:00:04:c0:0c:00:09:00:00:00:00:00:00:00:02:c0:0c:00:
03:00:00:00:00:00:00:00:03:c0:14:00:01:00:00:00:72:64:
70:64:72:00:00:00:00:00:80:80
```

CTU-7 was a `GET` request to that IP address for

```
t=1&s=2&m=50F8290AC57E77F533C2A3F\\1B4AB39E4
```

If we are looking for botnet behavior in a historical data set, then network flow is a common data format. This means that we must look outside of the data set for validation that the data contains a botnet.

Leading us to the next discussion point. Context matters. Without the context of the IRC commands, we wouldn't be able to say we found botnets. This applies to more than just network traffic. Finding a domain in DNS and calling it malicious requires more than just finding the domain. It also requires understanding why it is malicious.

Finally, we saw that a hypothesis can be wrong. This is why we hypothesize. We have a guess about what happened, and we want to prove ourselves right or wrong. In this case, we were wrong.

People tend to only report correct results, so we don't know what process they went through to reach them. This is an example of that process. Hypotheses can be wrong. The important lesson is to recognize when that occurs and to reformulate it. It is a very wrong thing to reformulate the environment to prove the hypothesis right.

Chapter 11

Malware Study

The term malware is not necessarily about the software but the behavior. This means that to determine if a given piece of software is malware, the behavior must be studied. For example, if a user downloads a game and doesn't like how it works, it isn't malware. If the software decides to communicate with a central server and steal bank information, then it is most likely malware.

There isn't a definitive definition of maliciousness. The behavior of some software has been deemed malicious by some and annoying by others, for example, adware. Adware is software that serves up advertisements when the user is online. A famous example of adware is Fireball (Perekalin, 2017). It hijacked web browsers to change the default search engine and serve ads. The danger in this type of software is that it may be malware masked as adware. Fireball included code that allowed the adware to run any code on the machine it wanted (Greenberg, 2017).

It's easy to see why this would be considered malware by some. It caused unwanted behavior in the computer and redirected computer traffic to a different location. It installed unwanted services and changed settings.

Clearly, there's a fine line between the two, and some researchers obliterate that line and consider all adware to be malware. Adware is also considered to be grayware, also known as potentially unwanted programss (PUPs) (Team, 2015).

Another example is spyware, which is designed to track a user's online behavior. An example is the Sony Rootkit (Halderman and Felten, 2006). By implementing copy protection, Sony wanted to make sure that the people listening to their CDs weren't sharing them. Unfortunately, that Digital Rights Management (DRM) software reported back to Sony on the user's activities, without the user's knowledge, thus fitting the definition of spyware. It also was a RootKit and did damage to the installed system.

It's easy to see how adware and spyware can be subverted. Since malware is defined by its behavior and spyware often has malicious behavior, it is also classified as malware.

Malware is an equal opportunity offender; it's found as windows executables, Portable Network Graphics (png), javascript, PHP: Hypertext Preprocessor (PHP), perl scripts, python scripts, and more. It's also not restricted to Windows. It has been found in Apple, Linux, and other operating systems, as well as mobile devices.

One goal of the malware author is to evade the malware defender. Every time a malware defender determines a new method to detect the malware, the malware author will work to hide themselves in a different way. This means that malware is constantly evolving, so the properties of malware from ten years ago will be completely different from the malware today.

Let's turn to the population of malware. We want to take a random sample of this population so that we can study it and make inferences about the entire population. Unfortunately, we have no idea what the population is. We only know what malware has been found. We have no idea how much malware is out there, nor do we have any way of knowing. If it evades detection completely, it could never be found. It's possible that the worst of the worst malware has never been detected, but we don't know that. We're also often dependent on other people declaring software to be malware. Unless we study the behavior ourselves, we don't know if this is true or not. We only know what others tell us. It's easy to imagine a scenario where a duplicitous researcher informs everyone that a certain piece of software isn't malware. It's also possible that a novice researcher does the same thing. If we rely upon others to annotate our data, we could be labeling malware as safe when the opposite is true.

We could also be labeling safe software as malware. When we rely on others to annotate our data, both situations could occur. The important takeaway is to always document from where the data came and how it was labeled.

Section 11.1 begins this chapter with a discussion of malware analysis in general. Skip to the next section on study design if you are already conversant with this area of research.

11.1 Discussion

Malware analysis often starts with a piece of software that someone deemed suspicious. Perhaps an end user reported it, an antivirus tagged it, or a researcher discovered it. As we discussed, it's the behavior of the software that makes it malware. The end user could report, "this software makes my computer run slow," where the problem is not the software but in the computer configuration. The researcher must verify that the software is performing unwanted acts.

In the interests of containment, we don't want to run potentially malicious software on computers that have access to the Internet. The software might attack other machines, spread itself, or cause other trouble. Instead, we run the malware in a sandbox. That's a system that has been set up without Internet access with the intent to watch the malware and determine its behavior. These sandboxes are instrumented to record network traffic, process table changes, registry changes, and more. For example, if the malware is designed to contact specific domains upon installation, we could see that in the traffic.

Since we don't want the malware to run on the Internet, we can set up our own network to mimic the network. This could include a name server that responds to any queries with a default IP address and other common network services.

Malware authors have evolved their software so that it tries to detect if it is in a sandbox and therefore won't run (Lindorfer *et al.*, 2011). For example, the malware might try to resolve www.google.com, and then exit if this fails. Since it is the behavior that makes it malware, the fact that it exits upon start up doesn't necessarily mean that it is malware. It could just be poorly written software.

In short, we want to know if the software is malware, and we want to know the probability that categorizing it as malware is correct. It's important to know the false positive rate, that is, how often something is tagged as malware that isn't, as well as the false negative rate, that is, how often malware is tagged as not malware.

Antivirus is a black box that uses its own methods to tag malware. This could be signatures, heuristics, behavior, or other methods that we don't know. All we do know is that the antivirus has tagged the software as malware, and we don't know the false positive nor false negative rates. If something is tagged as malware by an antivirus, we don't know if it really is malware or the probability that it isn't.

11.1.1   *Bad Behavior Evolves*

One of the first computer viruses was a boot record virus called The Brain (Cooney, 2012). Spread by floppies, it made them unusable by filling them up. It was called a "friendly virus" by its creators and was originally designed to protect their software, not cause trouble for others. The intent behind the software wasn't malicious, but the usage was.

A common attack today is Ransomware. It isn't a new attack; it started in 1989 with the AIDS Trojan (Simone, 2015). Instead of via the Internet, the AIDS Trojan was delivered by floppy disk. The ransomware was a failure since it required the disk, and the Internet wasn't widespread. Modern Ransomware got its start in 2005 with the Trojan.Gpcoder (Syamtec, 2015). It has completely evolved from its origins, so studying the original malware tells us nothing about the current threat.

Both of these are interesting because the attack they originated has evolved over time. Today, malware can send spam, DDoS, steal data, and more. Malware authors aren't interested in destroying the computer or the data. They want to steal information or money.

These behaviors are only a few of the possible behaviors, and they're also the obvious ones. There may be other behaviors out there, but since the malware hasn't been found, they aren't known, which makes it very difficult to generalize malware.

11.1.2   *Good Bad Behavior*

What is malicious or not is only determined by an organization's security policy. Since all organizations have different security policies, what is a violation for some is not a violation for others. An alternative way of thinking about finding a common malware detector is that it is searching for a useful and common implicit security policy. That tag line doesn't seem to sell products, but beware of anything that says it detects all malware unless it aligns with your security policy.

To make matters worse, malware can mimic good behavior. Further complicating things, behavior of benign software can, presumably via a software design mistake, appear malicious.

Bulk email is often seen as spam, even when the sender has good intentions. If a researcher is only going by the behavior of the software, then a bulk email sender could be tagged as malware.

The Microsoft forced upgrade to Windows 10 appeared to be malware behavior by some people (Gralla, 2016).

Another example is software that mimics botnet behavior. SETI@HOME (Korpela *et al.*, 2001) the software that looks for intelligent life, is an example of this. It communicates with a central server similarly to a botnet. It could also be malware if the behavior was the key and not intent.

PDFs with javascript are often tagged as malicious because javascript can be used maliciously. Even though it can be, it isn't always. Javascript is often used to assist users in filling out pdf forms, for example, inserting the current date.

11.1.3 *Obfuscating Behavior*

Malware authors are always attempting to hide from antivirus detection. There is no point in writing malicious software if it's immediately removed from the target computer, so hiding is their best bet. The longer that it can hide, the more effective it is.

Antiviruses can use signatures of the binary to block it, such as the MD5 or SHA256 hash. If the malware authors modify their source code slightly, then the signature could fail.

Another signature is the YARA (yara) signature. YARA is a regular expression that matches binary files. The YARA signature can be fragile to changes in the malware code (French, 2012). It can also find false positives, that is, software that seems to be malicious but isn't; it just has the same binary pattern that a piece of malware does.

Malware wants to avoid detection, so it can use timing techniques. It will look for certain behaviors by the user before it executes its commands or limit itself to running at certain times. For example, the malware may wait for the system to reboot or wait for a particular date to activate.

A goal for some researchers is to find the property of malware that will distinguish malware from good software without individual deep analysis of the software. Malware changes over time. The original malware was spread by floppy disks. Today malware is often spread through networks. The features chosen for malware from the late 1990s may not be the same features that would be applicable today.

It is also difficult, slow work to reverse-engineer malware or to determine its behavior in a sandbox. Researchers would like to speed up the classification by finding these features. Several factors come into play on this. First, the fact that malware changes over time. Second, malware is not a singular corpus. Ransomware has different features from worms, and worms have different features from rootkits. It's not possible to consider malware as a monolithic category.

11.2 Data

If the goal of the research is to separate malware from other software, then it requires two data sets, one that is malware and one that isn't. We'll call the set that isn't malware, *goodware*.

A study of malware needs a set of software that has been labeled malware. Github is a good source for this; there are repositories of malware that people have uploaded. Again, this is relying on someone else's label. That work is either repeated or accepted. VirusTotal will allow a user to upload a potential piece of malware and will attempt to determine if it is malware or not, but again, that's a third-party source.

A collection of malware samples was found on github (fabrimagic72, 2018). The owner of the collection says that the malware was found on several honeypots he manages. He used VirusTotal to determine if it was malware and also included several samples that could be malware, but weren't labeled by VirusTotal. This is a good set: the set details how it was collected, details how it was labeled, and it is categorized. It also contains unknown samples.

Another collection of malware samples on github (wolfvan, 2018) was also collected by honeypots. However, context is lacking for how the owner designated the files as malware. It's also unknown what kind of malware is in the repository. It's an interesting collection, a combination of windows executables and HTML documents, but with the exception of two files labeled as **mirai**, context is lacking.

A third collection of malware samples was also found on github (ytisf, 2018). The owners of this collection included both malware executables and malware source code. It is populated by people submitting samples, and other than that, the origins of the malware is missing. When someone submits a sample, they also add to the collection's database what kind of malware it is. It is interesting that source code for malware is available, but the origin of this malware is in question. The method used to determine what kind of malware submitted is also lacking. It's possible that an adversary submitted an invalid sample to confuse researchers. Further analysis is required.

A set of goodware is a difficult data set to create. If a set of goodware is collected, it is necessary to verify that it isn't malware. Antivirus, signature databases, and running the software to observe its behavior are all good methods to analyze it, but in the end, there's no method that will guarantee it isn't malware. It's impossible to prove a negative.

Suppose a researcher creates a fresh install of an operating system and decides that all of its executables will be the set of goodware. This is a reasonable set; however, it isn't perfect. The problem with that choice is that adware has been shipped with laptops before (Pagliery, 2015). In another case, PCs came with botnet software (World, 2012). It is assumed that a fresh install has no malware, but it has happened in the past. It's also possible to use software that purchased from a vendor; however, this has also been shipped with malware before. The Sony Rootkit mentioned previously is an example of this.

Another possibility is that the source code for a selection of programs is found and this is then compiled. Most programs compile using external libraries. For example, libtiff was written to handle TIFF image files. Assuming that the compiled software has no malware because we can look at the source code is reasonable, but that doesn't extend to the libraries.

Generating a set of goodware is a much harder problem than it seems. It is only known what malware has been found, not what malware could be found. The set could be tainted, but it is impossible to know.

11.2.1 *Exploring Malware*

Exploratory analysis on malware is useful but to begin, it is necessary to know what can be examined in malware. Rather than a single piece of malware, that is an anecdote, the study requires data, which is many copies of malware. It is necessary to find something that's present in all software that can be measured.

In the following, three features that have been used in malware studies will be considered and their goals examined.

Researchers (Deng et al., 2017) have done run-time analysis with limited connectivity to the Internet to analyze the environmental sensitivity of malware. They determined that 78% of their samples were sensitive to the environment that they were executed in. That doesn't mean that 78% of all malware is sensitive to the environment. It just means that 78% of their malware was. This is because their sample was a convenience sample and it isn't possible to project the results on the sample to the population. Their goal was to determine how much malware would be effectively analyzed in a sandbox environment versus how much wouldn't. From their analysis, they know that 78% of the malware they have wouldn't be effectively analyzed in a sandbox. It's a way of categorizing malware, but not a method of detecting it.

The feature in this case is a binary; "Does it work in a sandbox? Yes/No." It's a categorical variable. It's possible that it appears to work in a sandbox while the malware is obfuscating its behavior otherwise. It's also not possible to say if it doesn't work in a sandbox, it's malware.

The function call graph has been used to analyze malware. In this case, the malware is examined to determine which functions call other functions, and a graph is created from this information. The goal of researchers (Hu *et al.*, 2009) was not to determine if software is malware or not, but to classify the malware. The idea is to reduce the amount of work by classifying malware into groups and then to analyze only representatives of the group.

In this case, the measurement problem has been changed from one of malware directly to one of the graph. While this is interesting, using it is beyond the scope of this work.

Machine language is the binary code a compiler creates from a programming language. Opcodes are the human readable form of machine language. For example, **add** is the opcode to add two numbers together. **nop** is the operation to do nothing, and **sub** is the opcode to subtract two numbers. In this case, the opcode is a categorical variable. It isn't possible to compute the average of two opcodes. It's only possible to measure their frequency.

Opcodes have been used to study malware. For example, the sequence of opcodes could detect malware (Santos *et al.*, 2010). Another example is the distribution of opcodes to determine malware vs. goodware (Bilar, 2007). In this paper, the goal is to determine if the software is malware or not based on the distribution of the opcodes. Opcodes are categorical variables.

11.3   Study Design

Of the three malware analysis methods discussed, opcodes were used to separate goodware from malware. We're going to use this as the basis of our study.

We'll start with some exploratory data analysis, and then create a hypothesis and a method to test it. The tool to find opcodes is important, and we'll begin with using a common one.

11.3.1 Exploratory Data Analysis

Let's start by looking at opcodes in malware, study their frequency, and create distributions from them.

With the assistance of a second program, the binary of an executable can be translated into a list of opcodes. The program objdump is such a program. For example, it can be run on the Windows 7 executable winhlp32.exe, and returns 1,511 lines of information. The first 10 lines of this output look like:

```
winhlp32.exe: file format COFF-i386

Disassembly of section .text:
.text:
1001000: 9a b6 e2 77 1a c4 e3  lcalll $-7228, $444064438
1001007: 77 0c ja 12 <.text+0x15>
1001009: 06   pushl %es
100100a: e3 77   jecxz 119 <.text+0x83>
100100c: 9b   wait
100100d: 50   pushl %eax
100100e: e2 77   loop 119
```

The words lcalll, ja, pushl, jecxz, wait, pushl, and loop are all opcodes.

objdump (Free Software Foundation, Inc., 1991) has its issues, namely the assumption that everything in the binary is code when the -D option is used. It is useful for the initial exploratory analysis, though. Let's start by looking at the distribution of opcodes in winhlp32.exe.

The output from objdump gives us 95 opcodes to examine. Fig. 11.1 illustrates the frequency of the opcodes in that result.

From that figure, it's clear that the majority of opcodes appear five times or fewer in the results. Let's consider the top 14 opcodes. They appear in the results 25 or more times, in Fig. 11.2.

Turning to malware, consider the LoadMoney Trojan (Microsoft, 2017). There is a sample of it from theZoo collection. objdump returned 60 opcodes in the file. Repeating the frequency counts of opcodes, Fig. 11.3 shows that distribution for LoadMoney.

The distribution of counts in the LoadMoney Trojan is clearly different from the winhlp32.exe file, at least visually. The opcodes with counts be-

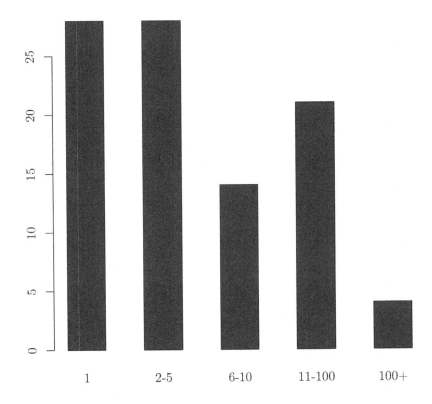

Fig. 11.1   Frequency Distribution of Opcodes in winhlp32.exe

tween 2 and 5 as well as 11 to 100 dominate the set overall, as opposed to the winhlp32.exe figure, where the counts for 1 and 2–5 dominate.

Now, let's consider the top 14 opcodes in the LoadMoney Trojan in Fig. 11.4. The sets of opcodes do intersect, but there are unique opcodes for each program. Using eyes as the analytical engine, the distributions appear different. There is a steeper climb in the LoadMoney figure while the increase in the winhlp32.exe is flatter.

The question is, is this difference just the two completely different programs or are the distributions completely different over all goodware and malware. Of course, that question is too broad for this analysis, the study is restricted to the samples at hand.

11.3.2   *Hypothesis*

Using what we've discussed so far, let's generate a hypothesis for the study.

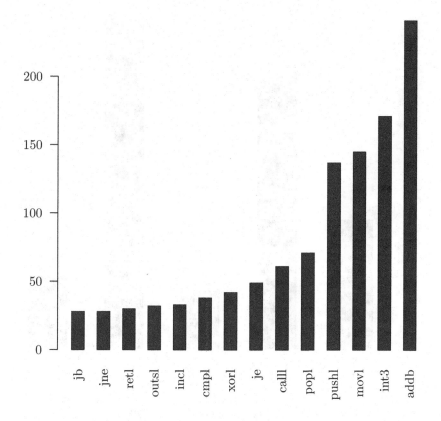

Fig. 11.2   Top 14 Opcodes in winhlp32.exe

Goodware and malware are different. This hypothesis is much too broad. Also, it's true by definition.

Goodware and malware act differently. Again, too broad. Also, it is also true by definition. Malware is defined to be software that acts in a manner that is harmful. The previous discussion concerned opcodes, so the hypothesis should be related.

Malware uses different opcodes from goodware. This is still a bit broad. Different isn't defined, at all. It's possible to just compare the sets, but a good hypothesis should suggest a means of testing it.

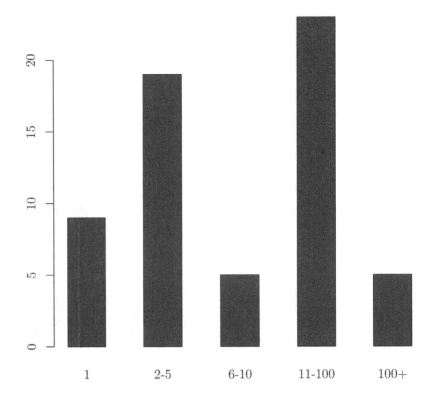

Fig. 11.3   Distribution of Opcodes in LoadMoney

In our samples of malware and goodware, the distribution of opcodes is different. This is a hypothesis that is focused, suggests an avenue of testing, and fits with the data available. The work is replicating the work (Bilar, 2007) done previously, so this paper will be the guide when creating the current study.

11.3.3 *Brainstorm Methods*

Once a hypothesis is generated, a method is needed. The first step is to list everything that could be needed.

- A sample of goodware to examine is required.

- A sample of malware is required.

- As discussed before, `objdump` will find opcodes, but it tends to look at data as code. Other tools should be considered.

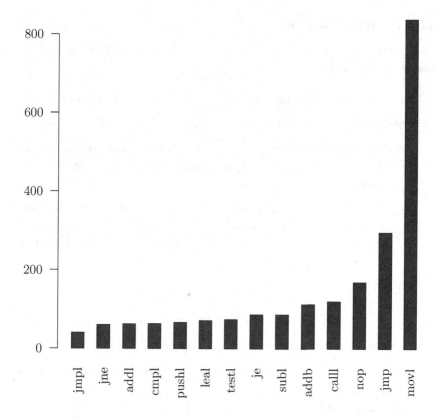

Fig. 11.4   Top 14 Opcodes in LoadMoney

- If the study will consider malware of different types, the sample should include that. Malware of different types has different functions, so it's logical to assume it would look different in opcodes.

No study ever considers all the potential problems. It is something of a matter of experience whether the study design considers the most important issues. Aspects of a study are can be considered to be not important if the change in the results is small enough it falls within an error that is much less than the effect size detected in the study. This is particularly difficult with malware studies, since the malware authors may read the public studies and think of clever ways to disrupt them. However, for a solid check list to start from, see Rossow *et al.* (2012).

11.3.4   *Actual Method*

Now, we'll take the methods we brainstormed in the previous section and create our method.

(1) Find tools other than `objdump` to find opcodes in PE executables.

(2) Find a malware sample that includes multiple malware types.

(3) The paper discussed previously binned Windows binaries by size, then took a stratified sample of that. That should be used for this study.

(4) For each piece of malware, create a distribution of opcodes found in it. Do the same for each piece of goodware. In the previous exploratory data analysis the top 14 opcodes had a good result, so that will be repeated.

(5) Create the following plots:

(a) A distribution of the top 14 opcodes in all malware

(b) A distribution of the top 14 opcodes in all goodware

(c) A distribution of the top 14 opcodes for each type of malware

11.3.5   *Assembly*

For the goodware sample, use a base install of Windows 7 Service Pack 1. Using this command:

```
dir /s *.exe
```

create a list of PE executables on the system. Then, bin the binaries by size into four categories: [0—10 KB), [10—100 K), [100—1 M) and [1—10 M].

The paper this study is following referenced an unpublished honors thesis as the source for the malware (Ries, 2005). This makes it difficult for an outside reader to duplicate the work done in the paper.

For this study, the malware from a repository of malware on github (fabrimagic72, 2018) could be used. This repository is useful because the owner explicitly says where it came from, how it was determined to be malware, and how it was classified. In this repository are 58 PE samples in 13 families. The problem with that malware is that 29 of the samples came

Table 11.1   Number of Opcodes

Executable	objdump	radare2	udcli
winhlp32.exe	95	13	104
LoadMoney	60	26	289

from Ransomware and the other categories had 1–3 samples from which to choose. This is a very small sample.

Instead, theZoo's samples will be used for the source of malware. This has 580 malware samples to choose from. To start, create random samples from the malware that included Toolkits, Rootkits, Botnets, APT, Ransomware, Trojans, and Banking Trojans. This can be followed up by examining the individual malware types.

For tools other than `objdump`, there are `udcli` (Thampi, 2009) and `radare2` (Radare Team, 2017). Each of the tools disassembles the binary to find opcodes, but each does it in a different manner. Both `objdump` and `udcli` are linear disassemblers; they run through the file directly looking for opcodes. `radare2` tries to be more intelligent by attempting to create a call graph and looks for opcodes in the code that will be executed. We'll create distributions using all three tools. The study should also start with exploratory data analysis with the three tools before the study to see what the initial differences are.

11.4   The Measurement Study

For a first step, start by running each tool on the two samples winhlp32.exe and the LoadMoney Trojan and counting the number of opcodes. Table 11.1 has the results.

There's a big difference in the number of opcodes for all three programs. For winhlp32.exe, `radare2` only found 13 opcodes while `udcli` found 104 and `objdump` found 95.

Now, consider the distribution of the top 14 opcodes, or in the case of winhlp32.exe and `radare2`, the top 13. `objdump` was already examined in a previous section. Fig. 11.5 has the distribution for winhlp32.exe using `radare2` and Fig. 11.6 has `udcli`.

As illustrated in Figs. 11.7 and 11.8, not only are the opcodes completely different, but the distributions are different as well.

Not only did `udcli` find more opcodes, it also found more instances of the opcodes it did find. The distributions between the goodware and

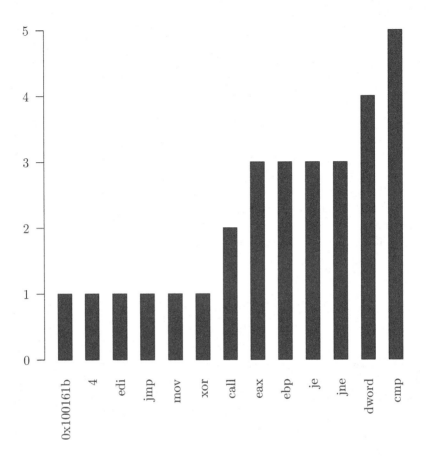

Fig. 11.5　Top 13 Opcodes in winhlp32 Using `radare2`

malware do look different, though for `udcli` there is a little similarity in appearance, but considering the opcodes themselves, they are different.

Again, this could be because of the singular nature of the program we chose. Extend the study by repeating it over all the malware samples and goodware samples. The study devised calls for this but doesn't state which tools to use.

The first results are for goodware. We've split these across three figures. Notice how the opcodes at the bottom of the figure, on the x-axis, change order between the three figures. This is because the figures are sorted by the number of opcodes detected. The fact the x-axis labels change order

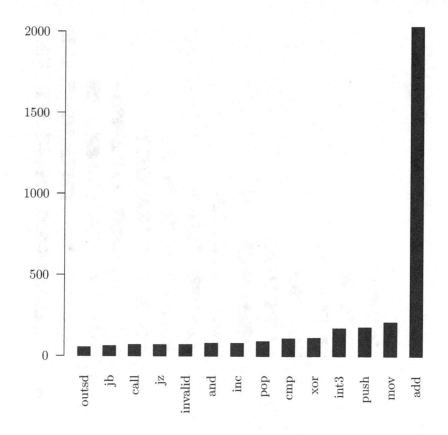

Fig. 11.6   Top 14 Opcodes in winhlp32 Using `udcli`

between each of the charts makes them hard to assess. As an exercise, try to compare how many `push` opcodes each disassembly method found.

Figs. 11.9, 11.10, and 11.11 have the distributions for `objdump`, `radare2` and `udcli` respectively. Visually, all three appear different, which, considering each uses a different method, that isn't necessarily concerning.

Now, consider the malware distributions over the three tools.

Figs. 11.12, 11.13, and 11.14 are the three bar graphs. The plots for `radare2` and `udcli` appear similar for malware, as opposed to goodware, which is interesting because the two tools are completely different.

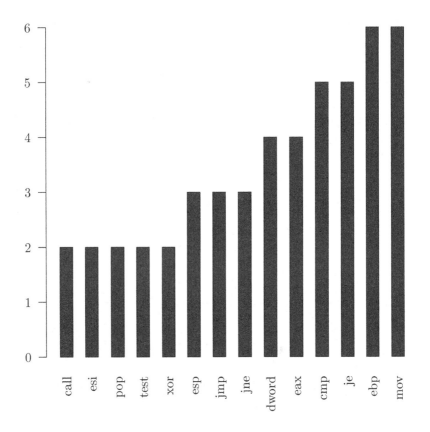

Fig. 11.7   Top 14 Opcodes in LoadMoney Using `radare2`

Comparing the goodware to the malware, the pictures look similar between the two `objdump` pictures. However, when examined closely, the opcodes are different. They've been sorted by size of opcode, not by name.

The problem here is that the comparison is not across equal things. The lists of opcodes are different in each image, which skews perception of the results, as shown in the `objdump` distributions.

Let's retry this with a slight change. Instead of the top 14 opcodes in each set of malware and goodware, pick the top 14 opcodes in goodware and then look at the distribution of those in malware. To make things easier, plot them on the same bar graph.

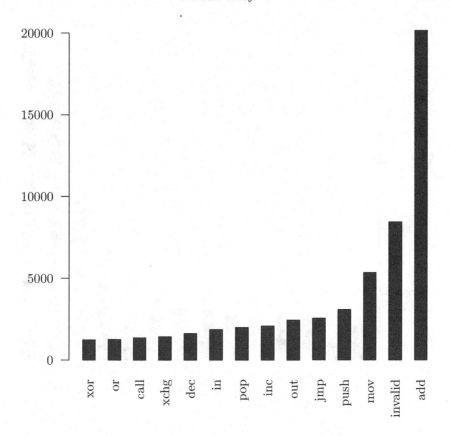

Fig. 11.8   Top 14 Opcodes in LoadMoney Using `udcli`

In Fig. 11.16 for **radare2**, it looks very different. Figure 11.17 for `udcli` also has very different distributions. However, Fig. 11.15 appears different but not as vibrantly different as the other two.

Notice that plotting two bars side-by-side makes it much easier to compare the number of **nop** opcodes, for example, between benign and malicious software within one disassembly method. These side-by-side bar charts still have the problem that comparing across methods, the sort order of the x-axis changes. What would Fig. 11.16 look like if the x-axis had the same sort order as Fig. 11.17? While neither the goodware or malware bars would be in ascending order, would it be easier or harder to read? Easier or harder to compare to the other figures?

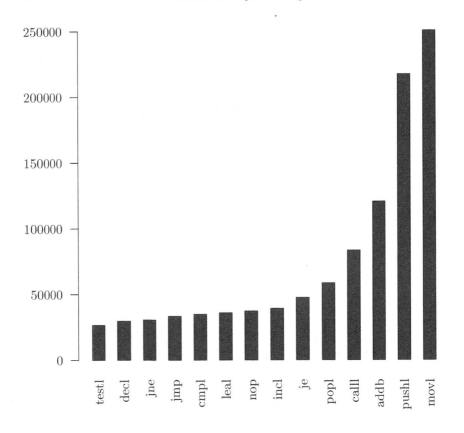

Fig. 11.9   Top 14 Opcodes in Goodware from `objdump`

This visual comparison isn't a proof of the hypothesis, it's just a guide to the next step. Statistical methods should be used to be sure.

The hypothesis is that the two distributions were drawn from the same distribution.

Understanding this requires further explanation. Suppose the population is a large amount of random numbers chosen from the normal distribution. If two samples from this population are chosen at random, they were drawn from the same population. This can be shown using statistics. If there is one sample that was pulled from the normal distribution another that is all 5's, then they weren't drawn from the same distribution. It's a method of looking at the similarity of the results that goes beyond the eyes.

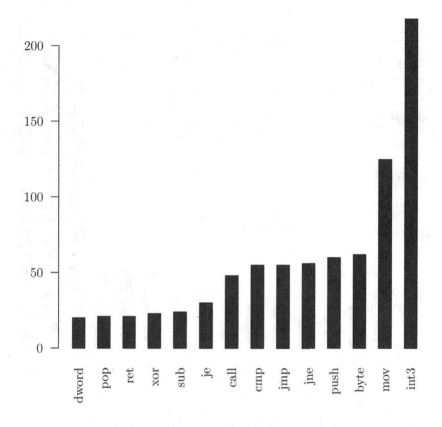

Fig. 11.10 Top 14 Opcodes in Goodware from `radare2`

In Fig. 11.18, we have an illustration of two distributions. These two distributions don't look all that similar, but it's still possible they might originate from the same distribution. In fact, that's the hypothesis.

One way to verify this is the Kolmogorov–Smirnov test (Massey Jr, 1951). This tests if the two underlying distributions of the frequencies differ. When used, this returns a value known as the p-value. If it is greater than 0.05, then it is believed that they originate from the same distribution. The p-value has been known to have problems, as mentioned in Chapter 4. p-hacking, discussed in Chapter 8, is a common problem in research. We'll try to avoid that in this study.

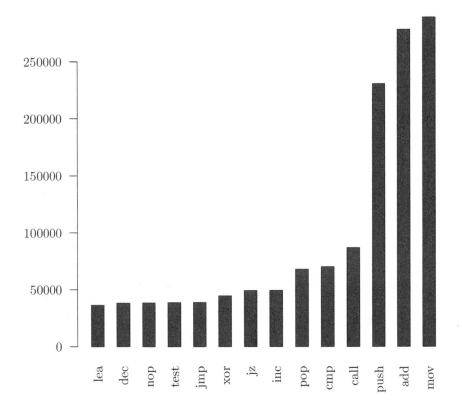

Fig. 11.11   Top 14 Opcodes in Goodware from `udcli`

Table 11.2   Kolmogorov–Smirnov
Test Results

Tool	p-value
objdump	0.05903
radare2	0.3338
udcli	0.001021

When it is computed for the two distributions in Fig. 11.18, the p-value is 0.722, which means the hypothesis is correct: they do originate from the same distribution even though, visually they seem quite different.

We can repeat the hypothesis for the distributions in Figs. 11.15, 11.16, and 11.17 to consider if the distributions of opcodes were drawn from the

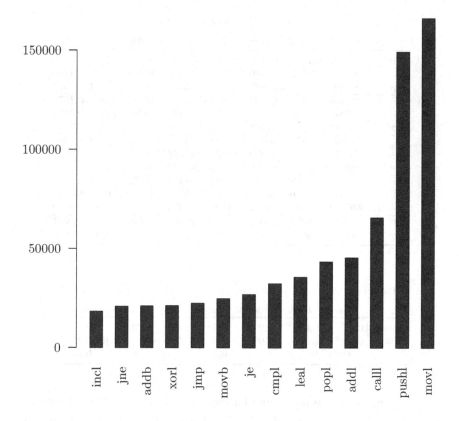

Fig. 11.12   Top 14 Opcodes in Malware from `objdump`

same parent. Table 11.2 has a compilation of the p-values. Remember, p values of greater than 0.05 are needed to accept the hypothesis that they were drawn from the same distribution. This means that they are statistically similar.

Interestingly, the hypothesis that they were drawn from the same distribution is true for `radare2` and `objdump`, but not true for `udcli`. This contradicts the guess from examining the visualization, which shows that while visualizations are useful, they aren't definitive.

Now, let's move to looking at the types of malware. Using `udcli`, Table 11.3 was created.

Table 11.3   Distribution of Opcodes Using `udcli`

	goodware	apt	bank	botnet	ransom	rootkit	toolkit	Trojan
add	278228	117461	69491	49081	372831	105795	38204	198919
call	86710	34022	19526	3091	40541	10739	5225	54287
cmp	69966	22639	52465	3837	45785	9766	7854	146858
dec	38235	5362	63507	3846	64763	10388	13593	183579
inc	49264	14766	64271	5356	74239	16709	21524	184899
jmp	38734	13175	25508	3252	23565	4393	2349	72853
jz	49069	15175	10213	1395	33788	6083	4613	25228
lea	36426	19715	7220	1227	19714	6896	2321	18901
mov	289039	81934	199465	13635	165136	46124	15879	587695
nop	38356	288	7931	465	144494	1872	1858	24134
pop	67743	20370	86656	7069	45275	15960	10678	248689
push	230602	69618	116752	11400	101685	39903	34618	328050
test	38617	10378	34969	2626	20657	5199	2775	100961
xor	44544	8975	54195	3537	62630	7865	14318	146047

Table 11.4   Kolmogorov–Smirnov Results for Malware vs. Goodware

	apt	bank	botnet	ransom	rootkit	toolkit	Trojan
`objdump`	0.0	0.0	0.0	0.0	0.0	0.0	0.0
`radare2`	0.0009	0.0009	0.0009	0.0	0.0146	0.000 18	0.0
`udcli`	0.000 16	0.1549	0.0	0.6355	0.000 16	0.0	0.1549

The same table can be created for `objdump` and `radare`. This is difficult to visualize because it is just columns of numbers. It's hard to imagine patterns in this data, so instead we use a mosaic plot (Hofmann, 2000). A mosaic plot lets us visualize proportions across contingency tables.

The size of the box is directly related to the amount of data found in the column. Fig. 11.19 illustrates the relative proportions of the data across the contingency table.

Let's start with the claim that the distributions from the malware types and goodware are statistically different. In Table 11.4 the results of the Kolmogorov–Smirnov test and the p-values for each type of malware when compared with goodware using the same tool. When the value 0.0 is given, it means that the p-value was so low as to be close to 0.

The p-values for `objdump` and `radare2` all imply that the hypothesis that the two distributions were drawn from the same distribution should be rejected, meaning they are statistically different. However, the results for udcli in the banking, Ransomware, and Trojan cases all prove that the

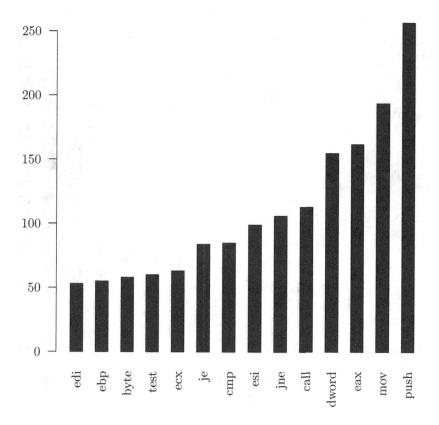

Fig. 11.13 Top 14 Opcodes in Malware from `radare2`

hypothesis is correct, that they were drawn from the same distribution and not statistically different. Otherwise, they are not.

Going back to the original hypothesis, that malware and goodware have different distributions of opcodes, it is clear that the results depend on the tool in question. In the first situation, where the comparison was all of malware to goodware, the `radare2` and `objdump` tools implied that our hypothesis was incorrect whereas the `udcli` tool said otherwise. Similarly, when types of malware were considered, the `radare2` and `objdump` tool proved our hypothesis, but the `udcli` tool proved it in some cases and disproved it in others.

Instead of the most common opcodes, it's possible to examine the rarest opcodes. In that case, there are opcodes that appear in some pieces of malware but not in others. There are also opcodes that appear in malware

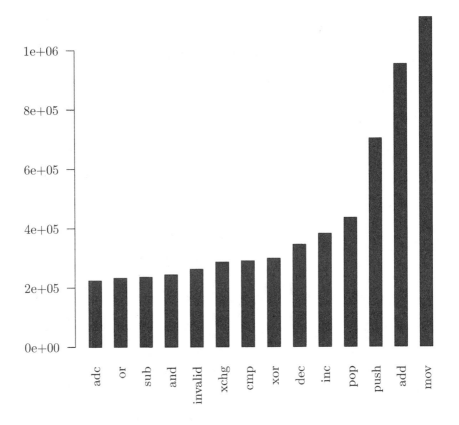

Fig. 11.14   Top 14 Opcodes in Malware from `udcli`

but not in goodware and vice versa. Comparing two different sets of objects is a difficult proposition.

11.5   Lessons Learned

Our study was to examine opcodes in malware and consider the distributions of them versus the distributions in goodware. In doing this, we discovered that the tool used can directly affect the results. We evaluated three tools, all open source, radare, `udcli` and `objdump`. Of the three, `radare` is designed to consider the flow of the executable while `udcli` and `objdump` go linearly through the code looking for opcodes. The difference in the tools is probably what made the results different, but without further study we don't know.

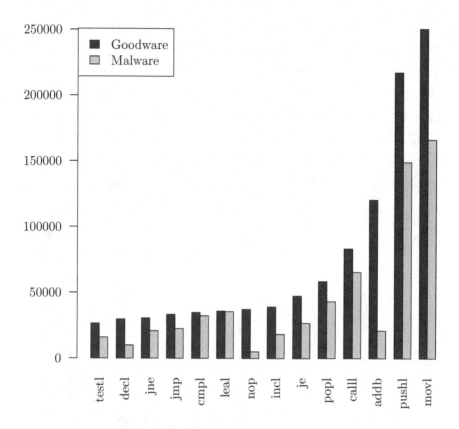

Fig. 11.15   Comparing Distributions with `objdump`

We also noticed the difficulty in comparing sets of different objects. If we want to compare the distributions of the opcodes between two programs, we need to consider the same opcodes and not a different set from each one.

Finally, we also saw that visualization can lead us down the wrong path. The bar plots looked different, but using the statistical Kolmogorov-Smirnov test showed otherwise. We shouldn't rely on our eyes as the sole arbiter. Statistical difference requires actual analysis beyond the bar plots that illustrate the data. Speaking of illustrating data, the mosaic plot is a visualization that illustrates the proportions of the table.

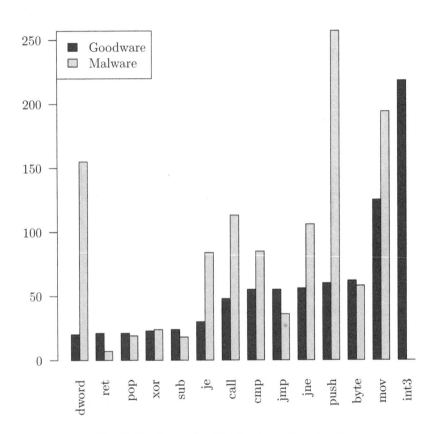

Fig. 11.16   Comparing Distributions with `radare2`

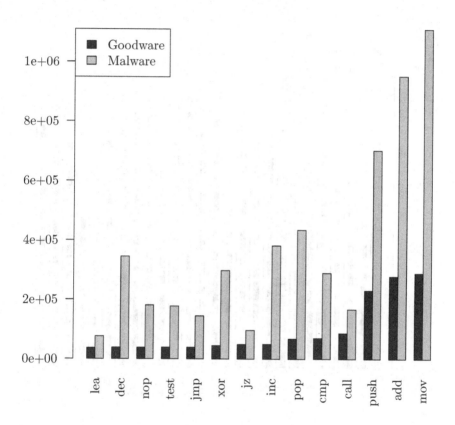

Fig. 11.17   Comparing Distributions with udcli

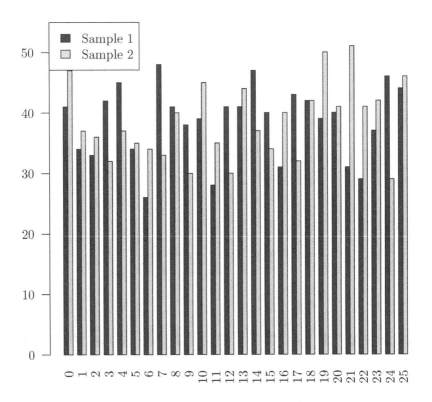

Fig. 11.18   Comparing two Distributions

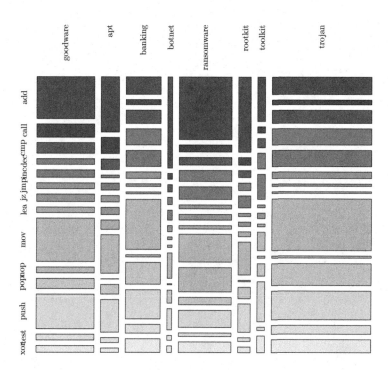

Fig. 11.19   A Mosaic Plot of the Malware Contingency Table

Chapter 12

Human Factors

The previous three chapters discussed case studies of DNS, network traffic, and malware. The three case studies have a similar theme, they are all artifacts found on computers. While they are all closely related to the technical operation of computers, those computers only operate because of and for humans. In order for a domain name to appear in passive DNS data, a resolution of the domain was done. This is often triggered by a human going to a website, sending email, or playing a game. If the resolution was part of an automated process, then some human created and initialized that automation.

The desirable study properties introduced in Chapter 4 apply just as well to the example studies for DNS, network traffic, and malware as they do to understanding human behavior and human choices. This chapter will introduce some example studies about humans in a cybersecurity context.

Human interaction may cause a cybersecurity incident directly or indirectly. A user must click on a link in a phishing email to activate it. Malware installation often requires that the user do something on their computer or access a website. Every security incident is also related to the decisions and mistakes of risk managers, software developers, system administrators, and network engineers: that is, the people who chose, created, managed, and interconnected the system. Attackers are also humans with their own decisions, mistakes, patterns, and interests; all of which a defender can take advantage of. While we study the resulting security events by examining malware, patterns in DNS or network traffic, it was the human factor that caused the issue.

This chapter introduces ways of studying humans that are commonly useful in cybersecurity. Entire libraries have been written on how to study humans, and there are many different expert perspectives which one might use. Experts in sociology, psychology, economics, criminology, and anthropology have contributed thousands of pages each to cybersecurity. One chapter in a cybersecurity book cannot provide enough information to allow you to create your own studies. This chapter will, however, allow you to understand the studies that have been done and to contribute to a study in collaboration with the appropriate experts.

We will discuss the potential questions these kinds of studies can ask (recall Chapter 3), the gathering and evaluation of study populations (recall Section 4.2.3), and how to put a study together (recall Chapter 7). Finally, we discuss study results and what you can expect (and not expect) to learn.

12.1 The Questions

Any research study on humans begins as any other topic, with a question to answer. In the prior three chapters, some examples were what's the pattern of domain resolutions, what's the pattern of network traffic that illustrates exfiltration, or what's the basis of the malware that makes it distinct from other malware. Some examples research questions about humans in cybersecurity include: Why are people clicking on phishing links? How do cybersecurity professionals accomplish their jobs well? What are the differences in attitudes towards cybersecurity among software developers? These are broad questions that need to be narrowed down for effective research on the human elements of cybersecurity.

As with other areas, a key research skill is how to narrow down these broad questions into a testable and useful research question. The best option will be an interrelated set of structured research questions, each of which is narrow enough to be answered but also just general enough to inform some of the other questions to study. For any given narrow research question, the results may provide unexpected answers that force the interrelated questions to adapt. This adaptation to achieve the broader research agenda is why understanding the difference between negative results and non-results is so important (see Section 8.5.2). Negative results let you adapt, but non-results don't let you make any progress whatsoever. A well-posed research question is testable, which is the first step in getting to a negative or positive result and avoiding a non-result.

Tackling a research agenda should be handled in much the same way developers write software. Decompose the problem into distinct parts or distinct actions and try to localize the big properties or outcomes into specific parts or actions (Bechtel and Richardson, 1993). Encapsulate how the part functions or the action is achieved. Basically, try to define the application programming interface (API) for each part of the research problem. Then you can worry about understanding how each component implements its respective API separately. If, after one iteration of this decomposition and localization process, some components are still too complex to describe a narrow and testable research question, repeat the process.

In this metaphor, one main difference between defining research questions and software development is direction, but the concepts are analogous. In research, you often start with a topic of interest and break it up, moving from the top down. In software development, while there is a functional top-level goal in mind, APIs are often designed from the bottom up, encapsulating a process when it has become well-understood enough to be reliable but complicated enough to be a distraction. Research questions should instead break a topic into smaller mechanistic parts to understand it better, as long as how the parts interact can be measured and understood (Craver, 2007).

Asking a broad question of "Who falls victim to phishing?" is a start, but it does not prove any testable advice. For that, one might ask about the demographics, attitudes, professional roles, level and kind of education, personality traits, available attention or effort, and economic incentives of those victims. If 10 people clicked on the link, that is a problem statement. To form a research question, ask what makes those 10 people different from the others and what you can do about it. For example: what about their thought processes will help devise ways to prevent the activity in the future?

The researcher will always bring their own perspectives into a study. One common theme in user-centered security research is studies that implicitly (and often wrongly) blame the user for security failures. There is a big difference between these two questions:

- "Why is this user at fault for this phishing attack?"

- "What part(s) of the socio-technical system failed that permitted this phishing attack?"

An example of the first kind of question is asking what personality traits are correlated with clicking on phishing links, such as in Halevi *et al.* (2013). The study used personality traits defined by the five factor model of personality assessment (McCrae and John, 1992). This is a method from psychology to create a model of personal traits. This study examines the risky behavior in cybersecurity in terms of psychology to determine what traits are more likely associated with risky behaviors. This kind of thinking can be dangerous, but there are some useful applications.

In jurisdictions where profiling based on personality traits is legal, knowing what personality traits are correlated with, say, insider threat behavior or accidental data loss may inform an organization's security configurations. Companies generally have cybersecurity policies in place to protect the company and its assets. For example, acceptable use is often spelled out, backup and retention policies are described, guest policies, and more. Employees are required to conform to these policies, sometimes through technological means, others through written agreements. Unfortunately, employees don't always follow the agreements. Understanding the motivations behind why can help organizations shape their reactions that best fit the likely reasons.

An example of a study that approaches the research with a mindset more like the second question is Beautement *et al.* (2009). The study examines what happens when a security policy was put in place without considering how people do their work. Understanding that case can help an organization reshape their policy to a more usable state.

Beautement *et al.* (2009) uses an interview format to consider why users do or don't follow a security policy. The result of the study is a broad examination of why users follow policies and why they don't, including attitudes towards encryption and risk. The study gives a more in depth understanding about what users are thinking about instead of a narrowly focused study. The results are a spectrum of opinions instead of a percentage of responses.

Another example of a well-posed research agenda is "What is the relationship between users and their passwords?" One smaller question that fits into this broad question is "Why do people choose poor passwords or poor strategies for remembering their passwords?" The first study to approach this question (Adams and Sasse, 1999) used a web survey focused mainly on password related behaviors. The goal in the study design is to elicit the "why" directly from the users to focus future research questions on testing the possible explanations.

Adams and Sasse (1999) identified four major factors effecting password behavior: multiple passwords, the password content, the perception of compatibility with work practices, and the perception of organization security. Each of these topics has been studied from multiple perspectives in the years since, leading the US (Grassi *et al.*, 2017, §10) and UK (National Cyber Security Centre (UK), 2018) national governments to change their password guidance in ways that take the burden off the user and on to more robust and better designed authentication and authorization systems.

Human factors research is not limited to studying lay users, as Section 12.2 will discuss. For example, various methods have been used to study and understand how a CSIRT functions best. Outsiders using surveys and interviews to analyze the inner workings of such group have failed. However, an anthropological approach, in which researchers have the skills and methodology to embed within a culture and gain trust, proved more successful (Sundaramurthy *et al.*, 2014).

There are many other important questions at the intersection of human behavior and cybersecurity. Your questions might range from "What will be the organizational cost of this new security control?" to "What do attackers want?" to "How does the sound of the alert affect SOC employee skills?" (for this last, see Axon *et al.* (2019)). All of these questions are related to the human factors in the socio-technical system that cybersecurity practitioners aim to secure.

12.2   Who to Study: Important Study Populations

In the Malware Study, Chapter 11, we began with discussing the types of malware you could study. We'll do something similar here for human factors studies.

We classify humans in this case based on their job and task. A person whose computer use is their job has a different view than someone who is not being paid to use the computer but rather is accomplishing some task in their personal life. The same person may often have different views in these two scenarios, so it is not just about personal knowledge, but context and purpose. Within the professional category, anyone whose primary task is security computers is a cybersecurity professional, and their concerns and viewpoints are markedly different than a software engineer or human resources specialist whose primary task is not cybersecurity but rather to deliver a product or service. Some general knowledge is transferable between these three groups, such as the neurological basis of memory. But in most ways directly relevant to cybersecurity outcomes, study design and the relevant results will be quite different among the three groups.

It is sometimes useful to further divide the non-cybersecurity professional group as IT professionals or non-IT professionals. An IT professional is often not a cybersecurity expert. Database administrators, network engineers, technical support, and software developers are all examples of IT professionals. These job roles are not automatically experts in cybersecurity, but they should have job tasks that intersect with providing cyber-security and can directly impact cybersecurity in ways that many non-IT professionals do not. There are plenty of non-IT job roles that also may intersect with cybersecurity, such as legal counsel, HR, and acquisitions. As an extreme example, a purchasing manager who decrees an organization will not pay for any software with a known vulnerability would certainly have a profound effect on cybersecurity posture. The IT and not-IT division should not be used as a proxy for the cybersecurity and not-cybersecurity division of professionals. But not-IT professionals describes a certain segment of the white collar work force that are important for organizations in some industry sectors to understand.

Suppose we want to know what non-IT professionals know about cybersecurity. This group is part of a corporate network's defense in depth strategy, so knowing its strengths and weaknesses is important for designing other security services. One study (Carlton *et al.*, 2019) approached this by creating a set of scenario-driven tasks in which they measure non-IT professionals on a set of skills. Cybersecurity experts crafted the list of skills to be what they expect to be applicable skills (though, if we were to critique this study, the fact that the skills improve workforce outcomes should be validated separately).

The corporate security team should be interested in these study results. Understanding the skills of the staff you are trying to protect is useful for understanding cybersecurity risk and designing complementary mitigations. And while a security team can read Carlton *et al.* (2019) and take the results as an assumption, this introduces a fair amount of unexamined sample bias. It would be much more applicable to take this kind of study style and conduct it on a sample of your corporate workforce that is representative of exactly the people you are protecting.

Understanding the workforce to be protected can only be done by studying that workforce. Asking cybersecurity experts what they know about cybersecurity doesn't answer this question. Asking lay people who don't work at the company doesn't help either. You want to know what the user that doesn't specialize in IT knows and understands. Any such study on professionals who are not tasked with cybersecurity is markedly different from studies of cybersecurity professionals. In the latter, you might be looking for how you can improve your own workflow or that of your colleagues. Consider pen testers, for example.

Penetration testing is a cybersecurity practice to probe the security posture of an organization. There are myriad tools and mechanisms for performing penetration testing, from open source to expensive licensed software suites. Understanding the commonly used tools helps us understand the methods available to pen testers, but what a good pen tester really wants to know is how to most efficiently think about breaking into a target. If a team or professional organization can describe this thought pattern, they can create training methods to teach effective pentesting. Since there is a huge shortage of qualified pen testers, effective training methods are a top priority.

A reliable study to describe these professional thought processes and methods—and filter out which aspects are actually what make for a good pen tester—is not a simple matter. If you use a search engine to search for tools you only learn what's available. But the research goal is what tools the professionals use and how they deploy them effectively. In this case, asking cybersecurity professionals as a whole isn't a good population. Not everyone who is a cybersecurity professional is knowledgeable about pen testing. To get the best results, we need to ask the right population. In this case it's pen testers, not malware researchers or other cybersecurity professionals.

Armstrong *et al.* (2018) relied on a self-identified population of pen testers to answer this question. Self-identification certainly has some weaknesses as far as a sampling method; it is essentially a convenient sample (Section 4.2.3). The study mitigates this problem by selecting participants who are attending the industry-standard events for pen testers, BlackHat and Def Con. This context makes the study population likely to be drawn from pen testers, and not from random liars on the internet. There are still the usual problems of convenient samples; for example, there is no way to know if the kind of pen tester who is too paranoid to talk to a researcher, or who would prefer not to travel to the United States and so is not attending the conference, will work in a systematically different way from those in the study. But as far as a strategy for gathering leads on a satisfactory set of pen testing tools to be verified by future studies, it's not a problem in this context.

In both of these examples it's the people you study who are important. The study should be directed at the group that best answers your research question. Asking lay people to describe pen testing isn't a useful way to learn how pen testing should be taught. With a different research goal— say, understanding pop culture influences of hacking—asking lay people to describe pen testing might be exactly the right approach.

12.3   Study Design Examples

There are several steps to putting a human factors study together. In this section we'll discuss the broad outline of this process. Deciding on a testable, narrow but interconnected research question is the first step (Section 12.1). These desirable question properties and how we ensure them are no different than studies in other topic areas like DNS or malicious software used as examples in Chapters 9, 10, and 11. Understanding the population type the study should draw on and examine was the second step (Section 12.2). For example, if your research question is "How does a SOC handle alerts" then the appropriate study participants are members of SOCs selected in a way that makes the representative of the population of interest (recall Section 4.2).

Once we have those two parts, we need to consider how we're going to go from the question and target population to answers. Chapter 7 introduced five types of structured observations. Like with any other part of cybersecurity, each of those five can be used to study the human aspect of cybersecurity. Their relative strengths and weaknesses are similar with some important differences. For example, a simulation-based study must demonstrate fidelity between the simulated model and real humans with more and more diverse evidence than you need to show that a simulated DNS server is comparable to a DNS server "in the wild."

Your first step is to understand and sample from the population. This information gathering is an iterative process; prior case studies or measurement studies provide information to design future studies, whether this means further case studies, interventions, or simulations depends on your goals. Sections 12.3.1 through 12.3.5 describe an example of each of these study types in the context of human factors in cybersecurity.

Determining the best method for approaching subjects is a difficult question that has no straightforward answer. It's best to find an expert in the field.

12.3.1   *Case Study*

Case study methods originated in the social sciences, and they are well developed in fields such as sociology and anthropology (Stake, 1995). In this book, we have used an expansive sense of the term case study that includes cybersecurity studies like attack papers and understanding the technical impact of a single vulnerability. But studying the human element of systems is the origin and core purpose of case study methods. Sundaramurthy *et al.*

(2014), discussed in Section 12.1, is an example of anthropological case study methods used to study a CSIRT.

The example set by Beautement *et al.* (2009) is not a classic case study; we discuss it here to press a bit on the boundaries between case studies and measurement studies. Beautement *et al.* (2009) uses semi-structured interviews to investigate users attitudes towards cybersecurity policies. The researchers conduct a series of interviews, each of which is a case study. A semi-structured interview has set questions the interviewer will ask, but they are free to prod the respondent to follow-up or expand their initial answer. Each of these cases is comparable to each other, since the questions are the same and the study participants each represent some aspect of the population of interest (Western, educated, adult technology users). Case studies are differentiated from measurement studies based on the richness and diversity of information collected, not how many people are in the study.

12.3.2 Measurement Study

Measurement studies may be the most common kind of research in cybersecurity presently, which creates a wide diversity of study designs based on what is being measured how. On the technology side, there is a well-established academic conference dedicated exclusively to network measurement studies: the Internet Measurement Conference. An example human-centric measurement study discussed in Chapter 7 was measuring the cost of cybercrime (Anderson *et al.*, 2012, 2019). A common measurement aim is to measure what is going on inside people's heads: their thoughts, attitudes, skills, knowledge, opinions, or decisions. Unlike technology or financial exchanges, these things are not directly observable. Surveys are commonly applied technique to measure these mental states.

Surveys may be commonly used, but they are rarely conducted properly. Subtle aspects of survey design can enormously influence the results (Diamond, 2011), such as the order of the questions, relationship between questions, and whether another person is in the room when the respondent fills out the survey. Published academic papers are far from immune to these survey design flaws. In fact, we suspect your marketing department is a better resource for survey design assistance than academics. Let's look at one academic example to see where things can go wrong in survey measurements.

Anwar *et al.* (2017) poses a research question about the relationship between gender and cybersecurity beliefs and behaviors. This study used

87 questions that are related to an individual's computer skills, perceptions about cybersecurity topics, and self-reported security behavior. Example questions include:

- What is your comfort level, when using computers?
- How comfortable are you with online shopping?
- I feel that my chance of receiving an email attachment with a virus is high.

The answers were a 7 point range from "strongly disagree" to "strongly agree." This kind of qualitative range for a survey response is know as a *Likert scale*. Psychologists have been using Likert scales for a long time to measure humans' opinions, and while there are certainly some dangers with misusing Likert scales these dangers can be managed (Jamieson, 2004; Norman, 2010).

This survey study strays from the start with its research question (recall Section 12.1). While the question of whether gender is linked to self-reported cybersecurity behavior is certainly testable, it's not useful. It's not useful for two reasons. It frames the question more as "why is this user at fault" rather than "what part(s) of the socio-technical system failed," as discussed in Section 12.1. Secondly, the question does not address how society treats different genders differently. It is already well-known that gender interacts with self-efficacy (Pajares, 2002).

Although Anwar *et al.* (2017) poses an impressive array of 87 questions to study participants, there is little evidence they did so in a way to avoids systematic problems. These problems start with participant recruitment. The authors sent a link to the online survey to employees at various organizations. This is a common but devastating recruitment error. The study population is worse than a convenient sample; the study population is some mix of the people who care very much about the topic and people who were bored at work that day. It is always bad when study participants *self-select* as to whether they will participate, rather than the study designer selecting participants. A better way to do this would be to solicit 1,000 volunteers and then the study designer selects 500 to take the survey, balancing the study participants' demographic characteristics. The fact that 66% of respondents were female suggest a sizeable impact of self-selection for this study. But there is no way to know how that impact should be handled when interpreting the results.

The design of the actual survey demonstrates further common mistakes. One issue is simply the length: 87 questions is longer than an unpaid volunteer can be expected to spend on an online survey. The method section doesn't state the order in which the questions were asked. The order is extremely important; for most surveys, the questions should be shown in a different, random order to each participant. For a Likert-scale set of responses, the order answers are presented in should stay the same. But for most surveys, the order of answers for each question should also be randomized rather than fixed across all participants. These techniques even out effects from the question ordering (Diamond, 2011).

Especially with a long survey, the survey method has to have a way to check participants are engaging in good faith. Often enough to mess with research results, people handle surveys by answering "3" (for example) to everything without reading any of the questions. Anwar *et al.* (2017) do not report doing any sort of check for this, which generally involves asking the same question in different ways and having a couple canary questions which have a correct answer and check comprehensive rather than participant opinions. The researcher can then remove all the responses from any participant who gets a canary question wrong.

Survey respondents, especially employees, often know when answers are more or less socially responsible. Even when no one else will specifically see their response, respondents will filter their self reports towards prosocial behavior. The respondent may not be lying consciously in these cases; human memory formation is not a photographic recording. People may remember themselves in a more positive light than was actually the case. Another confounding element is how respondents understand words like "virus" or "cybersecurity." Someone who doesn't know what a computer virus is may self-report their chances of receiving one via email are low. Therefore, any self-reporting survey is a combination of three surveys: what people did, what people think they should have done, and how people understand the jargon terminology used by the survey. It is nearly impossible to disentangle these three, which is why surveys that use self-reporting alone are a bad idea.

The questions themselves were largely drawn from prior research. This practice is quite helpful, as it increases the researcher's ability to connect their results to other published results. This design choice is one thing the authors did well. Unfortunately, with all the other problems, there is not much value in their results to make them worth connecting to other results.

12.3.3 *Intervention*

There are many kinds of interventions on human behavior in cybersecurity practice. Cybersecurity practice can be understood as a series of interventions which attempt to influence the behavior of one group of humans: attackers. Stoll (1989), discussed in Chapter 7, is a classic example of a series of interventions and their effect on attacker behavior. Cheswick (1992) is another classic example in this vein. When the goal of an intervention is to defend a system, it is often hard to measure the effect that intervention had on the attacker.

When you're designing an intervention—that is, responding to an incident—you should always have a hypothesis about what the attacker will do in response. Consider Mandiant's publication of its report on Peoples Republic of China (PRC) government espionage (Mandiant, 2013). The publication itself was an intervention in two ways. It provided information to companies to defend themselves, including specific indicators of compromise (IoCs). The publication also told the attackers that Mandiant knew these network addresses were in use by the attacker. If Mandiant were in a position to observe how the attackers' behavior changed based on this information reaching the attacker, they can use that observation to better understand the attackers' operations. As a simple example, Mandiant analysts learned how quickly the attackers heard about the publication of the report and the tempo of changes to operations the attackers could support. The information gathering and tempo capabilities of a group provide insight into how well resourced the group is.

12.3.4 *Randomized Control Trials*

The study design method of RCTs were primarily developed to study people in a medical context. Cybersecurity can use the concept of RCTs to study technology, such as with release engineering (see Section 7.2.4). But conducting an RCT on human factors in cybersecurity brings the study method back to its roots. One field that often conducts RCTs to test how small interventions change human behavior is around nudges, or "soft paternalism."

Acquisti *et al.* (2017) captures many examples of how user behavior can be nudged or influenced by choices in system design. One example example is how a population of users responds to changes to the default settings of their web browser. Unsurprisingly, most users stick with the default, whether the default is more or less secure. There are some exceptions;

people who self-identify as very privacy-conscious will usually take the time to change privacy settings in a browser, whatever the defaults.

Testing this for your population of users is fairly straightforward, at least as far as RCTs go. You need two comparable groups of users; the groups should be about the same size and have about the same proportion of job roles and demographic characteristics (age, gender, education, etc.). The IT department might achieve this by randomly assigning every new user at enrollment time into one of the two groups. One group gets HTTPS Everywhere, a browser extension that forces TLS connections whenever possible, installed by default, and the other does not.

The security team can measure a few properties of these two groups going forwards. The most basic one is to confirm the expected result and measure whether most users stick with the default they are given. But you could go further, and gather some information about what effect this default choice has on user behavior. Some measurements to help answer this question include whether one group creates more IT tickets than another, triggers more IDS alerts, or accomplishes more work-related tasks.

12.3.5 *Simulation*

Section 7.2.5 focused on mathematical models of computer systems, But several fields study humans and human decision making primarily through mathematical models and simulations, such as game theory (Alpcan and Başar, 2011). These simulations over-simplify some specific aspect of human decisions to describe the interaction precisely as a set of mathematical formulae. The benefit of this approach is that the outcomes of the simplified description can be simulated, testing the model and providing potential explanations for what elements are dominant in the real scenario.

Veksler *et al.* (2018) introduce several ways that cognitive modeling and simulations of human's thought processes have been used in cybersecurity. One important aspect is to create realistic training scenarios in which the virtual users in a training environment should be realistic simulations of the relevant user population.

Setting up a study to simulate users in a reliable way has two main phases. There is the technical phase of implementing the virtual environment and with an agent and corresponding cognitive model on each host. Then there is an evaluation phase, measuring whether the virtual users in aggregate produce traffic that is similar enough to a network of real users. "Similar enough" can be defined in different ways, but a reasonable test in a training environment is whether real human penetration testers can hide among the virtual users from the defenders being trained.

Training scenarios can also simulate attacker behavior using cognitive models, so the simulated attacker can respond to defender countermeasures. If the training simulation environment closely matches the production environment, simulating an attacker's behavior can lead directly to pragmatic changes in production. The main challenge is ensuring the model of the attacker is like relevant real attackers. Efforts to model attackers based on past incidents, such as the Diamond Model (Caltagirone *et al.*, 2013) or Adversarial Tactics, Techniques, and Common Knowledge (ATT&CK), can be used as input into the simulation to increase confidence in connection to real attackers.

In some sense, a defender doing incident response is mentally simulating what the attacker would have done or wanted. So it is a short step from simulating attacker behavior to simulating incident response options. While this technology is a ways away from production, there is research in directions that would allow simulation of what an attacker might have done in order to aid incident analysis (Spring and Pym, 2018; Al-Shaer *et al.*, 2020).

12.4 Interpreting Results

For a technology-focused practitioner, reading the results sections of human factors papers is often difficult. The results are informed and described by the terms found in social science fields and may use jargon specific to social sciences rather than have the conclusions translated into actionable advice in language a cybersecurity practitioner is used to. Better papers, such as (Adams and Sasse, 1999), will contain recommendations at the end of the paper that summarize the results in a useful form. There are enough venues at the intersection of humans and cybersecurity that a technology-focused person can rely to some extent on important results being translated into cybersecurity terms. Some example venues are Usable Security (USEC), the Symposium on Usable Privacy and Security (SOUPS), the Conference on Human Interaction (CHI), and the cybersecurity technical group at the Human Factors and Ergonomics Society (HFES).

A reader can take those results and implement the suggested changes in their organization.

Cybersecurity is inherently a practical field; we want to find use in the research done for the field. Human factors research can inform us about how best to create policies for users, best practices, assist in education, nudge user behavior, and in the end, make the system more secure.

Beautement *et al.* (2009) doesn't end with a plethora of statistics, rather it gives examples of user thinking based on the structured interviews the authors conducted. These include examples such as

> "I know very few people who run encrypted file systems on a laptop ... because they don't trust the file system. They want their data to be accessible."

Rather than assuming that users just don't want to encrypt their file systems, this illustrates the risk a user thinks they are taking by encrypting the file system. They want their data available, and in their opinion, encrypting a file system would create more risk that it wouldn't be available than they are willing to accept.

A good paper in this field will contain recommendations and lessons learned that can be adapted and utilized. This paper informs the reader that education is needed so that the user will understand better the risks and gains in encrypting file systems.

Some basic heuristics you can us to evaluate results in human factors studies include the following (Krol *et al.*, 2016):

- Did the study participants have a realistic or well-understood primary task? If not, the results may be an artifact of the study environment.

- Was the risk the study explores realistic? Did participants experience a realistic risk to which the study captures a response? If not, the results may be an artifact of the study environment.

- Were the participants primed towards one response or another by some aspect of the study procedure or environment? Were measurements (such as surveys) designed according to established best practices?

- For any study that tests the effect of a change (interventions, RCTs, some simulations, some case studies, and natural experiments), are the participants and researchers both *blinded* so they can't influence what they think the results should be?

- Certain jargon terms are always slippery, and need to be defined or have a definition cited. Did the study define the terms "threat model," "security," "privacy," and "usability"? If not, the different researchers or different participants likely have different understandings of what is being studied, likely muddling the results.

While this list is not a panacea, it will help you avoid the worst and most dubious results.

12.5   Recap

This chapter introduced you to studies of human factors in cybersecurity. We provided examples of forming research questions, important study populations, five types of study design, and some venues to check for relevant results.

The research question a study seeks to answer should be testable and useful. Unexpected results or negative results in response to a research question are an important part of research, and should be accepted. Non-results, in which a question was not actually answered because the research methods were flawed, should be avoided. Avoiding non-results and getting useful negative results starts with a testable and useful research question that is clearly interconnected to some things that are well-known and some other questions. Especially when studying users in cybersecurity, avoid research questions that implicitly blame the user before the study even begins.

Who you want to study has a big influence on how you study them. Lay or non-professional users of systems are a diverse group that often needs to be studied one sub-group at a time. Professionals whose job role is not cybersecurity are a common study target because they are one layer in any organizations defense-in-depth strategy; understanding employee motivation, skills, and tasks is important for designing integrated cybersecurity solutions. Cybersecurity professionals themselves are also a common subject of study, whether it is how to improve training, increase workflow efficiency, or reduce employee burnout.

Study designs related to human elements of cybersecurity are as diverse as any other area of cybersecurity. Case study methods from sociology and anthropology are well suited to collecting a rich and diverse set of data about a topic. Measurement study methods often include surveys, though Section 12.3.2 describes how a good survey is often harder to construct that it might appear. Interventions often target changing adversary behavior. RCTs can be used to evaluate how users respond to default settings or other system design choices with a goal to nudge them towards desired (secure) behaviors. Simulations of human cognitive models and behavior are used to enrich training environments or predict possible attacker actions.

Finally, we provided some heuristics you can use to evaluate the results of these kinds of studies. These are specific ways that connection, generalizability, and transparency often fail during studies of human factors in cybersecurity.

Acknowledgments

We are grateful to Josiah Dykstra, Kathryn Renae Metcalf, and Phil Groce for helpful comments on drafts of the book. We are also grateful to our publisher Rochelle Kronzek for her helpful guidance.

Dr. Spring thanks his parents and friends for their continued love and support, even when he disappears for a time to work on a textbook.

Dr. Metcalf thanks her parents and friends for their support and her co-workers, including Allen Householder, Edward Schwartz, Art Manion, Jeffrey Havrilla, Charles Hines, and Kyle O'Meara for many illuminating conversations on this topic.

Bibliography

abuse.ch (2018). abuse.ch zeus tracker, `https://zeustracker.abuse.ch/blocklist.php?download=baddomains`.

Acquisti, A., Adjerid, I., Balebako, R., Brandimarte, L., Cranor, L. F., Komanduri, S., Leon, P. G., Sadeh, N., Schaub, F., Sleeper, M., *et al.* (2017). Nudges for privacy and security: Understanding and assisting users' choices online, *ACM Computing Surveys (CSUR)* **50**, 3, pp. 1–41.

Adams, A. and Sasse, M. A. (1999). Users are not the enemy, *Commun. ACM* **42**, 12, pp. 40–46.

Akerlof, G. A. (1970). The market for "lemons": Quality uncertainty and the market mechanism, *The Quarterly Journal of Economics* **84**, 3, pp. 488–500.

Akiyama, M., Kawamoto, T., Shimamura, M., Yokoyama, T., Kadobayashi, Y., and Yamaguchi, S. (2007). A proposal of metrics for botnet detection based on its cooperative behavior, in *2007 International Symposium on Applications and the Internet Workshops* (IEEE), pp. 82–82.

Al-Shaer, R., Spring, J. M., and Christou, E. (2020). Learning the associations of MITRE ATT&CK adversarial techniques, in *Communications and Network Security* (IEEE, Virtual).

Alberts, C., Dorofee, A., Killcrece, G., Ruefle, R., and Zajicek, M. (2004). Defining incident management processes for CSIRTs: A work in progress, Tech. Rep. CMU/SEI-2004-TR-015, Software Engineering Institute, Carnegie Mellon University.

Albrecht, J. P. (2016). How the GDPR will change the world, *European Data Protection Law Review* **2**, p. 287.

Alpcan, T. and Başar, T. (2011). *Network Security: A Decision and Game-Theoretic Approach* (Cambridge University Press, Cambridge, UK).

Amazon (1997). Alexa, `https://www.alexa.com/`.

Amrhein, V., Trafimow, D., and Greenland, S. (2019). Inferential statistics as descriptive statistics: There is no replication crisis if we don't expect replication, *The American Statistician* **73**, sup1, pp. 262–270.

Anderson, R., Barton, C., Böhme, R., Clayton, R., Van Eeten, M. J., Levi, M., Moore, T., and Savage, S. (2012). Measuring the cost of cybercrime, in

. *Workshop on the Economics of Information Security* (Berlin), pp. 119–148.

Anderson, R., Barton, C., Bölme, R., Clayton, R., Gañán, C., Grasso, T., Levi, M., Moore, T., and Vasek, M. (2019). Measuring the changing cost of cybercrime, in *Workshop on the Economics of Information Security* (Boston, MA, USA).

Anderson, R. J. and Moore, T. (2006). The economics of information security, *Science* **314**, 5799, pp. 610–613, doi:10.1126/science.1130992.

Anklesaria, F., McCahill, M., Lindner, P., Johnson, D., Torrey, D., and Albert, B. (1993). *RFC1436: The Internet Gopher Protocol (a distributed document search and retrieval protocol)* (RFC Editor).

Antonakakis, M., Perdisci, R., Nadji, Y., Vasiloglou, N., Abu-Nimeh, S., Lee, W., and Dagon, D. (2012). From throw-away traffic to bots: Detecting the rise of DGA-based malware, in *Presented as part of the 21st {USENIX} Security Symposium ({USENIX} Security 12)*, pp. 491–506.

Anwar, M., He, W., Ash, I., Yuan, X., Li, L., and Xu, L. (2017). Gender difference and employees' cybersecurity behaviors, *Computers in Human Behavior* **69**, pp. 437–443.

Apt, K. R. (1981). Ten years of Hoare's logic: A survey—Part I, *ACM Transactions on Programming Languages and Systems (TOPLAS)* **3**, 4, pp. 431–483.

Armstrong, M. E., Jones, K. S., Namin, A. S., and Newton, D. C. (2018). The knowledge, skills, and abilities used by penetration testers: Results of interviews with cybersecurity professionals in vulnerability assessment and management, *Proceedings of the Human Factors and Ergonomics Society Annual Meeting* **62**, 1, pp. 709–713, doi:10.1177/1541931218621161.

Axelsson, S. (2000). The base-rate fallacy and the difficulty of intrusion detection, *ACM Transactions on Information and System Security (TISSEC)* **3**, 3, pp. 186–205.

Axon, L., Happa, J., van Rensburg, A. J., Goldsmith, M., and Creese, S. (2019). Sonification to support the monitoring tasks of security operations centres, *IEEE Transactions on Dependable and Secure Computing* **early access**.

Babyak, M. A. (2004). What you see may not be what you get: A brief, nontechnical introduction to overfitting in regression-type models, *Psychosomatic Medicine* **66**, 3, pp. 411–421.

Balmer, B. (2013). *Secrecy and Science: A Historical Sociology of Biological and Chemical Warfare* (Ashgate Publishing, Ltd.).

Bambenek Consulting (2017). Domain feed of known DGA domains from −2 to +3 days, `http://osint.bambenekconsulting.com/manual/dga-feed.txt`.

Bano, S., Richter, P., Javed, M., Sundaresan, S., Durumeric, Z., Murdoch, S. J., Mortier, R., and Paxson, V. (2018). Scanning the internet for liveness, *SIGCOMM Computer Communications Review* **48**, 2, p. 2–9, `https://doi.org/10.1145/3213232.3213234`.

Bates, T., Gerich, E., Joncheray, L., Jouanigot, J.-M., Karrenberg, D., Terpstra, M., and Yu, J. (1995). *RFC1786: Representation of IP1 Routing Policies in a Routing Registry (ripe-81++)* (RFC Editor).

Beautement, A., Sasse, M. A., and Wonham, M. (2009). The compliance budget: Managing security behaviour in organisations, in *New Security Paradigms Workshop* (ACM), pp. 47–58.

Bechtel, W. and Richardson, R. C. (1993). *Discovering Complexity: Decomposition and Localization as Strategies in Scientific Research*, 1st edn. (Princeton University Press, Princeton, NJ).

Beckman, J., Bari, S., Chen, Y., Dark, M., and Yang, B. (2017). The impacts of representational fluency on cognitive processing of cryptography concepts, in *Learning from Authoritative Security Experiment Results (LASER)* (USENIX, Washington, DC), pp. 59–67.

Beringer, L., Petcher, A., Ye, K. Q., and Appel, A. W. (2015). Verified correctness and security of openssl hmac, in *USENIX Security*, SEC'15 (Washington, D.C.), ISBN 9781931971232, p. 207–221.

Beyer, B., Murphy, N. R., Rensin, D. K., Kawahara, K., and Thorne, S. (2018). *The site reliability workbook: Practical ways to implement SRE* (O'Reilly Media, Inc., Sebastopol, CA), https://landing.google.com/sre/workbook/toc/.

Bickle, J. (2008). Real reduction in real neuroscience: Metascience, not philosophy of science (and certainly not metaphysics!), in J. Hohwy and J. Kalestrup (eds.), *Being reduced: New essays on reduction, explanation, and causation* (Oxford University Press), pp. 34–51.

Bilar, D. (2007). Opcodes as predictor for malware, *International Journal of Electronic Security and Digital Forensics* **1**, 2, pp. 156–168.

Bilge, L., Kirda, E., Kruegel, C., and Balduzzi, M. (2011). EXPOSURE: Finding malicious domains using passive DNS analysis, in *Network and Distributed System Security (NDSS)* (San Diego, CA).

Bogen, J. and Woodward, J. (1988). Saving the phenomena, *The Philosophical Review* **XCVII**, 3, pp. 303–352.

Boolos, G. S., Burgess, J. P., and Jeffrey, R. C. (2002). *Computability and Logic*, 4th edn. (Cambridge University Press, Cambridge).

Bornat, R. (2000). Proving pointer programs in Hoare logic, in *Mathematics of Program Construction*, no. 1837 in LNCS (Springer), pp. 102–126.

Broman, K., Cetinkaya-Rundel, M., Nussbaum, A., Paciorek, C., Peng, R., Turek, D., and Wickham, H. (2017). Recommendations to funding agencies for supporting reproducible research, in *American Statistical Association*, Vol. 2.

Brown, M. D. and Pande, S. (2019). Is less really more? Towards better metrics for measuring security improvements realized through software debloating, in *12th {USENIX} Workshop on Cyber Security Experimentation and Test ({CSET} 19)*.

Brunton, F. (2013). *Spam: A Shadow History of the Internet* (MIT Press, Cambridge, MA).

Caesar, M. and Rexford, J. (2005). BGP routing policies in isp networks, *IEEE Network* **19**, 6, pp. 5–11.

Caglayan, A., Toothaker, M., Drapaeau, D., Burke, D., and Eaton, G. (2009). Behavioral analysis of fast flux service networks, in *Proceedings of the 5th Annual Workshop on Cyber Security and Information Intelligence Research:*

Cyber Security and Information Intelligence Challenges and Strategies, pp. 1–4.

Calcagno, C., Distefano, D., O'Hearn, P. W., and Yang, H. (2011). Compositional shape analysis by means of bi-abduction, *J. ACM* **58**, 6, pp. 26:1–26:66.

Caltagirone, S., Pendergast, A., and Betz, C. (2013). The diamond model of intrusion analysis, Tech. rep., Center for Cyber Intelligence Analysis and Threat Research, http://www.threatconnect.com/methodology/diamond_model_of_intrusion_analysis.

Carlton, M., Levy, Y., and Ramim, M. (2019). Mitigating cyber attacks through the measurement of non-it professionals' cybersecurity skills, *Information & Computer Security* **27**, 1.

Cartwright, N. (1983). *How the Laws of Physics Lie* (Clarendon Press, Oxford).

Cartwright, N. (1991). Replicability, reproducibility, and robustness: Comments on Harry Collins, *History of Political Economy* **23**, 1, pp. 143–155.

Carvey, H. (2005). The windows registry as a forensic resource, *Digital Investigation* **2**, 3, p. 201–205.

Caulfield, T., Spring, J. M., and Sasse, M. A. (2019). Why Jenny can't figure out which of these messages is a covert information operation, in *New Security Paradigms Workshop* (ACM, San Carlos, Costa Rica), pp. 118–128, doi: 10.1145/3368860.3368870.

CERT/NetSA at Carnegie Mellon University (2002–2016). SiLK (System for Internet-Level Knowledge), http://tools.netsa.cert.org/silk, [Accessed: Feb 4, 2014].

CERT/NetSA Security Suite (2019). The SiLK provisioning spreadsheet. https://tools.netsa.cert.org/releases/SiLK-Provisioning-v3.3.xlsx.

Chalmers, T. C., Smith Jr, H., Blackburn, B., Silverman, B., Schroeder, B., Reitman, D., and Ambroz, A. (1981). A method for assessing the quality of a randomized control trial, *Controlled Clinical Trials* **2**, 1, pp. 31–49.

Cheswick, B. (1992). An evening with berferd: In which a cracker is lured, endured, and studied, in *USENIX Winter Technical Conference* (San Francisco), pp. 20–24.

Cichonski, P., Millar, T., Grance, T., and Scarfone, K. (2012). Computer security incident handling guide, *NIST Special Publication* **800**, 61, pp. 1–147.

Cohen, A., Gilad, Y., Herzberg, A., and Schapira, M. (2015). One hop for RPKI, one giant leap for BGP security, in *Proceedings of the 14th ACM Workshop on Hot Topics in Networks*, pp. 1–7.

Combs, G. *et al.* (2008). Wireshark-network protocol analyzer, *Version 0.99* **5**.

Cooney, M. (2012). Security history: Nothing like an old-fashioned boot sector virus, https://www.networkworld.com/article/2184961/security/security-history--nothing-like-an-old-fashioned-boot-sector-virus.html.

Craver, C. F. (2007). *Explaining the Brain: Mechanisms and the Mosaic of Unity of Neuroscience* (Oxford University Press, Oxford).

Creath, R. (2014). Logical empiricism, in E. N. Zalta (ed.), *The Stanford Encyclopedia of Philosophy*, spring 2014 edn. (Metaphysics Research Lab, Stanford University).

Cronbach, L. J. and Meehl, P. E. (1955). Construct validity in psychological tests. *Psychological Bulletin* **52**, 4, p. 281.

Cruz, R. (2017). Dangers of overfitting in predictive analytics, *Society of Actuaries: Predictive Analytics and Futurism* **16**.

Darden, L. and Maull, N. (1977). Interfield theories, *Philosophy of Science* **44**, pp. 43–64.

Davidson-Pilon, C. (2020). *Probabilistic Programming & Bayesian Methods for Hackers* (GitHub), https://camdavidsonpilon.github.io/Probabilistic-Programming-and-Bayesian-Methods-for-Hackers/.

De Millo, R. A., Upton, R. J., and Perlis, A. J. (1979). Social processes and proofs of theorems and programs, *Communications* **22**, 5, pp. 271–280, doi:10.1145/359104.359106.

Dear, P. (2006). *The Intelligibility of Nature: How Science Makes Sense of the World* (University of Chicago Press, Chicago and London).

DeLaRosa, A. (2018). Log monitoring: Not the ugly sister, https://pandorafms.com/blog/log-monitoring/.

Deng, X., Shi, H., and Mirkovic, J. (2017). Understanding malware's network behaviors using fantasm authors, *Laser Washington DC: USENIX* **2017**.

Diamond, S. S. (2011). *Reference guide on survey research*, 3rd edn. (National Acadamies Press, Washington, DC), https://www.fjc.gov/sites/default/files/2012/SciMan3D09.pdf.

Dietrich, C. J., Rossow, C., Freiling, F. C., Bos, H., Van Steen, M., and Pohlmann, N. (2011). On botnets that use dns for command and control, in *2011 Seventh European Conference on Computer Network Defense* (IEEE), pp. 9–16.

Dittrich, D. and Dietrich, S. (2008). P2P as botnet command and control: a deeper insight, in *2008 3rd International Conference on Malicious and Unwanted Software (MALWARE)* (IEEE), pp. 41–48.

Dittrich, D. and Kenneally, E. (2012). The Menlo Report: Ethical Principles Guiding Information and Communication Technology Research, Tech. rep., U.S. Department of Homeland Security, http://www.caida.org/publications/papers/2012/menlo_report_actual_formatted/.

Dowling, B., Günther, F., Herath, U., and Stebila, D. (2016). Secure logging schemes and certificate transparency, in I. Askoxylakis, S. Ioannidis, S. Katsikas, and C. Meadows (eds.), *Computer Security – ESORICS 2016* (Springer International Publishing, Cham), pp. 140–158.

Dunning, B. (2010). Some new logical fallacies, https://skeptoid.com/episodes/4217.

Durumeric, Z., Li, F., Kasten, J., Amann, J., Beekman, J., Payer, M., Weaver, N., Adrian, D., Paxson, V., Bailey, M., *et al.* (2014). The matter of heartbleed, in *Proceedings of the 2014 Conference on Internet Measurement Conference*, pp. 475–488.

Dwork, C., Feldman, V., Hardt, M., Pitassi, T., Reingold, O., and Roth, A. (2015). The reusable holdout: Preserving validity in adaptive data analysis, *Science* **349**, 6248, pp. 636–638.

Dykstra, J. (2015). *Essential Cybersecurity Science: Build, Test, and Evaluate Secure Systems* (O'Reilly Media, Inc.).

Edgar, T. W. and Manz, D. O. (2017). *Research Methods for Cyber Security* (Syngress).

Ellis, P. D. (2010). *The Essential Guide to Effect Sizes: Statistical Power, Meta-analysis, and the Interpretation of Research Results* (Cambridge University Press).

Eslahi, M., Abidin, W. Z., and Naseri, M. V. (2017). Correlation-based http botnet detection using network communication histogram analysis, in *2017 IEEE Conference on Application, Information and Network Security (AINS)* (IEEE), pp. 7–12.

Etengoff, A. (2009). Nefarious donbot spews url-shortened spam, https://www.tgdaily.com/web/security/43802-nefarious-donbot-spews-url-shortened-spam/.

Evron, G. (2017). Art into science: A conference on defense, `http://artintoscience.com/`, accessed Apr 2017.

fabrimagic72 (2018). fabrimagic72/malware-samples. 7 25, `https://github.com/fabrimagic72/malware-samples`.

Faircloth, J. (2016). *Penetration Tester's Open Source Toolkit* (Syngress).

Fanelli, D. (2012). Negative results are disappearing from most disciplines and countries, *Scientometrics* **90**, 3, pp. 891–904.

Faugier, J. and Sargeant, M. (1997). Sampling hard to reach populations, *Journal of Advanced Nursing* **26**, 4, pp. 790–797.

Fei, B., Eloff, J., Olivier, M., and Venter, H. (2006). Analysis of web proxy logs, in *IFIP International Conference on Digital Forensics* (Springer), pp. 247–258.

Feitelson, D. G. (2015). From repeatability to reproducibility and corroboration, *ACM SIGOPS Operating Systems Review* **49**, 1, pp. 3–11.

Floyd, S. and Paxson, V. (2001). Difficulties in simulating the Internet. *IEEE/ACM Transactions on Networking* **392-403**.

Franceschi-Bicchierai, L. (2015). The feds and their partners share details of the operation that took down GameOver Zeus, Motherboard: Tech by Vice.

Free Software Foundation, Inc. (1991). objdump(1) —linux man page, `https://linux.die.net/man/1/objdump`.

French, D. (2012). Writing effective yara signatures to identify malware, `https://insights.sei.cmu.edu/sei_blog/2012/11/writing-effective-yara-signatures-to-identify-malware.html`.

Friston, K. J., Rotshtein, P., Geng, J. J., Sterzer, P., and Henson, R. N. (2006). A critique of functional localisers, *Neuroimage* **30**, 4, pp. 1077–1087.

Galison, P. (2010). Trading with the enemy, in M. E. Gorman (ed.), *Trading Zones and Interactional Expertise. Creating New Kinds of Collaboration*, chap. 3 (MIT Press, Cambridge, MA), pp. 25–52.

Garcia, S., Grill, M., Stiborek, H., and Zunino, A. (2014). An empirical comparison of botnet detection methods, *Computers and Security Journal* **45**, pp. 100–123.

Gates, C., Collins, M. P., Duggan, M., Kompanek, A., and Thomas, M. (2004). More netflow tools for performance and security. in *LISA*, Vol. 4, pp. 121–132.

Gavrilut, D. T., Popoiu, G., and Benchea, R. (2016). Identifying dga-based botnets using network anomaly detection, in *2016 18th International Symposium on Symbolic and Numeric Algorithms for Scientific Computing (SYNASC)* (IEEE), pp. 292–299.

Gelman, A., Carlin, J. B., Stern, H. S., Dunson, D. B., Vehtari, A., and Rubin, D. B. (2020). *Bayesian Data Analysis*, 3rd edn. (CRC press).

Genç, Z. A., Lenzini, G., and Sgandurra, D. (2019). Case study: Analysis and mitigation of a novel sandbox-evasion technique, in *Proceedings of the Third Central European Cybersecurity Conference*, pp. 1–4.

Girard, J.-Y. (1987). Linear logic, *Theoretical Computer Science* **50**, 1, pp. 1–101.

Glennan, S. and Illari, P. (eds.) (2017). *The Routledge Handbook of Mechanisms and Mechanical Philosophy*, Handbooks in Philosophy (Routledge, London, UK).

Godefroid, P., Klarlund, N., and Sen, K. (2005). Dart: Directed automated random testing, in *Proceedings of the 2005 ACM SIGPLAN conference on Programming language design and implementation*, pp. 213–223.

Goel, V. (2014). Facebook tinkers with users' emotions in news feed experiment, stirring outcry, *The New York Times* **29**.

Gorunescu, F. (2011). *Data Mining: Concepts, Models and Techniques*, Vol. 12 (Springer Science & Business Media).

Graham, D. W. (2019). Heraclitus, in E. N. Zalta (ed.), *The Stanford Encyclopedia of Philosophy*, fall 2019 edn. (Metaphysics Research Lab, Stanford University).

Gralla, P. (2016). How windows 10 became malware, `https://www.computerworld.com/article/3080102/operating-systems/how-windows-10-became-malware.html`.

Grassi, P. A., Fenton, J. L., Newton, E. M., Periner, R. A., Regensheid, A. R., Burr, W. E., Richer, J. P., Lefkovitz, N. B., Danker, J. M., Choong, Y.-Y., Greene, K. K., and Theofanos, M. F. (2017). Digital identity guidelines: Authentication and lifecycle management, Tech. Rep. SP 800-63-b, US Dept of Commerce, National Institute of Standards and Technology, Gaithersburg, MD.

Greenberg, A. (2017). Hack brief: Dangerous 'fireball' adware infects a quarter billion pcs, `https://www.wired.com/2017/06/hack-brief-dangerous-fireball-adware-infects-quarter-billion-pcs/`.

Halderman, J. A. and Felten, E. W. (2006). Lessons from the sony CD DRM episode. in *USENIX Security Symposium*, pp. 77–92.

Halevi, T., Lewis, J., and Memon, N. (2013). A pilot study of cyber security and privacy related behavior and personality traits, WWW '13 Companion (Association for Computing Machinery, New York, NY, USA), ISBN 9781450320382, p. 737–744, doi:10.1145/2487788.2488034, `https://doi.org/10.1145/2487788.2488034`.

Hatleback, E. and Spring, J. M. (2014). Exploring a mechanistic approach to experimentation in computing, *Philosophy & Technology* **27**, 3, pp. 441–459.

Hatleback, E. and Spring, J. M. (2018). A refinement to the general mechanistic account, *European Journal for Philosophy of Science* **9**, 2, p. 19.

Henrich, J., Heine, S. J., and Norenzayan, A. (2010). Beyond WEIRD: Towards a broad-based behavioral science, *Behavioral and Brain Sciences* **33**, 2-3, p. 111.

Herley, C. and van Oorschot, P. (2017). SoK: Science, security, and the elusive goal of security as a scientific pursuit, in *Symposium on Security and Privacy (Oakland)* (IEEE, San Jose, CA).

Hertzberg, H., Daniels, G. S., and Churchill, E. (1954). Anthropometry of flying personnel-1950, Tech. rep., Antioch Coll Yellow Springs OH.

Heuer, R. J., Jr. (1999). *Psychology of Intelligence Analysis* (US Central Intelligence Agency).

Hill, K. (2016). How an internet mapping glitch turned a random kansas farm into a digital hell, `http://fusion.net/story/287592/internet-mapping-glitch-kansas-farm/fusion`.

Hofmann, H. (2000). Exploring categorical data: Interactive mosaic plots, *Metrika* **51**, 1, pp. 11–26.

Holdener, A. T. (2011). *HTML5 Geolocation* (O'Reilly Media, Inc.).

Householder, A. D., Chrabaszcz, J., Novelly, T., Warren, D., and Spring, J. M. (2020). Historical analysis of exploit availability timelines, in *Workshop on Cyber Security Experimentation and Test* (USENIX, Virtual).

Householder, A. D., Wassermann, G., Manion, A., and King, C. (2019). The CERT guide to coordinated vulnerability disclosure, Tech. Rep. 2017-SR-022, Software Engineering Institute, Carnegie Mellon University, Pittsburgh, PA.

Hu, X., Chiueh, T., and Shin, K. G. (2009). Large-scale malware indexing using function-call graphs, in *Proceedings of the 16th ACM conference on Computer and Communications Security* (ACM), pp. 611–620.

Hu, X., Jang, J., Stoecklin, M. P., Wang, T., Schales, D. L., Kirat, D., and Rao, J. R. (2016). Baywatch: robust beaconing detection to identify infected hosts in large-scale enterprise networks, in *2016 46th Annual IEEE/IFIP International Conference on Dependable Systems and Networks (DSN)* (IEEE), pp. 479–490.

Hubbard, D. (2016). Cicso umbrella 1 million, `https://umbrella.cisco.com/blog/2016/12/14/cisco-umbrella-1-million/`.

Hume, D. (1902). *Enquiries Concerning the Human Understanding, and Concerning the Principles of Morals*, Vol. 2 (Oxford University Press), `https://www.gutenberg.org/files/9662/9662-h/9662-h.htm`.

ICANN (2011). ICANN approves historic change to internet's domain name system — board votes to launch new generic top-level domains, `https://www.icann.org/news/announcement-2011-06-20-enxx`.

ICANN (2013). Centralized zone data service (CZDS), `https://www.icann.org/resources/pages/czds-2014-03-03-en`.

Israel, G. D. (1992). Determining sample size, University of Florida.

Jacobson, V., Leres, C., and McCanne, S. (2003). Tcpdump public repository, http://www.tcpdump.org.

Jamieson, S. (2004). Likert scales: How to (ab) use them, *Medical education* **38**, 12, pp. 1217–1218.

Kabisch, M., Ruckes, C., Seibert-Grafe, M., and Blettner, M. (2011). Randomized controlled trials: Part 17 of a series on evaluation of scientific publications, *Deutsches Ärzteblatt International* **108**, 39, p. 663.

Kadane, J. B. (2011). *Principles of uncertainty* (Chapman & Hall).

Kartaltepe, E. J., Morales, J. A., Xu, S., and Sandhu, R. (2010). Social network-based botnet command-and-control: emerging threats and countermeasures, in *International Conference on Applied Cryptography and Network Security, Heidelberg*, Vol. 6123 (Springer, Berlin), pp. 510–528.

Kennedy, C., McGeeney, K., and Keeter, S. (2016). The twilight of landline interviewing, Tech. rep., Pew Research Center, Washington, DC.

Kfoury, A. (1982). *A Programming Approach to Computability*, 1st edn., The AKM Series in Theoretical Computer Science (Springer New York, New York, NY), ISBN 1-4612-5749-2.

Khattak, S., Ramay, N. R., Khan, K. R., Syed, A. A., and Khayam, S. A. (2013). A taxonomy of botnet behavior, detection, and defense, *IEEE Communications Surveys & Tutorials* **16**, 2, pp. 898–924.

Klausen, J. (2015). Tweeting the jihad: Social media networks of western foreign fighters in syria and iraq, *Studies in Conflict & Terrorism* **38**, pp. 1–22.

Koch, M. (2018). Implementing full packet capture, SANS Reading Room.

Kolkman, O. and Gieben, R. (2006). DNSSEC operational practices, Tech. rep., RFC 4641, September.

Korpela, E., Werthimer, D., Anderson, D., Cobb, J., and Lebofsky, M. (2001). Seti@ home—massively distributed computing for seti, *Computing in Science & Engineering* **3**, 1, pp. 78–83.

Kripke, S. A. (1965). Semantical analysis of intuitionistic logic I, *Studies in Logic and the Foundations of Mathematics* **40**, pp. 92–130.

Krol, K., Spring, J. M., Parkin, S., and Sasse, M. A. (2016). Towards robust experimental design for user studies in security and privacy, in *Learning from Authoritative Security Experiment Results* (IEEE, San Jose, CA), pp. 21–31.

Kuhn, T. S. (2012). *The Structure of Scientific Revolutions*, 4th edn. (University of Chicago Press, Chicago and London), introductory essay by Ian Hacking.

Lasota, K. and Kozakiewicz, A. (2011). Analysis of the similarities in malicious DNS domain names, in *FTRA International Conference on Secure and Trust Computing, Data Management, and Application* (Springer), pp. 1–6.

Lawrence Berkeley National Laboratory (2007). ftp://ita.ee.lbl.gov/html/traces.html.

Letier, E., Stefan, D., and Barr, E. T. (2014). Uncertainty, risk, and information value in software requirements and architecture, in *Proceedings of the 36th International Conference on Software Engineering*, ICSE 2014 (ACM, Hyderabad, India), ISBN 978-1-4503-2756-5, pp. 883–894, http://doi.acm.org/10.1145/2568225.2568239.

Levine, J. (2010). RFC 5782 DNS blacklists and whitelists, RFC Editor.

Lindorfer, M., Kolbitsch, C., and Comparetti, P. M. (2011). Detecting environment-sensitive malware, in *International Workshop on Recent Advances in Intrusion Detection* (Springer), pp. 338–357.

Liu, C. (2002). *DNS and Bind Cookbook: Solutions & Examples for System Administrators* (O'Reilly Media Inc.).

m3aawg (2011). Email metrics program: The network operators' perspective, https://www.m3aawg.org/sites/default/files/document/MAAWG_2011_Q1-4_Metrics_Report15Rev.pdf.

Mackenzie, P. (2019). Wannacry aftershock, https://www.sophos.com/en-us/medialibrary/PDFs/technical-papers/WannaCry-Aftershock.pdf.

Majestic (2016). The majestic million, https://majestic.com/reports/majestic-million.

Mak, I. W., Evaniew, N., and Ghert, M. (2014). Lost in translation: Animal models and clinical trials in cancer treatment, *American Journal of Translational Research* **6**, 2, p. 114.

Mandiant (2013). APT1: Exposing one of China's cyber espionage units, Tech. rep.

Manès, V. J. M., Han, H., Han, C., Cha, S. K., Egele, M., Schwartz, E. J., and Woo, M. (2019). The art, science, and engineering of fuzzing: A survey, *IEEE Transactions on Software Engineering* **early access**.

Manna, Z. and Pnueli, A. (1992). *The Temporal Logic of Reactive and Concurrent Systems* (Springer-Verlag, New York).

Mars, R. (2020). The natural experiment, in *99% Invisible*, 401 (Oakland, CA), https://99percentinvisible.org/episode/the-natural-experiment/transcript.

Massey Jr, F. J. (1951). The kolmogorov-smirnov test for goodness of fit, *Journal of the American Statistical Association* **46**, 253, pp. 68–78.

McCrae, R. R. and John, O. P. (1992). An introduction to the five-factor model and its applications, *Journal of Personality* **60**, 2, pp. 175–215.

Meng, W., Duan, R., and Lee, W. (2013). DNS changer remediation study, Talk at M3AAWG 27th.

Metcalf, L. (2018a). Cache poisoning of mail handling domains revisited, https://insights.sei.cmu.edu/cert/2018/06/cache-poisoning-of-mail-handling-domains-revisited.html.

Metcalf, L. (2081b). DGA domains with ssl certificates? why? https://insights.sei.cmu.edu/cert/2018/12/dga-domains-with-ssl-certificates-but-why.html.

Metcalf, L. and Casey, W. (2016). *Cybersecurity and Applied Mathematics* (Syngress, Cambridge, MA, USA).

Metcalf, L. and Spring, J. (2013a). A ccTLD case study: .tv, https://insights.sei.cmu.edu/cert/2013/07/a-cctld-case-study-tv.html.

Metcalf, L. B., Ruef, D., and Spring, J. M. (2017). Open-source measurement of fast-flux networks while considering domain-name parking, in *Learning from Authoritative Security Experiment Results* (USENIX, Arlington, VA, USA), pp. 13–24.

Metcalf, L. B. and Spring, J. M. (2013b). Everything you wanted to know about blacklists but were afraid to ask, Tech. Rep. CERTCC-2013-39, Software Engineering Institute, Carnegie Mellon University, Pittsburgh, PA.

Metcalf, L. B. and Spring, J. M. (2015). Blacklist ecosystem analysis: Spanning Jan 2012 to Jun 2014, in *The 2nd ACM Workshop on Information Sharing and Collaborative Security* (Denver), pp. 13–22.

Microsoft (2017). Pua:win32/loadmoney. july 11, https://www.microsoft.com/ en-us/wdsi/threats/malware-encyclopedia-description?Name=PUA: Win32/LoadMoney.

Mitchell, S. D. (2003). *Biological Complexity and Integrative Pluralism* (Cambridge University Press, Cambridge, UK).

MITRE Corporation (2010). Science of cyber-security, Tech. Rep. JSR-10-102, JASON Office, McLean, VA.

MITRE Corporation (2012). Common vulnerability enumeration, http://cve. mitre.org, last access Apr 2, 2012.

Morey, R. (2019). How to use honeypot traps to fight email and wordpress spam, https://www.mailpoet.com/blog/email-honeypot-traps.

Morgan, M. S. (2014). Resituating knowledge: Generic strategies and case studies, *Philosophy of Science* **81**, 5, pp. 1012–1024.

Mozilla (2007). Public suffix list, https://publicsuffix.org/.

Murphy, S. (2006). RFC 4272: BGP security vulnerabilities analysis, RFC Editor.

Nagel, E. (1979). *The Structure of Science: Problems in the Logic of Scientific Explanation*, 2nd edn. (Routledge & Kegan Paul, London).

National Cyber Security Centre (UK) (2018). Password guidance: Updating your approach, https://www.ncsc.gov.uk/collection/passwords/ updating-your-approach.

National Science Foundation (2001). Federal Cyber Service: Scholarship for Service (SFS). A federal cyber service training and education initiative, Tech. Rep. NSF 01-167, NSF, Directorate for education and human resources, Division of undergraduate education, Arlington, VA.

Nielsen, M., Haun, D., Kärtner, J., and Legare, C. H. (2017). The persistent sampling bias in developmental psychology: A call to action, *Journal of Experimental Child Psychology* **162**, pp. 31–38.

Noble, S. U. (2018). *Algorithms of Oppression: How Search Engines Reinforce Racism* (NYU Press).

Norman, G. (2010). Likert scales, levels of measurement and the "laws" of statistics, *Advances in Health Sciences Education* **15**, 5, pp. 625–632.

Norton, J. D. (2010). There are no universal rules for induction, *Philosophy of Science* **77**, 5, pp. pp. 765–777.

O'Neil, C. (2016). *Weapons of Math Destruction: How Big Data Increases Inequality and Threatens Democracy* (Broadway Books).

Open Science Collaboration (2015). Estimating the reproducibility of psychological science, *Science* **349**, 6251, p. aac4716.

Pagliery, J. (2015). Lenovo slipped 'superfish' malware into laptops, https://money.cnn.com/2015/02/19/technology/security/ lenovo-superfish/index.html.

Pajares, F. (2002). Gender and perceived self-efficacy in self-regulated learning, *Theory into Practice* **41**, 2, pp. 116–125.

Pantic, N. and Husain, M. I. (2015). Covert botnet command and control using twitter, in *Proceedings of the 31st Annual Computer Security Applications Conference*, pp. 171–180.

Parkkinen, V.-P., Wallmann, C., Wilde, M., Clarke, B., Illari, P., Kelly, M. P., Norell, C., Russo, F., Shaw, B., and Williamson, J. (2018). *Evaluating Evidence of Mechanisms in Medicine Principles and Procedures* (Springer).

Perekalin, A. (2017). Fireball: Adware with potential nuclear consequences, https://www.kaspersky.com/blog/fireball-adware/17015/.

Piscitello, D. (2018). ICANN GDPR and WHOIS users survey: A joint survey by the anti-phishing working group (apwg) and the messaging, malware and mobile anti-abuse working group (m3aawg), https://docs.apwg.org/reports/ICANN_GDPR_WHOIS_Users_Survey_20181018.pdf.

Pohl, R. and Pohl, R. F. (2004). *Cognitive Illusions: A Handbook on Fallacies and Biases in Thinking, Judgement and Memory* (Psychology Press).

Polska, C. (2013). NASK shuts down dangerous virut botnet domains, https://www.cert.pl/en/nask-shuts-down-dangerous-virut-botnet-domains/.

Popper, K. R. (1959). *The Logic of Scientific Discovery* (Hutchinson, London).

Porras, P., Saidi, H., and Yegneswaran, V. (2009a). An analysis of conficker's logic and rendezvous points, SRI International Technical Report.

Porras, P., Saidi, H., and Yegneswaran, V. (2009b). Conficker C analysis, *SRI International* **1**, pp. 1–1.

Pym, D. (2018). The origins of cyberspace, in *Oxford Handbook of Cyber Security*.

Pym, D., Spring, J. M., and O'Hearn, P. (2018). Why separation logic works, *Philosophy & Technology* **32**, pp. 483–516, doi:10.1007/s13347-018-0312-8.

Radare Team (2017). Radare2 github repository, https://github.com/radareorg/radare2.

Ravin, E., O'Reilly, T., Dougherty, D., and Todino, G. (1996). *Using & Managing UUCP* (O'Reilly & Associates, Inc.).

Rekhter, Y., Li, T., Hares, S., *et al.* (1994). A border gateway protocol 4 (BGP-4), ISI, USC Information Sciences Institute.

Ries, C. (2005). Automated identification of malicious code variants, BA CS Honors Thesis (unpublished), Colby College, ME, May.

Roesch, M. (1999). Snort: Lightweight intrusion detection for networks, in *Large Installation Systems Admin* (USENIX, Seattle, WA), pp. 229–238.

Rossow, C., Dietrich, C. J., Grier, C., Kreibich, C., Paxson, V., Pohlmann, N., Bos, H., and Van Steen, M. (2012). Prudent practices for designing malware experiments: Status quo and outlook, in *Symposium on Security and Privacy* (IEEE), pp. 65–79.

Saad, S., Traore, I., Ghorbani, A., Sayed, B., Zhao, D., Lu, W., Felix, J., and Hakimian, P. (2011). Detecting P2P botnets through network behavior analysis and machine learning, in *2011 Ninth Annual International Conference on Privacy, Security and Trust* (IEEE), pp. 174–180.

Santos, I., Brezo, F., Nieves, J., Penya, Y. K., Sanz, B., Laorden, C., and Bringas, P. G. (2010). Idea: Opcode-sequence-based malware detection, in *Interna-

tional Symposium on Engineering Secure Software and Systems (Springer), pp. 35–43.

Schreuder, D. A. (2014). *Vision and Visual Perception : The Conscious Base of Seeing* (Archway Publishing, Bloomington, IN).

Security, K. (2019). Prioritization to prediction volume 2: Getting real about remediation, https://www.kennasecurity.com/prioritization-to-prediction-report-volume-two/.

Silberzahn, R., Uhlmann, E. L., Martin, D. P., Anselmi, P., Aust, F., Awtrey, E., Bahník, Š., Bai, F., Bannard, C., Bonnier, E., *et al.* (2018). Many analysts, one data set: Making transparent how variations in analytic choices affect results, *Advances in Methods and Practices in Psychological Science* **1**, 3, pp. 337–356.

Silva, S. S., Silva, R. M., Pinto, R. C., and Salles, R. M. (2013). Botnets: A survey, *Computer Networks* **57**, 2, pp. 378–403.

Simon, H. A. (1996). *The Sciences of the Artificial*, 3rd edn. (MIT press, Cambridge, MA).

Simone, A. (2015). The strange history of ransomware, https://medium.com/un-hackable/the-bizarre-pre-internet-history-of-ransomware-bb480a652b4b.

Solomon, F. (1987). *Probability and stochastic processes* (Prentice Hall).

Spring, J. (2014). Domain blocking: The problem of a googol of domains, https://insights.sei.cmu.edu/cert/2014/10/domain-blocking-the-problem-of-a-googol-of-domains.html.

Spring, J., Fallon, J., Galyardt, A., Horneman, A., Metcalf, L. B., and Stoner, E. (2019). Machine learning in cybersecurity: A guide, Tech. rep., Software Engineering Institute, Carnegie Mellon University, Pittsburgh, PA.

Spring, J. M. (2013). A notation for describing the steps in indicator expansion, in *eCrime Researchers Summit (eCRS), 2013* (IEEE, San Francisco), pp. 1–6.

Spring, J. M., Hatleback, E., Householder, A. D., Manion, A., and Shick, D. (2020). Prioritizing vulnerability response: A stakeholder-specific vulnerability categorization, in *Workshop on the Economics of Information Security* (Brussels, Belgium).

Spring, J. M. and Huth, C. L. (2012). The impact of passive DNS collection on end-user privacy, in *Securing and Trusting Internet Names: SATIN* (National Physical Laboratory, Teddington, UK).

Spring, J. M. and Illari, P. (2018a). Building general knowledge of mechanisms in information security, *Philosophy & Technology* **32**, 4, pp. 627–659, doi: 10.1007/s13347-018-0329-z.

Spring, J. M. and Illari, P. (2018b). Review of human decision-making during incident analysis, *arXiv*, 1903.10080.

Spring, J. M., Moore, T., and Pym, D. (2017). Practicing a science of security: A philosophy of science perspective, in *New Security Paradigms Workshop* (Santa Cruz, CA, USA).

Spring, J. M. and Pym, D. (2018). Towards scientific incident response, in *GameSec*, LNCS 11199 (Springer, Seattle, WA).

Spring, J. M. and Stoner, E. (2015). CND equities strategy, Tech. Rep. CERTCC-2015-40, Software Engineering Institute, Carnegie Mellon University, Pittsburgh, PA.

Stake, R. E. (1995). *The Art of Case Study Research* (Sage, Thousand Oaks, CA).

Sterne, J. A., Sutton, A. J., Ioannidis, J. P., Terrin, N., Jones, D. R., Lau, J., Carpenter, J., Rücker, G., Harbord, R. M., Schmid, C. H., *et al.* (2011). Recommendations for examining and interpreting funnel plot asymmetry in meta-analyses of randomised controlled trials, *British Medical Journal* **342**, d4002.

Stodden, V. (2015). Reproducing statistical results, *Annual Review of Statistics and Its Application* **2**, pp. 1–19.

Stoll, C. (1989). *The Cuckoo's Egg: Tracking a Spy through the Maze of Computer Espionage* (Pan Books, London).

Stoner, E. (2010). Finding malicious activity in bulk DNS data, Tech. rep., Software Engineering Institute.

Sundaramurthy, S. C., McHugh, J., Ou, X. S., Rajagopalan, S. R., and Wesch, M. (2014). An anthropological approach to studying CSIRTs, *IEEE Security & Privacy* **12**, 5, pp. 52–60.

Syamtec (2015). The evolution of ransomware,
http://www.symantec.com/content/en/us/enterprise/media/
security_response/whitepapers/the-evolution-of-ransomware.pdf.

Tankard, C. (2016). What the GDPR means for businesses, *Network Security* **2016**, 6, pp. 5–8.

Tarski, A. and Vaught, R. L. (1956). Arithmetical extensions of relational systems, *Compositio Mathematica* **13**, pp. 81–102.

Team, N. (2015). What is grayware? https://uk.norton.com/norton-blog/
2015/08/what_is_grayware.html.

Tedre, M. and Moisseinen, N. (2014). Experiments in computing: A survey, *The Scientific World Journal* **2014**, pp. 1–11.

Thampi, V. (2009). Udis86: Disassembler library for x86 and x86-64, .

Turing, A. M. (1936). On computable numbers, with an application to the Entscheidungsproblem, *Proceedings of the London Mathematical Society* **2**, 1, pp. 230–265.

Uebel, T. (2016). Vienna circle, in E. N. Zalta (ed.), *The Stanford Encyclopedia of Philosophy*, spring 2016 edn. (Metaphysics Research Lab, Stanford University).

University of Victoria (2016). ISOT dataset overview. https://www.uvic.ca/
engineering/ece/isot/assets/docs/isot-datase.pdf.

VadeSecure (2019). Anti spam & graymail to stop non-priority emails,
https://www.vadesecure.com/en/solutions/
anti-spam-and-email-classification/.

Van Vleet, J. E. (2012). *Informal Logical Fallacies: A Brief Guide* (University Press of America).

Veksler, V. D., Buchler, N., Hoffman, B. E., Cassenti, D. N., Sample, C., and Sugrim, S. (2018). Simulations in cyber-security: A review of cognitive modeling of network attackers, defenders, and users, *Frontiers in Psychology*

9, p. 691, https://www.frontiersin.org/article/10.3389/fpsyg.2018.00691.

Vincenti, W. G. (1990). *What Engineers Know and How They Know It: Analytical Studies from Aeronautical History*, Johns Hopkins Studies in the History of Technlogy (Johns Hopkins University Press, Baltimore and London).

Vissers, T., Joosen, W., and Nikiforakis, N. (2015). Parking sensors: Analyzing and detecting parked domains, in *Proceedings of the ISOC Network and Distributed System Security Symposium (NDSS)* (San Diego, CA), pp. 53–53, http://www.internetsociety.org/sites/default/files/01_2_2.pdf.

Wasserstein, R. L., Schirm, A. L., and Lazar, N. A. (2019). Moving to a world beyond "p < 0.05", *The American Statistician* **73**, supl, pp. 1–19, doi:10.1080/00031305.2019.1583913, https://doi.org/10.1080/00031305.2019.1583913.

Weimer, F. (2005). Passive DNS replication, in *17th Annual FIRST Conference on Computer Security Incident Handling*.

Wiki, B. (2017). Good uses for botnets, https://jpdias.me/botnet-lab//history/good-uses-for-botnets.html.

Winding, R., Wright, T., and Chapple, M. (2006). System anomaly detection: Mining firewall logs, in *2006 Securecomm and Workshops*, pp. 1–5.

wolfvan (2018). some-samples, https://github.com/wolfvan/some-samples.

Woodward, J. (2003). *Making Things Happen: A Theory of Causal Explanation* (Oxford University Press, Oxford, UK).

World, P. (2012). Your pc may come with malware pre-installed, https://www.pcworld.com/article/262325/your_pc_may_come_with_malware_pre_installed.html.

yara (2008). yara, https://virustotal.github.io/yara/.

ytisf (2018). thezoo. july 25, https://github.com/ytisf/theZoo.

Zhang, J., Luo, X., Perdisci, R., Gu, G., Lee, W., and Feamster, N. (2011). Boosting the scalability of botnet detection using adaptive traffic sampling, in *Proceedings of the 6th ACM Symposium on Information, Computer and Communications Security*, pp. 124–134.

Zhang, L., Jajodia, S., and Brodsky, A. (2007). Information disclosure under realistic assumptions: Privacy versus optimality, in *Proceedings of the 14th ACM conference on Computer and communications security*, pp. 573–583.

Zou, J. and Schiebinger, L. (2018). AI can be sexist and racist —it's time to make it fair, Nature Publishing Group.

Glossary

Index

Printed in the United States
by Baker & Taylor Publisher Services